IMAGES
of America

Downtown Knoxville

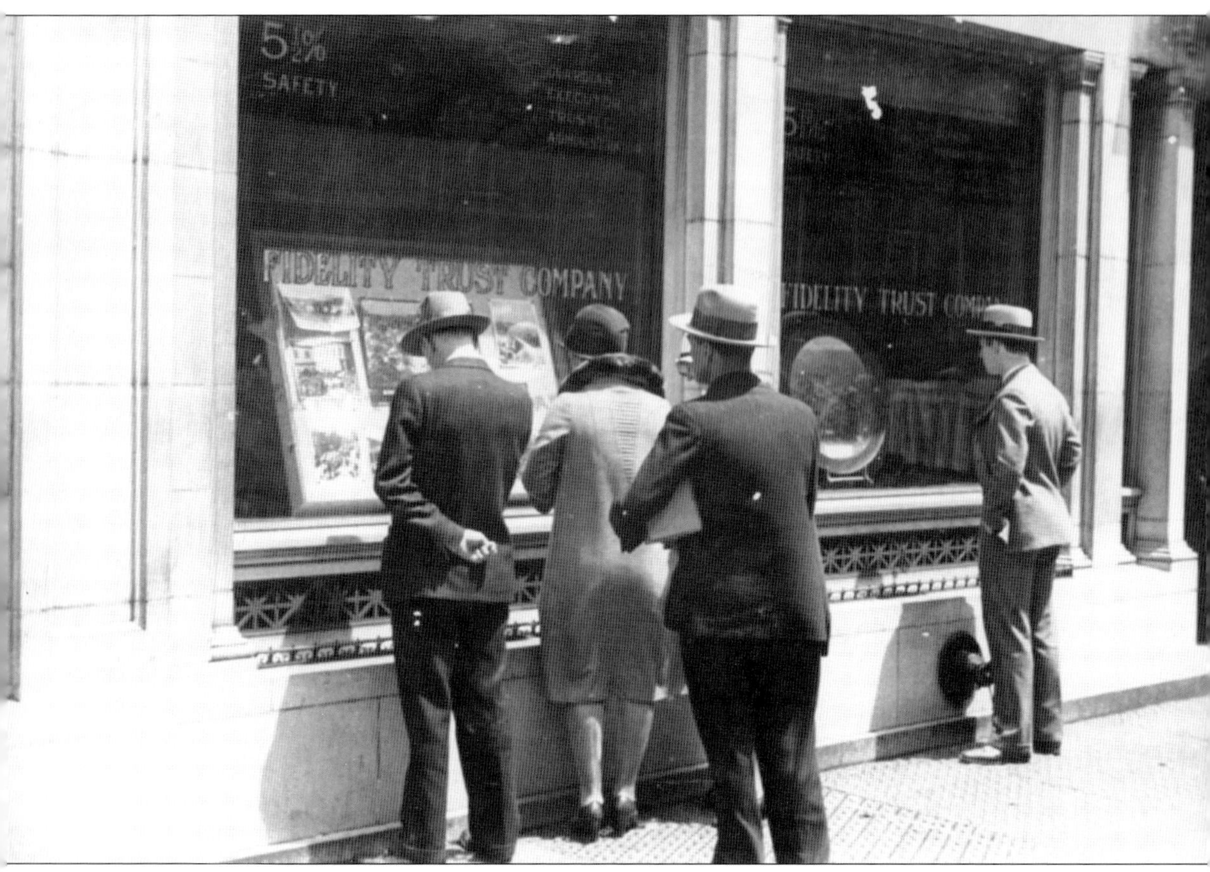

At the Fidelity Trust Building on Gay Street at Union Avenue around the 1920s, these men and one woman are curiously studying old photographs of Knoxville. At least two of the photographs, prize steers on Gay Street in 1877 and the circus parade of 1886, are included in this book. (Calvin M. McClung Historical Collection, Knox County Public Library.)

On the Cover: Around 1925, crowds await the next sensation at the Bijou Theatre, known for vaudeville shows and dramatic performances by the local Peruchi Players. Across the street, the Cumberland Hotel, at right, hosted a piano and phonograph store. Originally known as Schubert's, the well-known Victorian-era hostelry burned down in a fatal fire in early 1945. But the nearly acoustically perfect 1909 Bijou thrives today as one of downtown's liveliest attractions. (Calvin M. McClung Historical Collection, Thompson Photograph Collection, Knox County Public Library.)

IMAGES
of America

DOWNTOWN KNOXVILLE

Paul James and Jack Neely

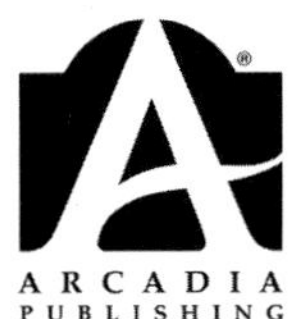

ISBN 978-1-4671-0772-3

Published by Arcadia Publishing
Charleston, South Carolina

Printed in the United States of America

Library of Congress Control Number: 2021946104

For all general information, please contact Arcadia Publishing:
Telephone 843-853-2070
Fax 843-853-0044
E-mail sales@arcadiapublishing.com
For customer service and orders:
Toll-Free 1-888-313-2665

Visit us on the Internet at www.arcadiapublishing.com

This book is dedicated to all those photographers from across the decades, famous and unknown, who captured the visual history of Knoxville.

Contents

ACKNOWLEDGMENTS

Knoxville is blessed with photographic archives that preserve the history of the city. Except where noted, photographs and illustrations in this book were selected from the Calvin M. McClung Historical Collection, part of the Knox County Public Library (noted as "McClung"). The authors particularly wish to thank Joanna Bouldin, archivist, and Steve Cotham, manager, at the McClung Historical Collection for their extensive assistance with this project. Photographs from individual collections within the McClung Historical Collection are noted with the captions.

Thanks also to helpful staff at other collections and museums who also supplied interesting historical photographs, some of which have never been published, including Laura Romans and Kyle Hovious, University of Tennessee Libraries; Rev. Renée Kesler and Janine Winfree, Beck Cultural Exchange Center; Pat Ezell, Tennessee Valley Authority; Eric Dawson, Tennessee Archive of Moving Image and Sound, McClung Historical Collection, Knox County Public Library; Dave Hearnes, Blount Mansion Association; and Clark Gillespie, Knoxville Museum of Art.

Individuals who helped with research, shared other historical images, or assisted in the production of this book include James D. Baeske, Robert Booker, Bob Davis, Charles Fels, Ernie Freeberg, Duane Grieve, David Harris, Patrick Hollis, Meredith James, Shawn Poynter, Cindy and Mark Proteau, Alec Riedl, Alan Sims, and Erin Slocum.

Introduction

Downtown Knoxville today, in an era of urban revival, attracts visitors like never before. Its new hotels are humming, as every day strangers are afoot on its sidewalks exploring, pointing at buildings and statues, and taking their own new photographs. As other photographers discovered more than a century ago, it is a striking place, presenting scenes not exactly like those in any other city. Although downtown includes the region's tallest modern skyscrapers, a majority of its buildings are more than 100 years old, reflecting a complicated history of idealistic dreams and catastrophic war, of boom years and depressions, of festivals and fatal fires.

Knoxville's photographs tell a vivid story. In this book we have taken pains to present a combination of well-known photographs that are hard to improve on—like the image of rough customers on a rustic Gay Street in 1869, Knoxville's earliest known street scene—but also numerous lesser-known photographs that have never been published in book form.

Photographs are limited in some respects, in that we have to rely on what photographers chose to capture at any given time. The resulting images often reflected what photographers were being paid to depict. There were some parts of town, and some communities, much less photographed than others. However, with study, photographs also bring out surprises that aren't always obvious in the written records.

Downtown's story is partly the typical story of an American city, but Knoxville's own narrative departs from the usual patterns in several respects.

The town was born in 1791 to sudden fame and temporary importance as the capital of the Southwest Territory, when it made sense to put a city up on top of a 60-foot bluff, not only to prevent flooding by the wild river but also to make it less vulnerable to attack when relations with multiple Native American tribes were uncertain. During that era, Knoxville became the birthplace and then the first capital of the new state of Tennessee.

By 1820, though, the legislature had sensibly migrated to the middle part of the state, and Knoxville lost its original reason for being. By then, a second generation of citizens found other reasons Knoxville might be important. The arrival of steamboats in 1828 helped, but not nearly as much as the arrival 30 years later of two significant railroads. The city's resources in marble, lumber, iron, and coal suddenly became profitable, and Knoxville's population tripled.

The Civil War divided the city or highlighted the divisions already there. Knoxville was home to Unionists, Confederates, enslaved African Americans, free people of color, and immigrants from Ireland, England, Germany, Switzerland, and Italy just finding their footing in a strange new land. Confederates occupied the city for the first half of the war, but the Battle of Knoxville came during Union occupation, when a weeks-long siege by Confederate forces ended with a desperate and costly charge on Fort Sanders.

War knocked the city backward, but by the 1870s, Knoxville was realizing its railroad-enabled industrial promise. Dozens of factories opened, producing a diverse array of products from machinery to textiles, and between 1870 and 1900, the booming city quadrupled in size, suddenly offering many of the amenities of a metropolis: a public library, concert halls, an electric streetcar system, street vendors, baseball grounds, and music festivals.

By the early 20th century, Knoxville was hosting significant expositions, notably the two-month National Conservation Exposition of 1913. But it also suffered many of the blights of an American city, including violent crime, slum districts, epidemics, exploitation of children, racial exclusion, and drug and alcohol abuse. Those extremes spawned new Progressive campaigns to improve life in Knoxville; some were successful. Temperance campaigns, part of the Progressive movement, closed Knoxville's 106 saloons at the end of 1907, changing the streetscape radically. At the same time, a brand-new sort of business called the cinema came to the fore, and movie theaters enlivened some blocks more than saloons ever could.

Knoxville in the 1920s and 1930s was a different sort of place, still aspiring but much more outward-looking, when hundreds of Knoxvillians were volunteering to work on the Great Smoky Mountains National Park and thousands were working for the Tennessee Valley Authority, planning dams, reservoirs, and recreation areas. Knoxville's creative people were excited more about the region than the city, mostly focusing their energies far from downtown.

The Knoxville area played a major role on the home front during World War II, with war-related factories—including previously little-known Oak Ridge and its sudden and secret nuclear-materials plants. After the war, as was the case with many American cities, many citizens abandoned the downtown for a quieter, greener life in the rapidly expanding suburbs. Neglected, downtown declined, inspiring best-selling travel writer John Gunther to call Knoxville the "ugliest city in America" in 1947, the most infamous of several perhaps creditable insults the city received in the mid-20th century.

After about 1930, little was built downtown until urban renewal in the 1960s, followed by the skyscraper era—and then one of the biggest surprises of Knoxville's history, the 1982 World's Fair, which brought 11 million people downtown. Forty years later, historians seem uncertain about how to assess its impact, but it did alter Knoxville's habits and left downtown with a large and useful park, now home to a city convention center, two hotels, a STEM academy, and an art museum.

Those impressive projects may not have convinced the world to welcome Knoxville into the front rank of cities, but around the beginning of the 21st century, the city witnessed a municipal renaissance driven in large part by a newfound fascination with what remained of the city's old downtown. Many of these mostly late-Victorian and early-20th-century structures that remain now host new businesses run by young people. With that fascination also came a fresh curiosity about architecture and institutions that were lost, many beyond living memory. This book presents many images of both, ranging from the commercial work of legendary photographer and conservationist Jim Thompson, who spent about 80 years taking pictures in Knoxville, to the fresh perspective of extraordinary visitors like the French journalist Annemarie Schwarzenbach, who was here for only a few days in 1937, to many images by photographers now unknown.

The authors hope this collection of photographs might add more clues to the ever-shifting mystery of Knoxville and maybe even answer some questions—the sort of questions people are asking now more than ever. For any city, curiosity is a good sign.

One

Knoxville on the Frontier

Around the time of the Revolutionary War, the land that would soon become the city of Knoxville was part of a vast frontier that stretched seemingly endlessly to the west. Land speculators and surveyors, keen to profit and expand their personal wealth, looked upon this territory, initially part of North Carolina, as a huge opportunity to develop the fledgling nation.

The first settlers came from several eastern states, including Revolutionary War veteran James White (1747–1821), a native of a rural section north of Charlotte, North Carolina. White came here around 1785 with his wife, Mary Lawson, following a short involvement in the abortive state of Franklin, and settled along a creek later dubbed White's Creek (now First Creek). White's fortified log cabin, later expanded into a stockade, was located where the State Street Parking Garage is today. No images of James White are known to exist.

Soon to join White was a curious traveling preacher named Rev. Samuel Carrick from Pennsylvania. Carrick created the first Presbyterian church here and became a leader in the area's earliest college, later to become the University of Tennessee.

The man who most influenced Knoxville's growth was William Blount (1749–1800), a native of North Carolina and a signer of the US Constitution. Appointed by Pres. George Washington to become governor of the Territory of the United States South of the River Ohio (commonly known as the Southwest Territory), the forerunner to the state of Tennessee, Blount came to James White's fort in the summer of 1791 to negotiate the Treaty of Holston with 41 Cherokee leaders. Later that year, with the help of White and others, Blount founded a new city to serve as the capital of the territory. He named the town Knoxville in honor of his superior, Gen. Henry Knox, Washington's secretary of war.

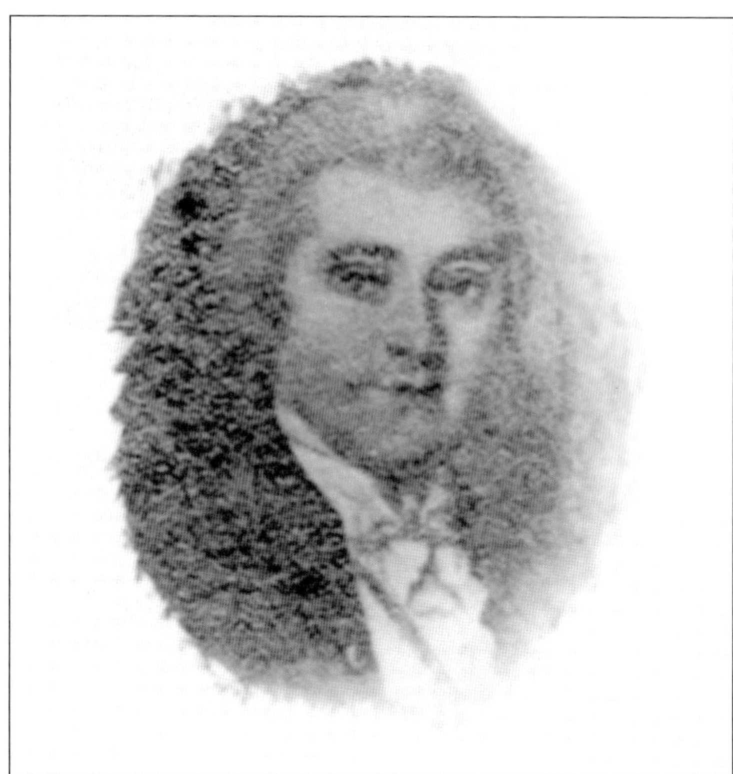

William Blount appears innocent in this portrait, but he was always working deals. A Revolutionary War veteran, he represented North Carolina as a signer of the US Constitution. In 1791, he placed the capital of the Southwest Territory at James White's fort, thereby founding the city of Knoxville. In 1796, he was president of the convention that founded the state of Tennessee. The following year, he was facing charges of treason as a US senator.

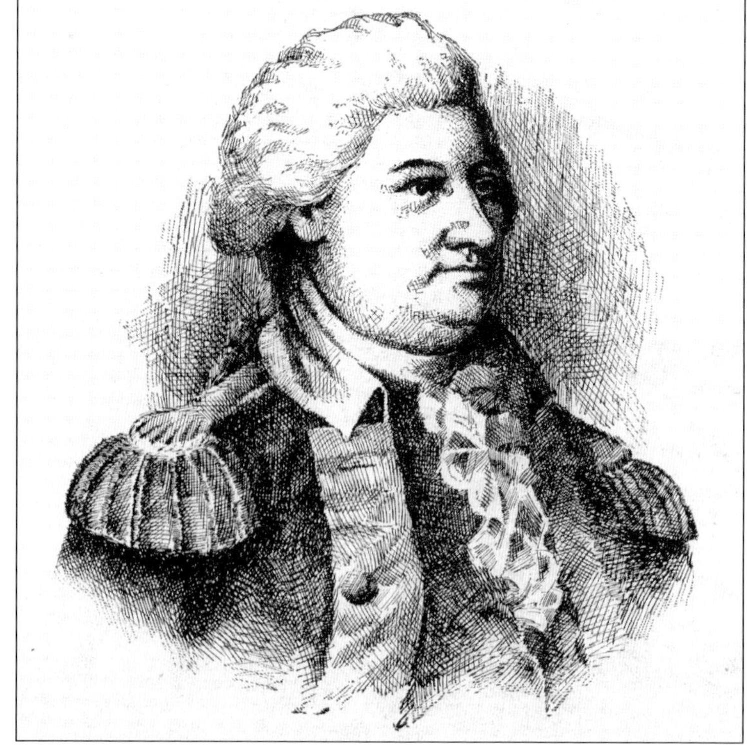

President Washington's secretary of war, Gen. Henry Knox, was a former Boston bookseller who became one of the youngest major generals of the Revolutionary War. He never visited the city named for him but certainly heard a lot about it. He was the cabinet member to whom Gov. William Blount reported. When Knoxville was only four years old, Knox retired from public life and settled in Maine. (Knoxville History Project.)

There is no reliable image of Knoxville's first settler, James White, who built a fortified settlement downtown in 1786. This stone was placed on the almost-forgotten site of his later home east of town, now off Riverside Drive. (Knoxville History Project.)

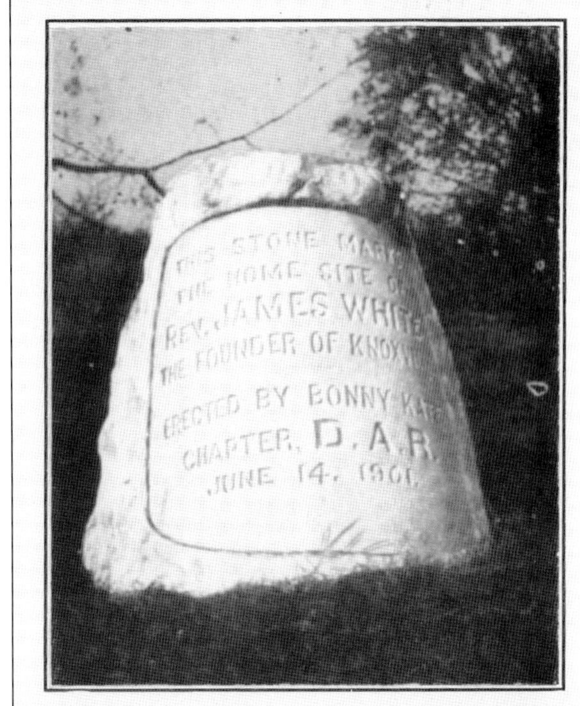

One of the earliest known images of James White's original cabin, it is almost unrecognizable as part of this ramshackle house owned at the time by James Kennedy Jr., which by 1900 was on the fringe of the saloon district along Central Street. Three children pose in the yard. (University of Tennessee Libraries.)

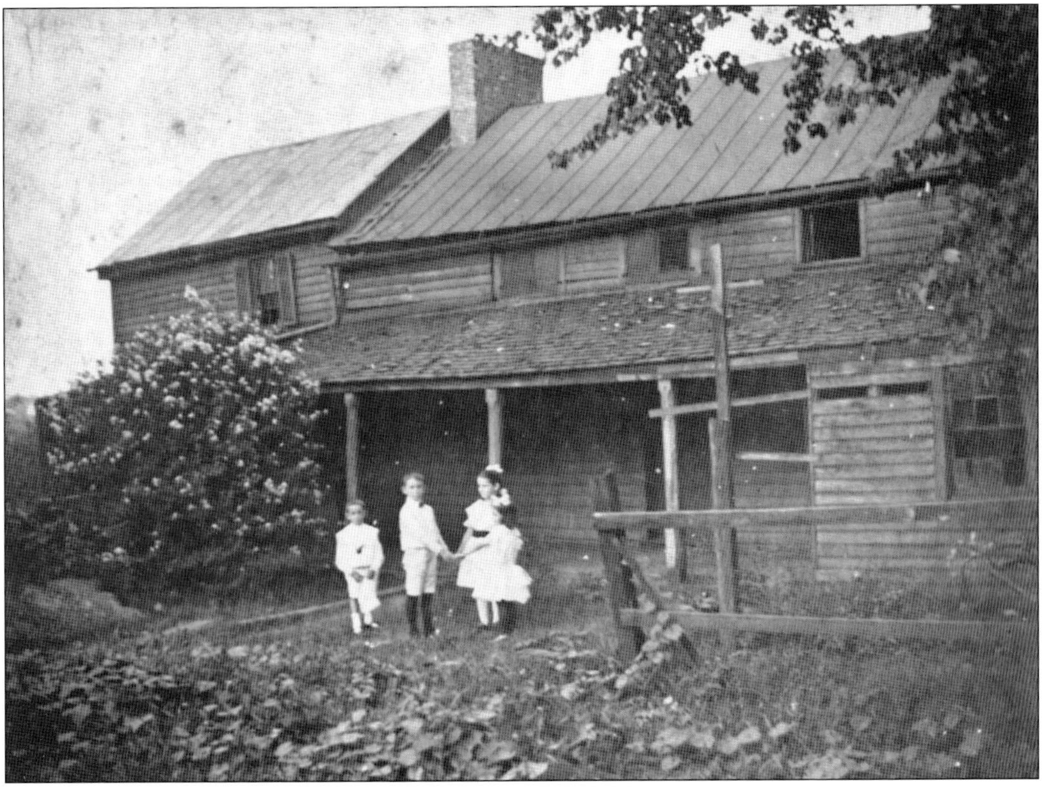

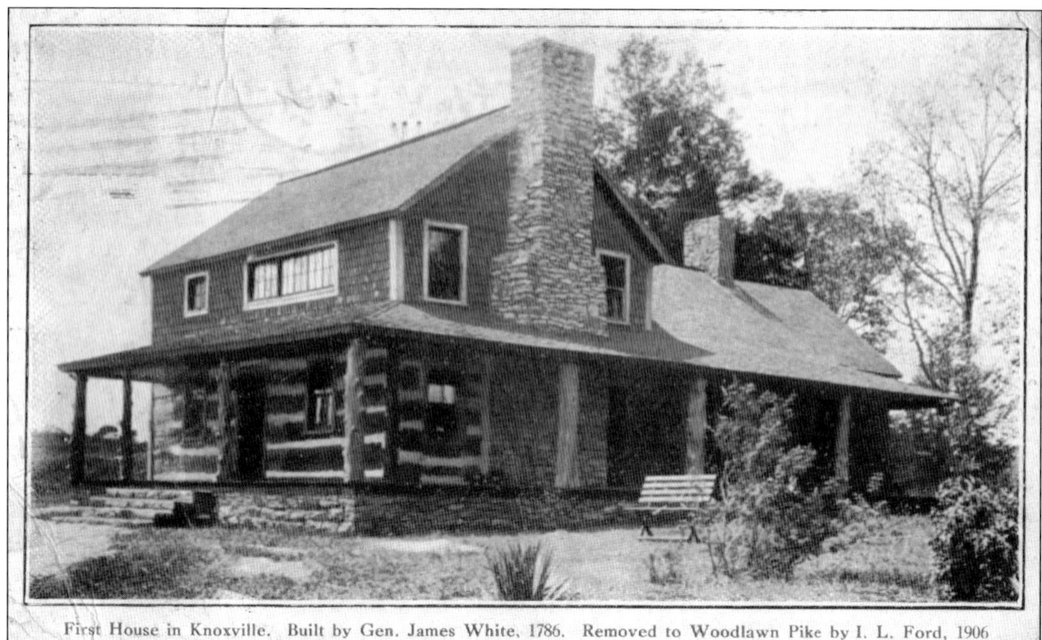

In 1906, Isiah Ford, one of the very few Knoxvillians familiar with pioneer James White's house, disassembled the structure, meticulously numbering the logs, and incorporated them into a new suburban house with a wraparound porch on Woodlawn Pike in South Knoxville, where it stood for 60 years. In the 1960s, the city reclaimed the relic and relocated it to a new location made available by urban renewal downtown, about a third of a mile southeast of its original location, with a reconstructed "fort" and some period structures to educate the public and celebrate the original settlement's early years. (Above, Knoxville History Project; below, McClung, Knox County Two Centuries Collection.)

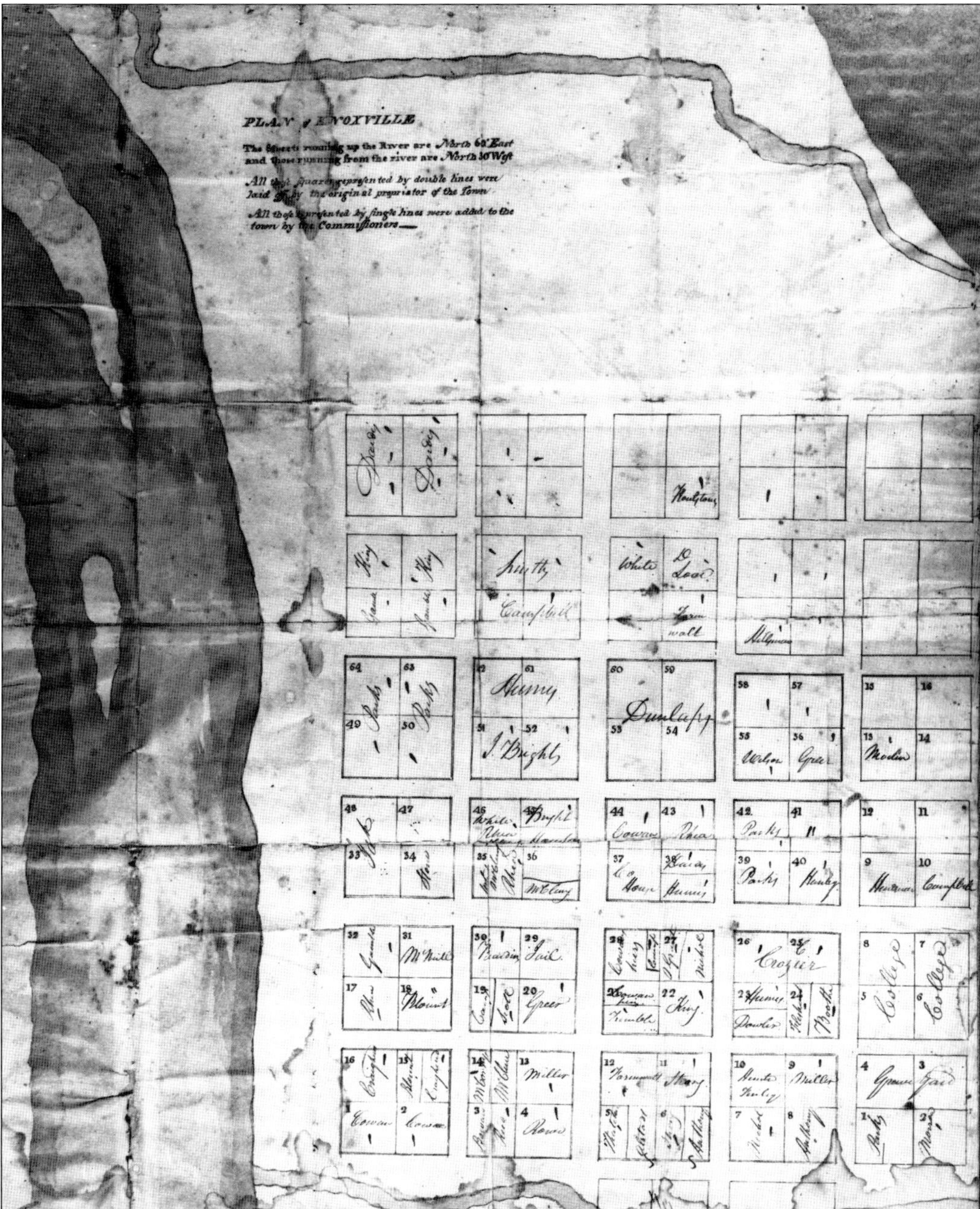

This "Plan of Knoxville" from the early 1800s shows the city's grid as it existed from 1795 to 1815. Today, this is the southern half of downtown Knoxville, with Clinch Avenue suggesting its northern limits. Note that on this unconventional map, north is to the right, and the river is at left. Under William Blount's guidance, the town was laid out by James White and White's son-in-law Charles McClung, a surveyor from Pennsylvania. Sixty-four equally sized lots on the high ground above the river adjacent to what is known today as First Creek were offered by way of a lottery system. The date of the lottery, October 3, 1791, signifies the founding of Knoxville. (University of Tennessee Libraries.)

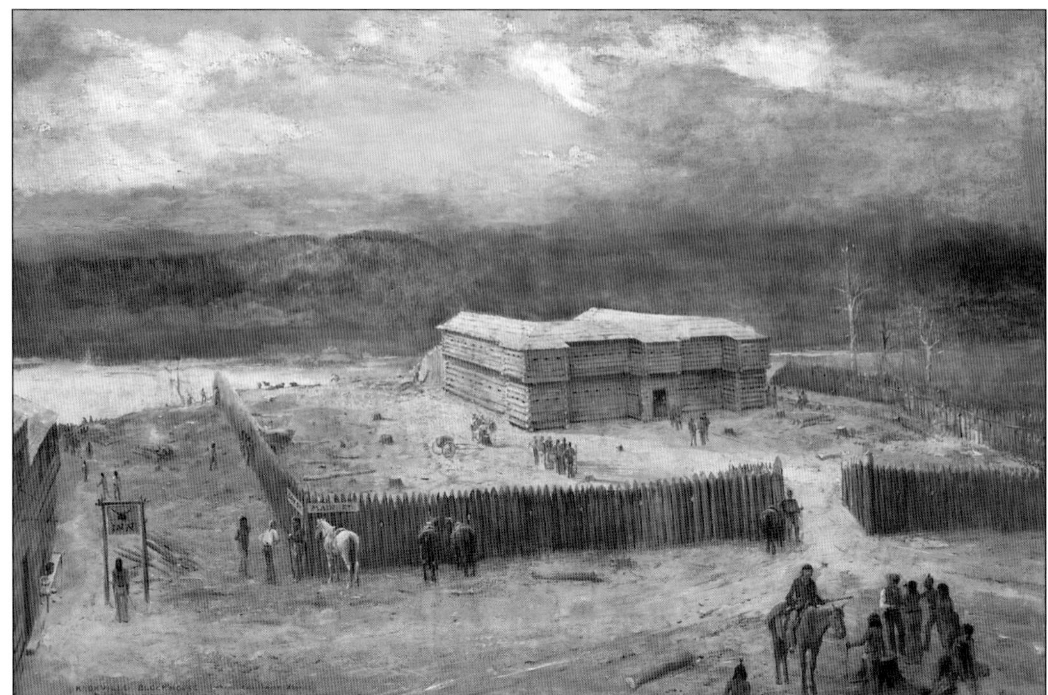

This federal fort, or blockhouse, stood in the 1790s at the site now occupied by the old courthouse. The fort was never attacked directly but played a role in discouraging a Chickamaugan assault in 1793. This painting, created a century later around 1900, is artist Lloyd Branson's educated guess as to how it appeared. (Knoxville History Project.)

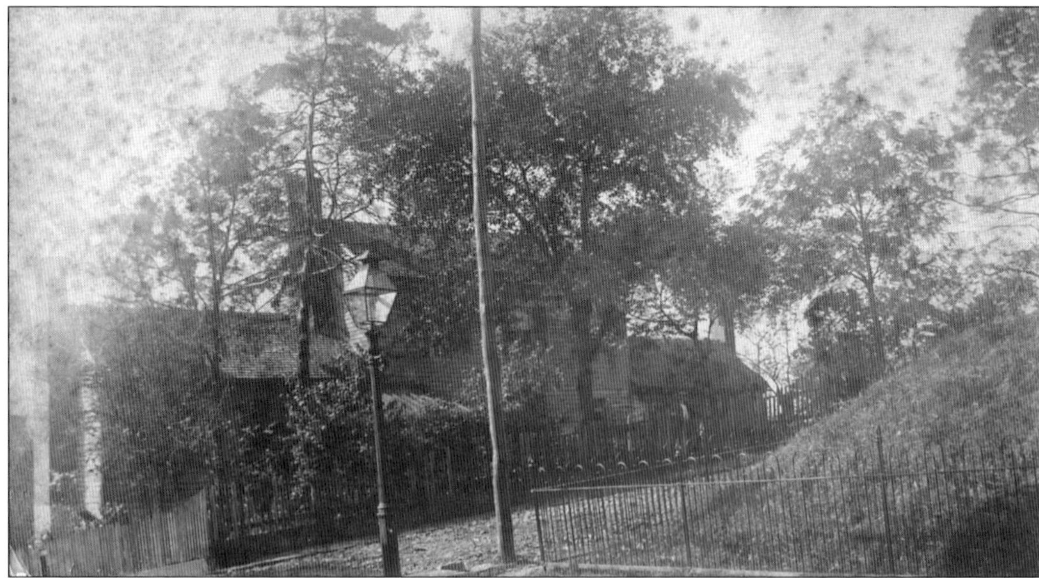

This rare image of what is now known as Blount Mansion dates from the late 1880s, when it was just considered the Boyd House. A bit of a surprise is the mound to the right, later removed by further development. The modern design of William Blount's gubernatorial residence was believed to be influenced by his strong-willed wife, Mary. When it was built around 1792, frame houses with glass windows were extraordinarily unusual on the frontier. (Lynn Tarpy/Blount Mansion.)

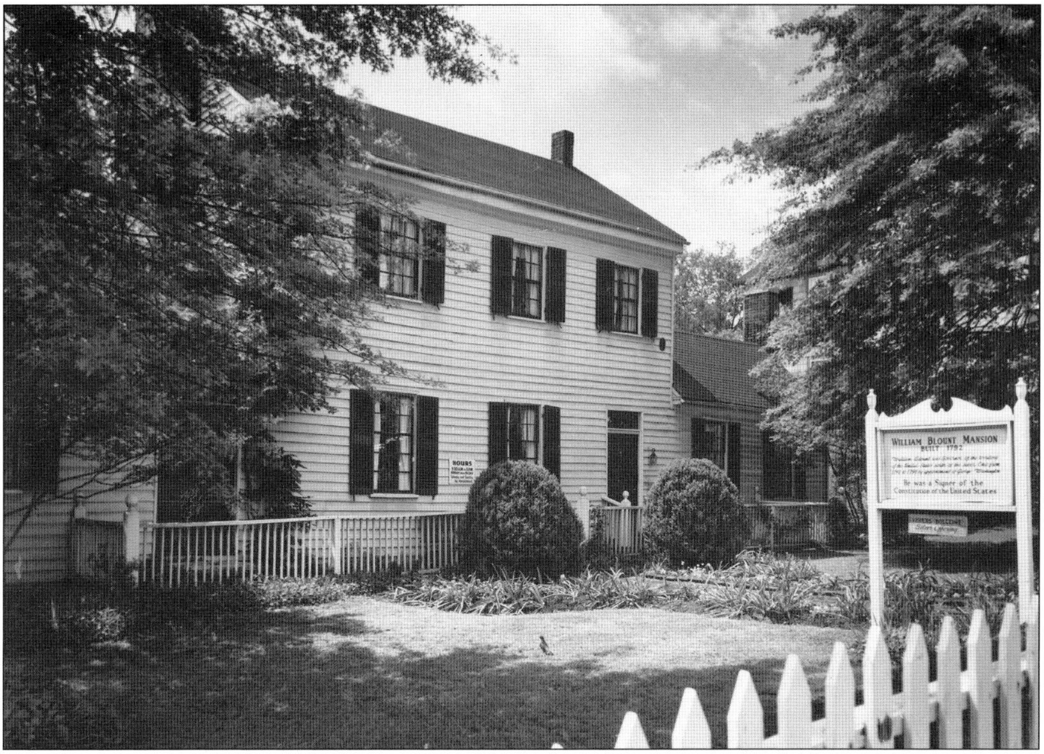

After a practical proposal to tear it down for the neighboring hotel project, Blount Mansion was renovated as a historic site in 1925, and has hosted tours and historical events ever since. Although not large by modern standards, it was termed a mansion in retrospect, honoring the fact that it was home to a sitting governor. Today, Blount Mansion is Knoxville's only national historic landmark.

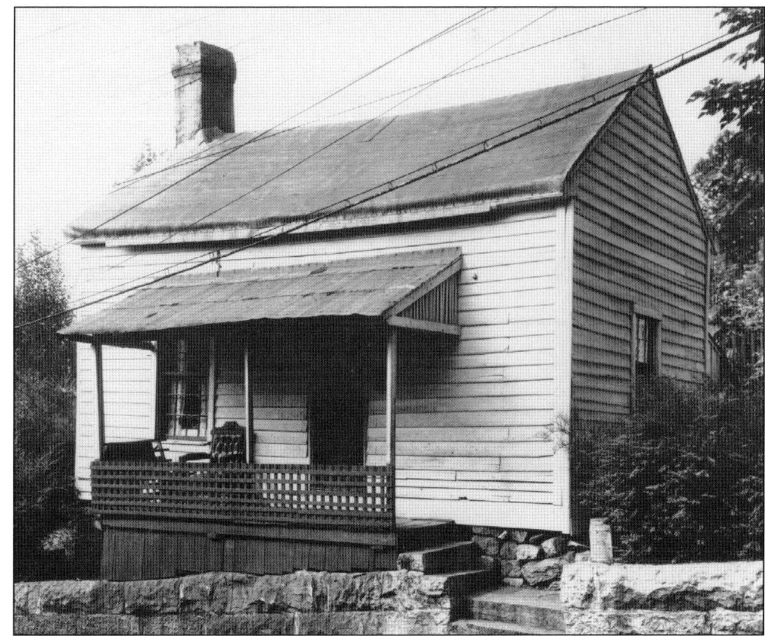

Blount's office, a freestanding building behind his home, is believed to have played a significant role in the founding of the state of Tennessee in 1796, when 55 delegates from across the Southwest Territory met in Knoxville to create a new state constitution. The desk on which the constitution was signed can be seen at Blount Mansion. (University of Tennessee Libraries.)

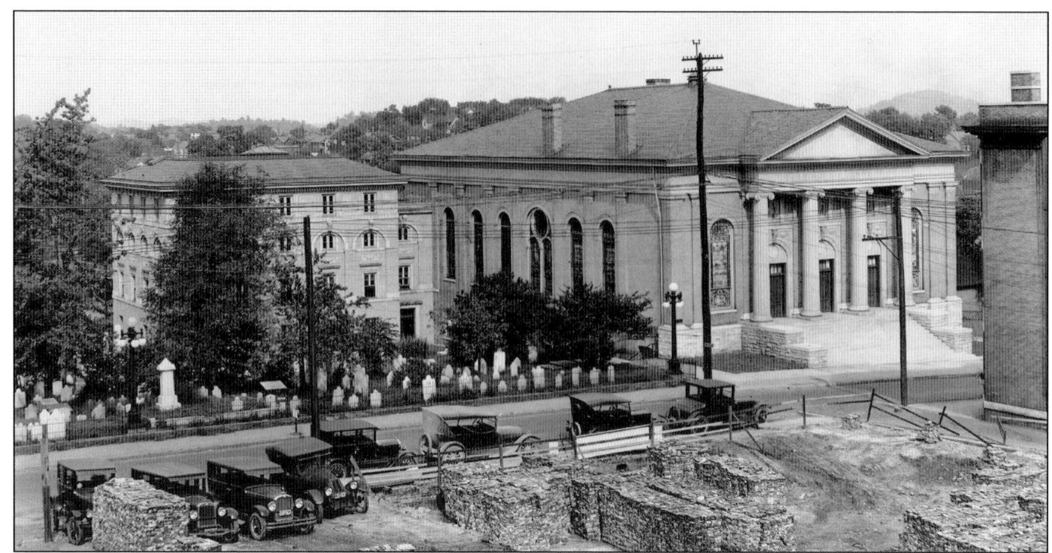

First Presbyterian Church and its 1790s graveyard are seen during the early stages of the construction of the Tennessee Theatre in the mid-1920s. The last of three church buildings constructed here since 1816, the columned church was built in 1901. The churchyard includes the graves of pioneers, including James White and William Blount, and three US senators, including Hugh Lawson White, a nationally prominent figure who ran for president in 1836. (McClung, Thompson Photograph Collection.)

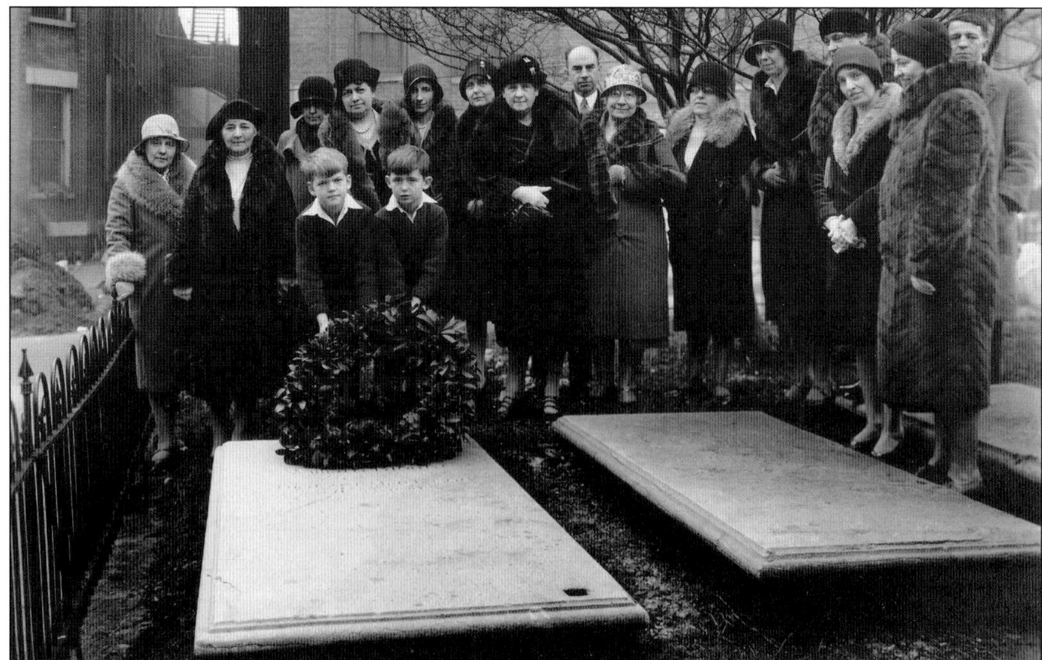

A reverent crowd gathers around the graves of William and Mary Blount, the oldest legible graves in the cemetery, in the 1920s, as Blount Mansion was being renovated. Among those attending were key preservationist Mary Boyce Temple (seventh from left), who started the effort to save Blount Mansion, and behind her, pastor Samuel Glasgow, who led First Presbyterian from 1919 to 1930. (Tennessee State Library & Archives.)

Two

War, Peace, and a New Destiny

The 19th century began with Knoxville serving as the first capital of the state of Tennessee, but after it lost that status in 1818 when the capital moved to Murfreesboro and later Nashville, the city's claim to any sort of importance was speculative. A decision to build a statewide school for the deaf here in the 1840s helped Knoxville recapture a semblance of relevancy, but the city's main focus at mid-century was the prospect of a railroad. After several false starts, including a convention of national railroad investors in 1836 that ultimately came to naught, Knoxville's first train arrived downtown in June 1855.

A year earlier, two Knoxvillians, William Swan (later mayor) and Joseph Mabry, developed an enterprising plan to purchase vacant land in town and donate the central part of it to the city for use as a farmers' market. Market Square was born, and remains one of downtown's liveliest spots.

The Civil War upended regular life for almost everyone, but natural events could be just as devastating. The flood of 1867 swept factories and houses downriver and left downtown completely surrounded with water. Most of the downtown area was protected from flooding because of the city's locale on the high bluff above the river—something the city's founding fathers likely considered to prevent surprise attacks from Cherokee raiders.

The Civil War divided the city into multiple factions. The Confederate army controlled the city during the war's first two years, but the Union army occupied it in 1863. The Siege of Knoxville was an attempt by the Confederates to retake the city.

After the 1867 flood, a proper bridge across the river connected downtown to the remote region that locals jokingly called "South America."

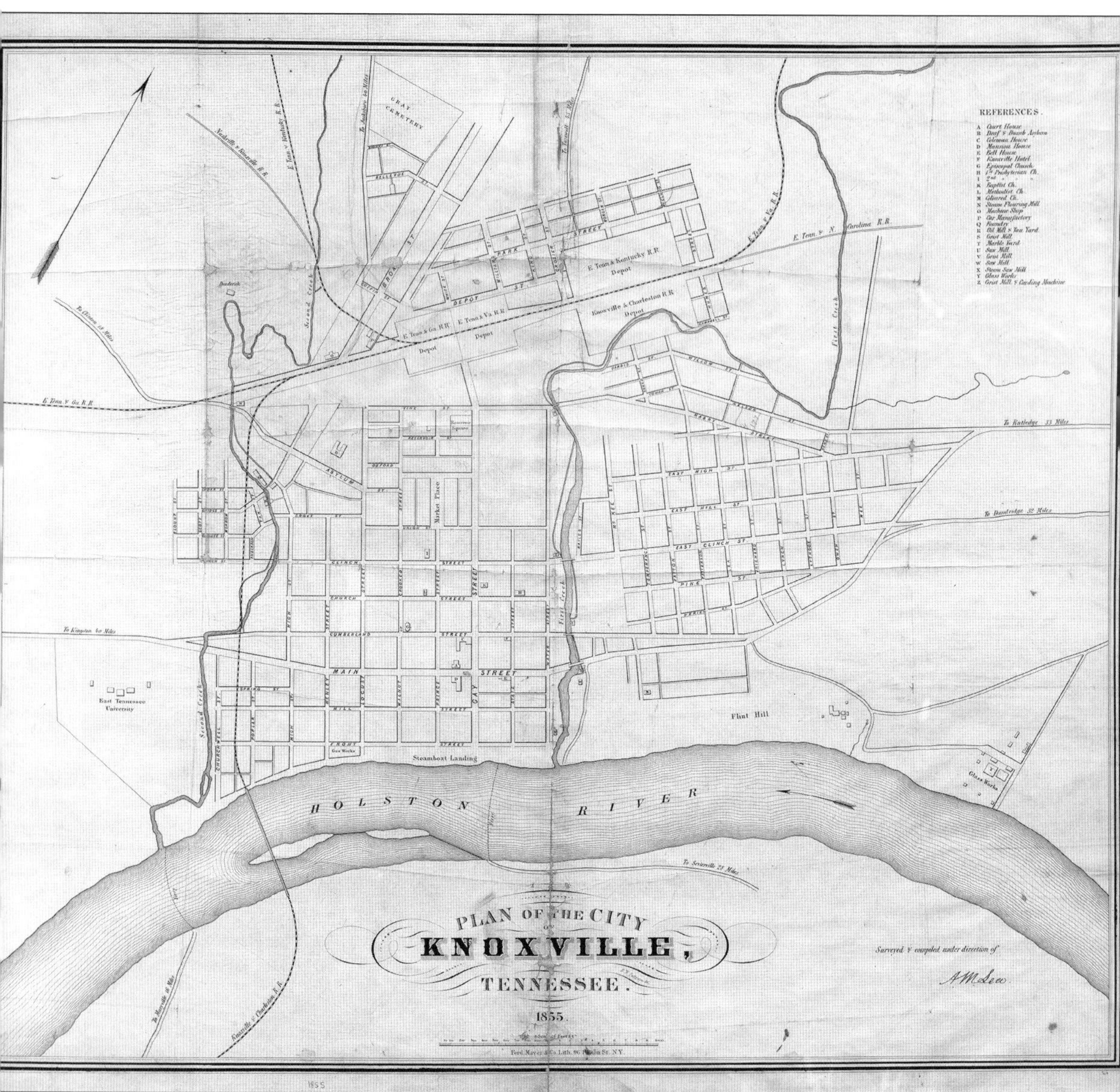

This 1855 map shows a growing city still clustered on the river bluff but beginning to expand on all sides except across the natural border of the Tennessee River (until the 1870s, the river at Knoxville was considered part of the Holston). The northern boundary is marked by the first rail depot, which arrived the same year. To the east an early suburb is developing, and to the west is the University of Tennessee on its famous "Hill." The location of the new Market Place, now known as Market Square, is also identified. Along the river front are the Knoxville Gas Works and the Steamboat Landing. At this point in the city's development, no bridge exists across the river here.

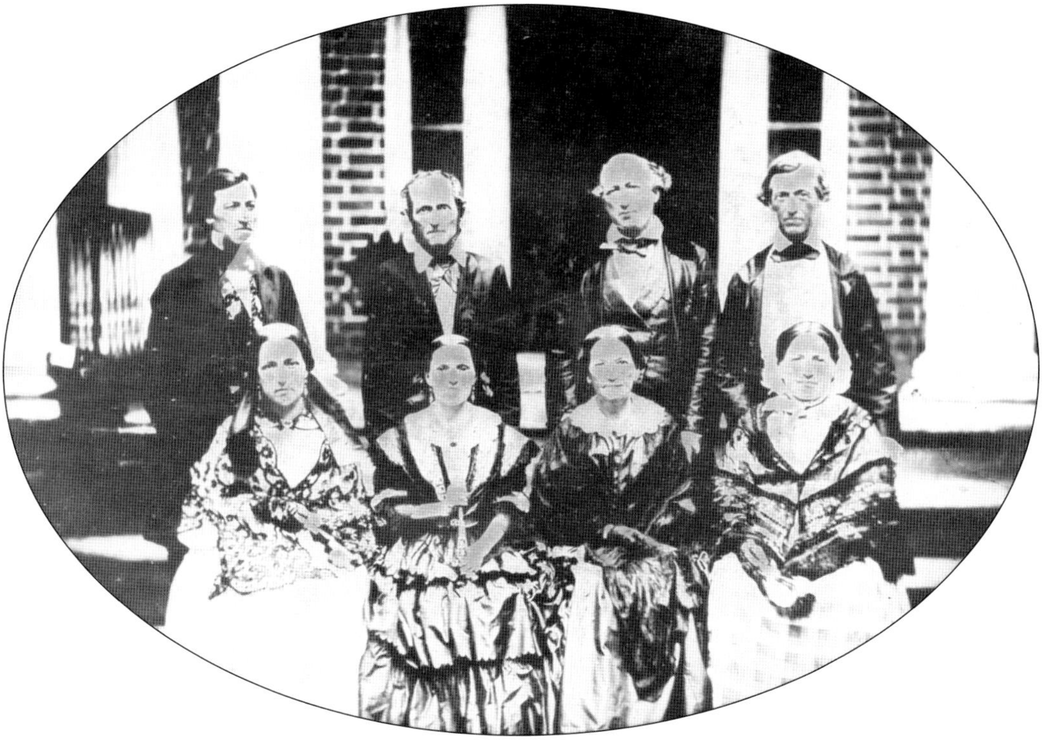

John Hervey Crozier (1812–1889), seen here with his family, served as the city's second postmaster for more than 30 years. One of his daughters was noted activist and suffrage leader Lizzie Crozier French. From left to right are (first row) Mary Ann Crozier, Hannah Crozier, Elizabeth Crozier, and Margaret Crozier; (second row) John Hervey Crozier, Arthur Crozier, Hugh Crozier, and Dr. Carrick Crozier. (McClung, Russell Harrison Collection.)

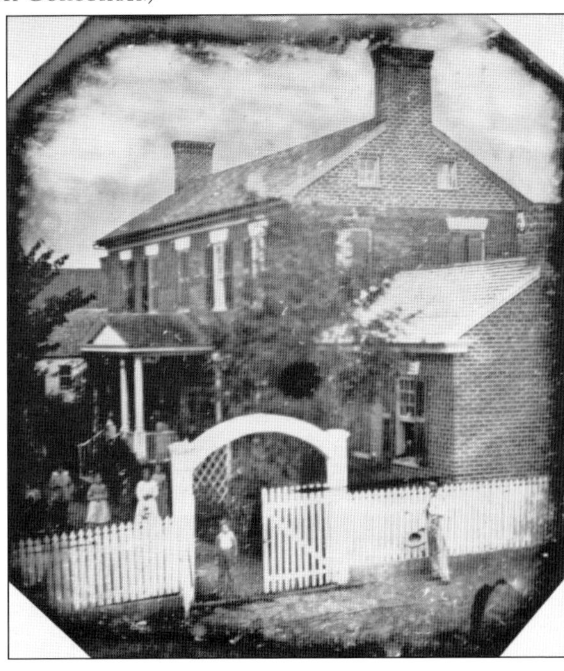

This very early photograph shows the Crozier home in the 1850s on the future site of the Farragut Hotel at Gay Street and Clinch Avenue. The Croziers' remarkable library was appreciated by Gen. Ambrose Burnside when he commandeered the house for a time in 1863 during Union occupation. (McClung, Russell Harrison Collection.)

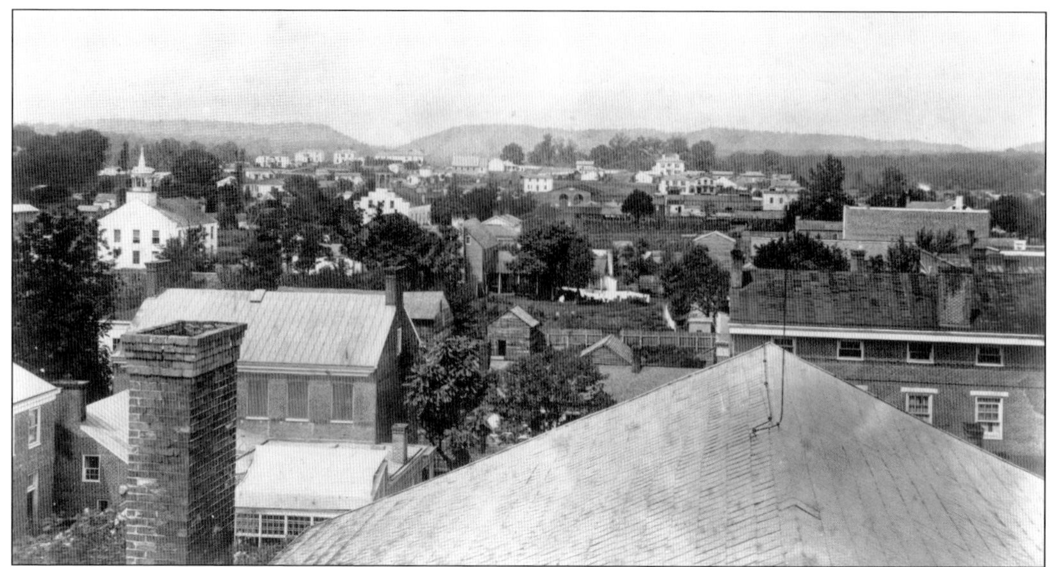

Thomas Harkness Smiley (1804–1866), originally from Springfield, Vermont, was one of Knoxville's earliest photographers. Smiley's Photographic Gallery was on Gay Street. This shot, taken in 1859 from the cupola atop the Knox County Courthouse on Main Street, shows a view across the rooftops looking north toward Market Square. The church on the left is the First Methodist Episcopal Church. Sharp's Gap is visible on the horizon.

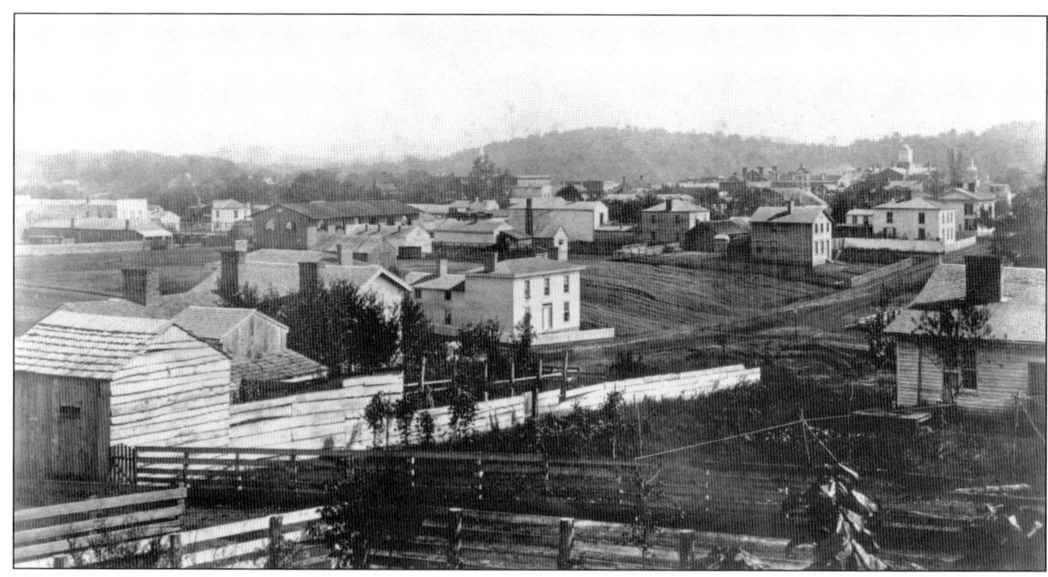

This view by Smiley, again from 1859, looks the other way, southeast toward the Knox County Courthouse. Smiley took the photograph from where he lived on the corner of Locust Street on Summit Hill. The long rectangular building at upper left appears to be the first Market House on still-developing Market Square.

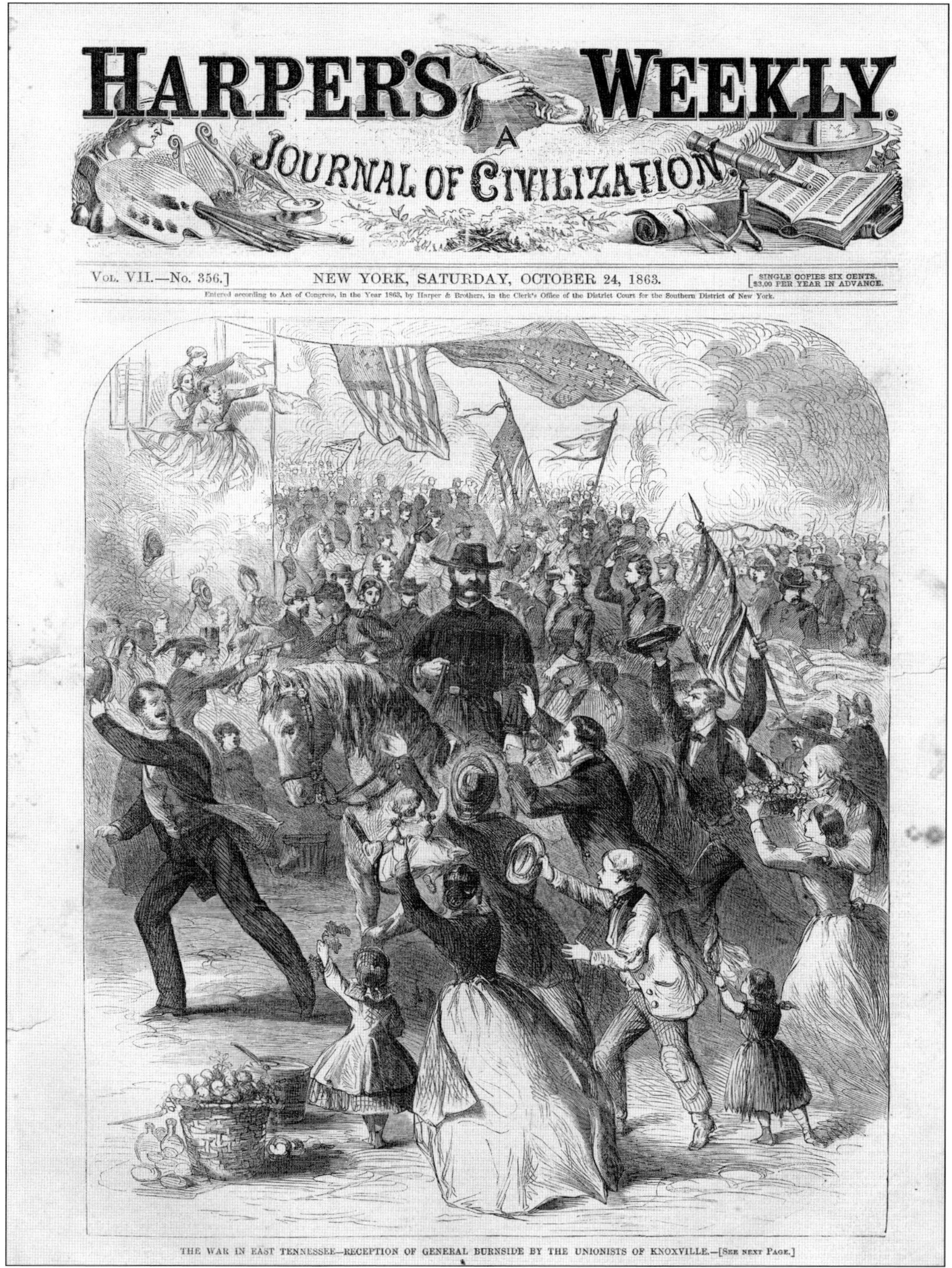

HARPER'S WEEKLY.

A JOURNAL OF CIVILIZATION.

Vol. VII.—No. 356.] NEW YORK, SATURDAY, OCTOBER 24, 1863. [SINGLE COPIES SIX CENTS. $3.00 PER YEAR IN ADVANCE.

Entered according to Act of Congress, in the Year 1863, by Harper & Brothers, in the Clerk's Office of the District Court for the Southern District of New York.

THE WAR IN EAST TENNESSEE—RECEPTION OF GENERAL BURNSIDE BY THE UNIONISTS OF KNOXVILLE.—[See next Page.]

Gen. Ambrose Burnside takes center stage on this cover of *Harper's Weekly* from October 24, 1863, following the Union army's takeover of Knoxville from the Confederates, who had controlled the city from 1861 to 1863. The scene captures the ebullient reception Burnside received upon his arrival in Knoxville, where he was afforded a hero's welcome by hundreds of Union sympathizers crowding the streets and waving US flags for days.

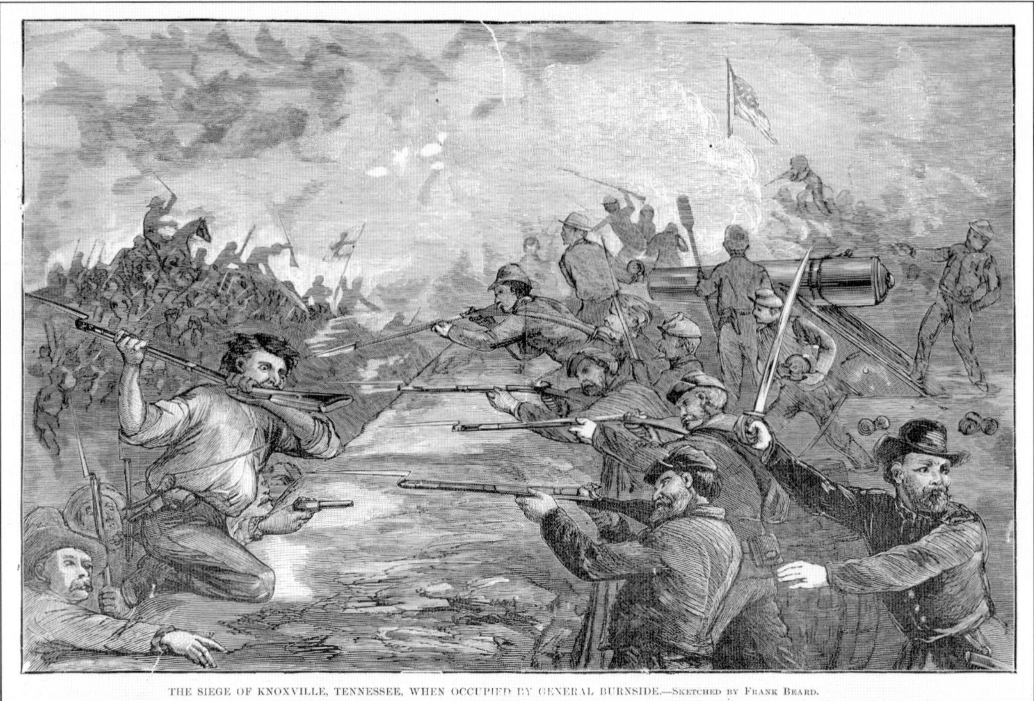
THE SIEGE OF KNOXVILLE, TENNESSEE, WHEN OCCUPIED BY GENERAL BURNSIDE.—SKETCHED BY FRANK BEARD.

Almost three months after General Burnside arrived in Knoxville, the Union army defeated a Confederate charge led by Gen. James Longstreet in a short but catastrophic assault on November 29, 1863—known forever afterwards as the Battle of Fort Sanders. Army sketch artist Frank Beard illustrated what has been described as "the bloodiest 20 minutes of the Civil War," when 129 Confederate soldiers were killed, with many more injured or declared missing, compared to a mere handful of Union casualties.

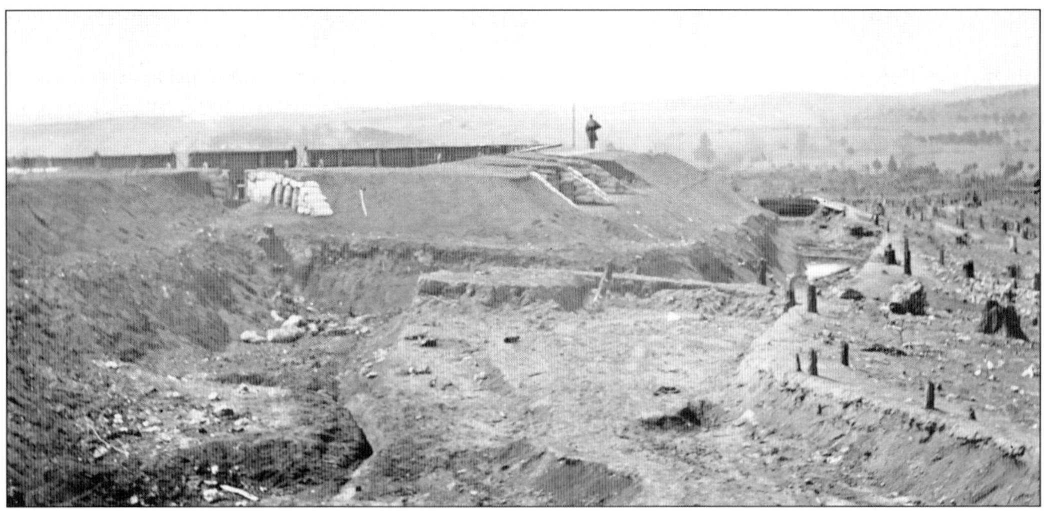
Union Fort Sanders, immediately west of downtown, started out as a Confederate fort. Experienced Union engineer Gen. Orlando Poe was charged with strengthening the fort, which was renamed after the recently slain Gen. William Sanders. In addition to soldiers, locals, including numerous African American residents, worked to quickly fortify the structure and make it battle-ready. This photograph was taken in March 1864, several months after the battle. (Library of Congress.)

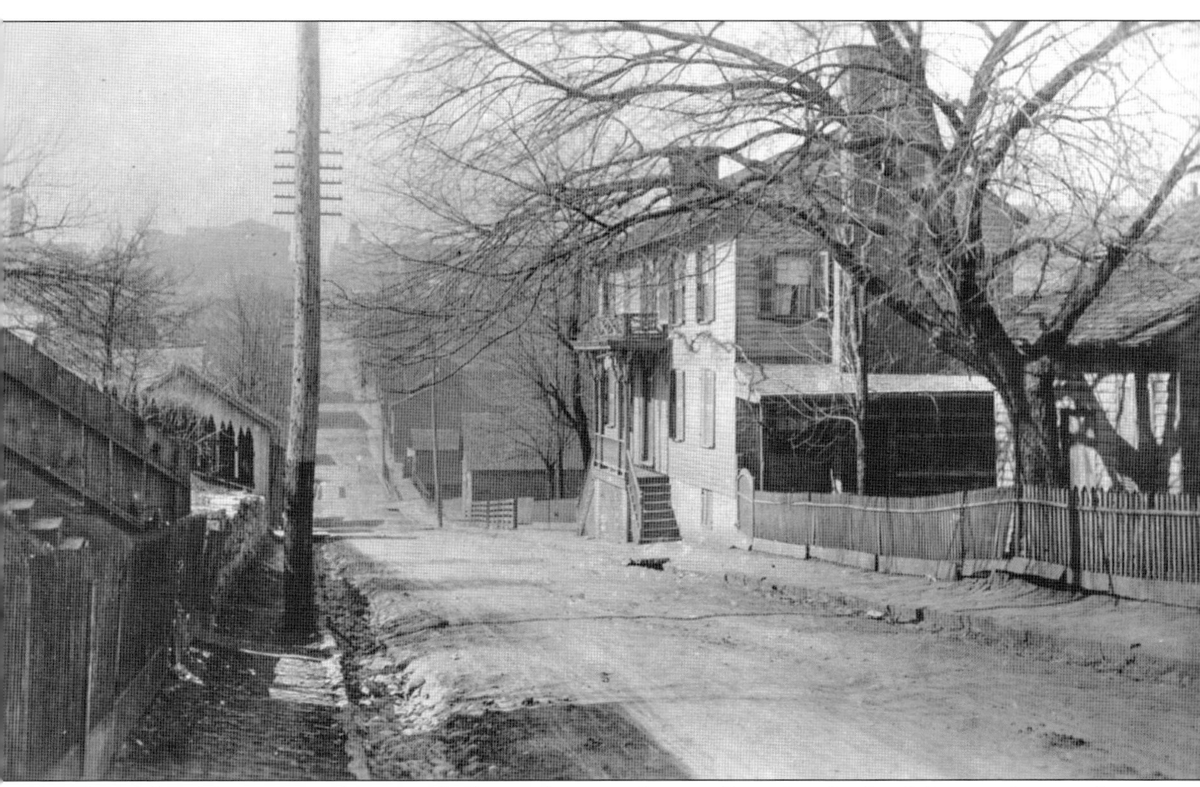

This early-20th-century photograph shows the once-famous East Cumberland Avenue home of "Parson" W.G. Brownlow (1805–1877). The most complicated leader of his era, Brownlow was a Methodist preacher who became the opinionated editor of the pro-slavery but fiercely pro-Union *Knoxville Whig*. He defiantly flew his US flag above this house during Confederate occupation while still publishing the *Whig*. Jailed by Confederates, he was banished to the north. He turned Republican and abolitionist during the war and was elected the unlikely governor of Union-controlled Tennessee. Governor Brownlow manhandled an often-reluctant legislature to extend civil rights and voting privileges to African Americans. After his death in 1877, five Republican presidents, including Teddy Roosevelt, visited his widow, Eliza, in their old home. She died here in 1914 and probably still lived here when young photographer Jim Thompson took this photograph. The house was torn down in the 1920s.

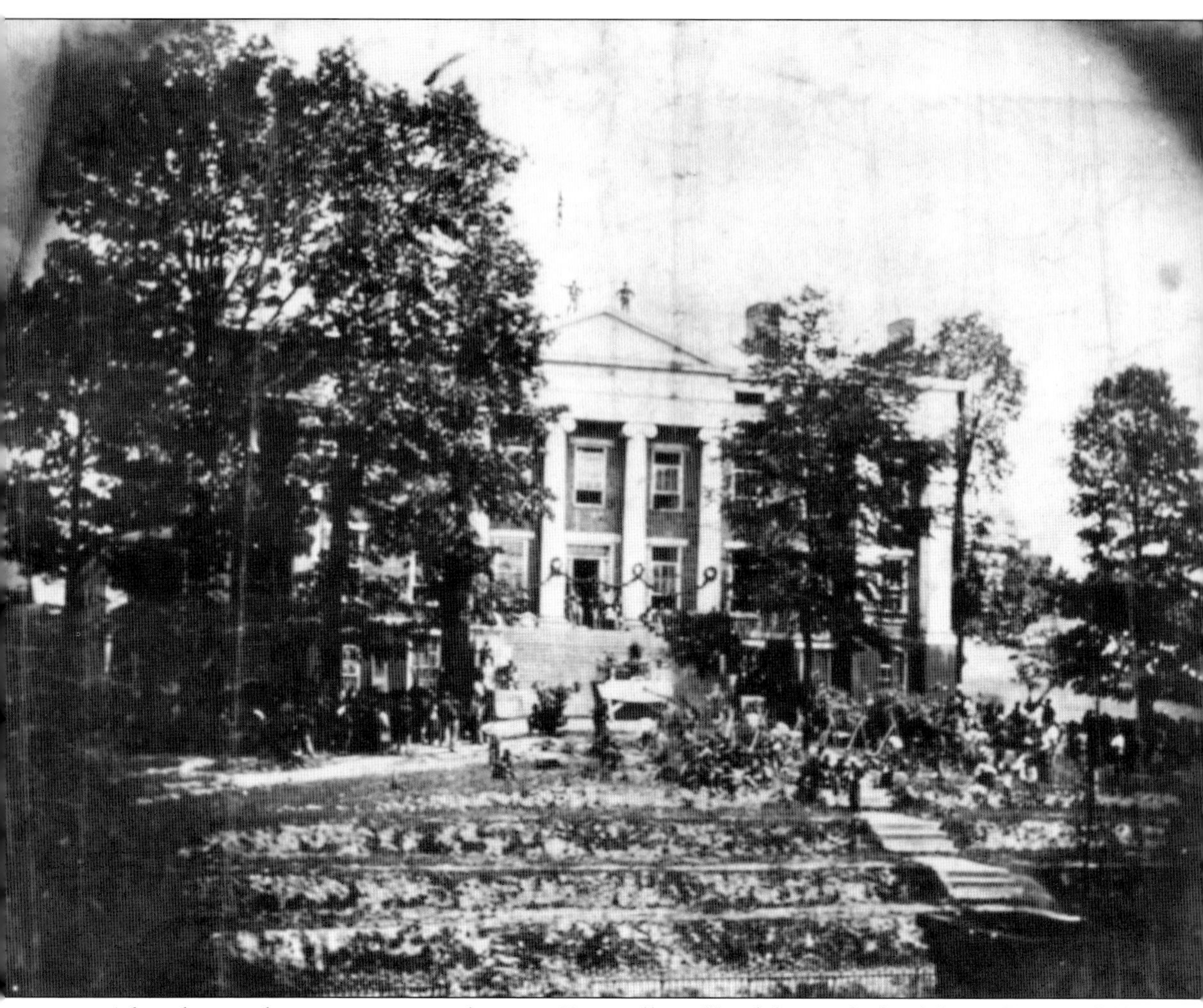

After the city lost its state capital status, Knoxville suffered from a lack of focus. But in 1848, Knoxville made it back on the map when it was chosen for the site of a statewide mental institution, the Deaf and Dumb Asylum, later renamed the Tennessee School for the Deaf. During the Civil War, the asylum ceased operating as a school and transitioned into a hospital to tend to injured soldiers. Seen here around 1863, Confederate soldiers are convalescing on the steps and around the school grounds. The Union army took over the hospital during the last two years of the war. Union soldiers who died here would have been transported for burial at the Knoxville National Cemetery behind Old Gray Cemetery, a few blocks to the north. Today, the building hosts Lincoln Memorial University's law school.

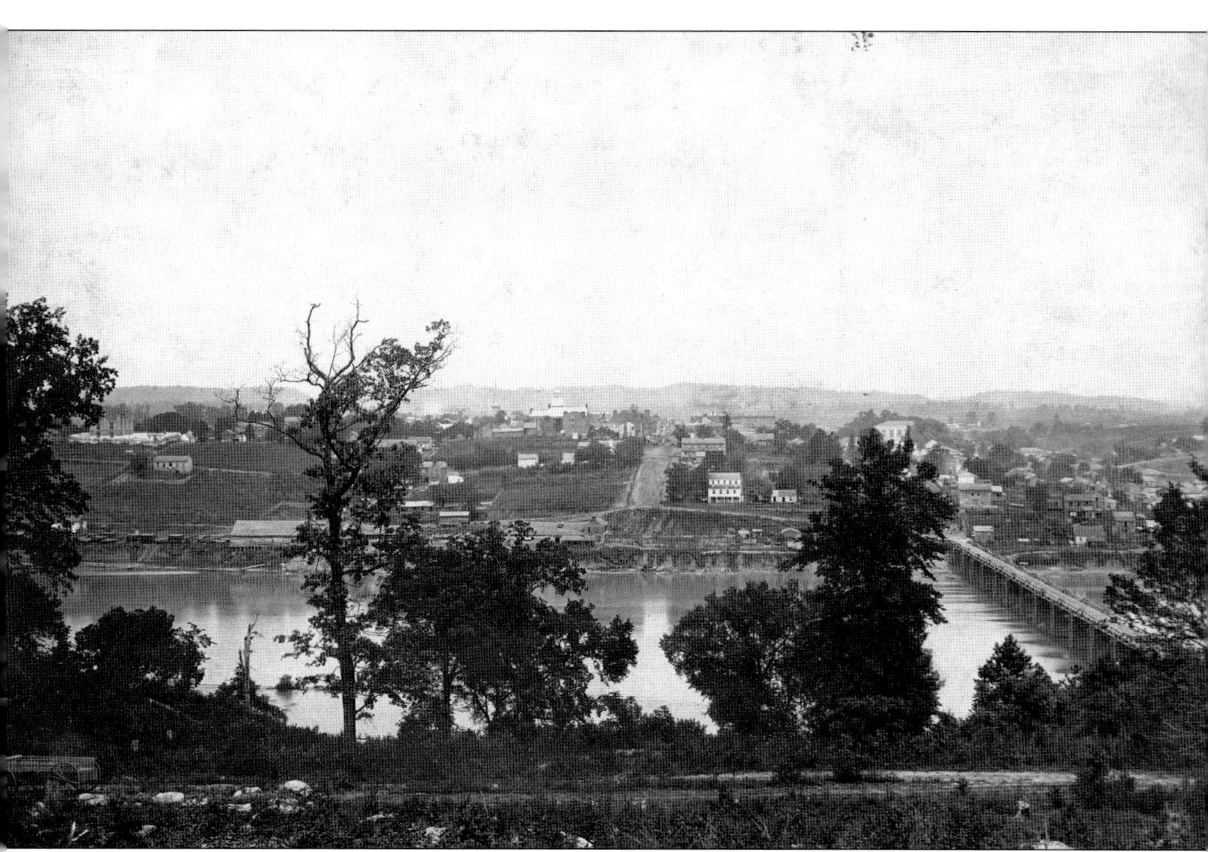

This view of downtown was captured from the southern shore of the Tennessee River during the Civil War. To the right is the first proper bridge, built by Union engineers and soldiers, replacing an earlier pontoon bridge. Note that it is not aligned with Gay Street, like the Gay Street bridge is today, but rather to the east, nearer the mouth of First Creek. In the center of the photograph, the old courthouse with its cupola can be seen on Main Street, surrounded by a cluster of buildings. On the far left is the old turreted military prison, once known as Castle Fox, which was demolished by the mid-1870s. (Library of Congress.)

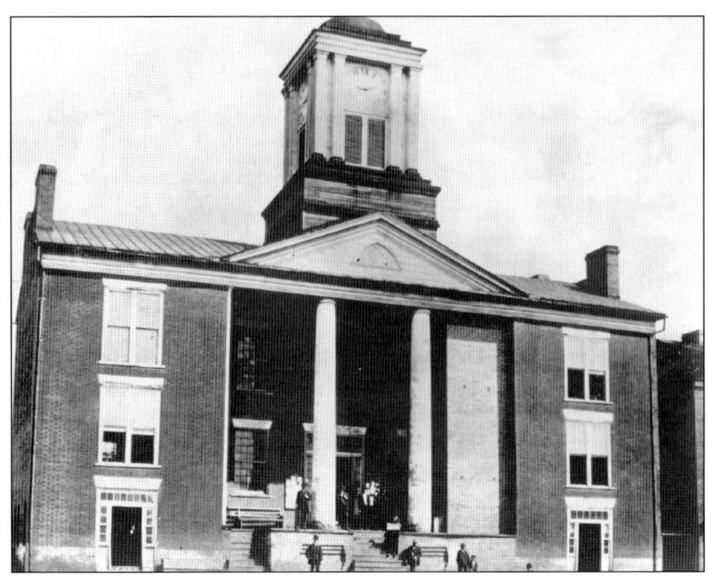

Over the years, Knoxville has seen four different county courthouses situated around the corner of Gay and Main Streets. This substantial third iteration, completed in 1842, was designed and built by John Dameron, who sold land north of downtown to form Old Gray Cemetery in 1850. It was Knox County's courthouse throughout the Civil War era. Its site is now occupied by the eastern wing of the federal courthouse. (University of Tennessee Libraries.)

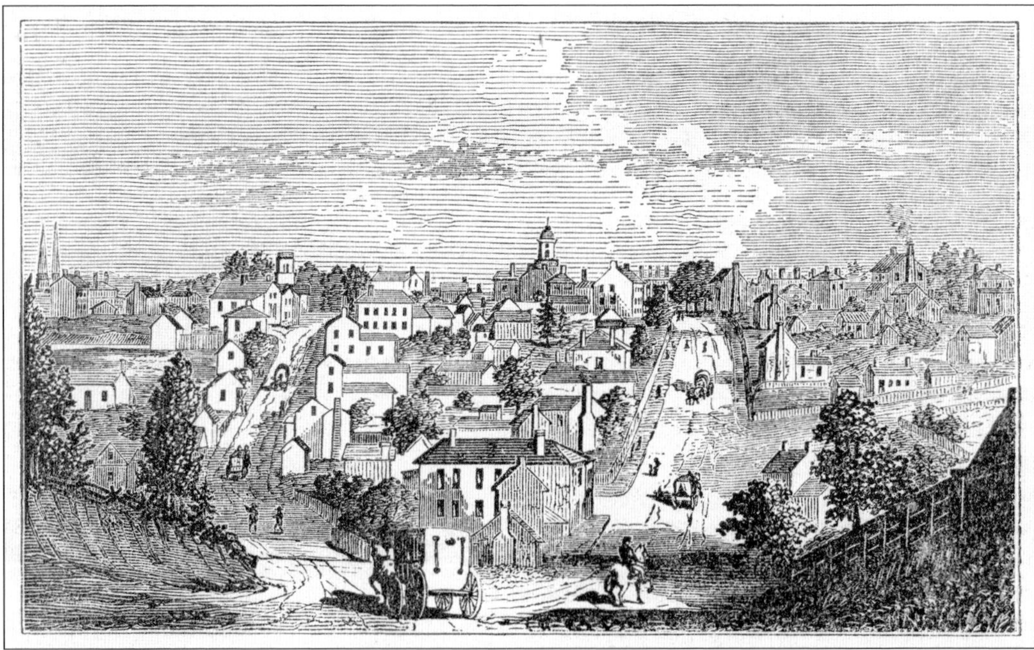

This mid-19th-century illustration, *Southwestern View of Knoxville*, shows the view of downtown from the foot of the university hill on Cumberland Avenue. The courthouse cupola can be seen on the horizon at center, while the fork where Cumberland Avenue and Main Street (to the right) meet is about where Eleventh Street and Cumberland Avenue intersect today. (Knoxville History Project.)

Unceasing rain led to the "Great Freshet" of 1867, when much of downtown was under water for several days. First and Second Creeks swelled their banks, and for a time, joined Flag Pond adjacent to the railroad tracks in the north section, leaving downtown an island surrounded by swirling water. The city's first bridge across the river washed away, as did houses and factories along the waterfront, including the gas works.

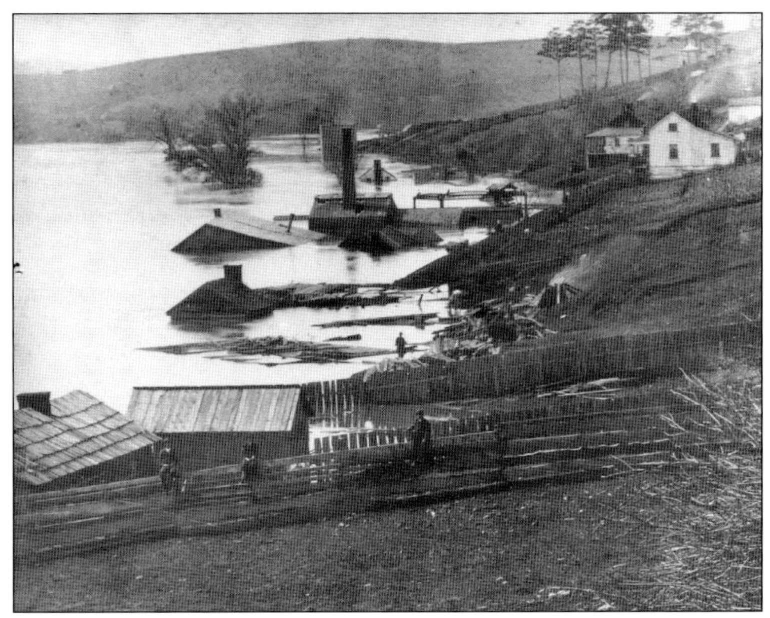

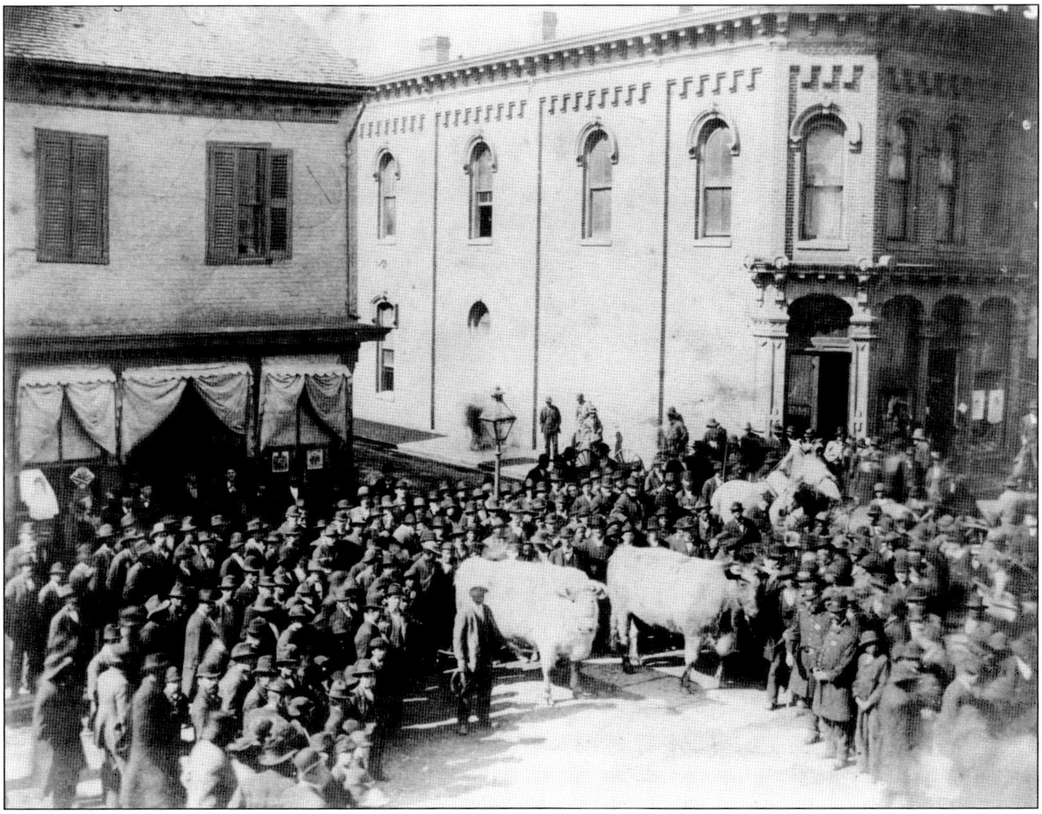

This photograph, taken in 1877 in front of the Fouché Building on the corner of Gay Street and Clinch Avenue, shows a crowd gathered around two prize steers owned by wealthy Massachusetts-born businessman Perez Dickinson. That same year, Dickinson purchased a massive 408-pound hog, which he hoped to further fatten on his Island Home farm across the river.

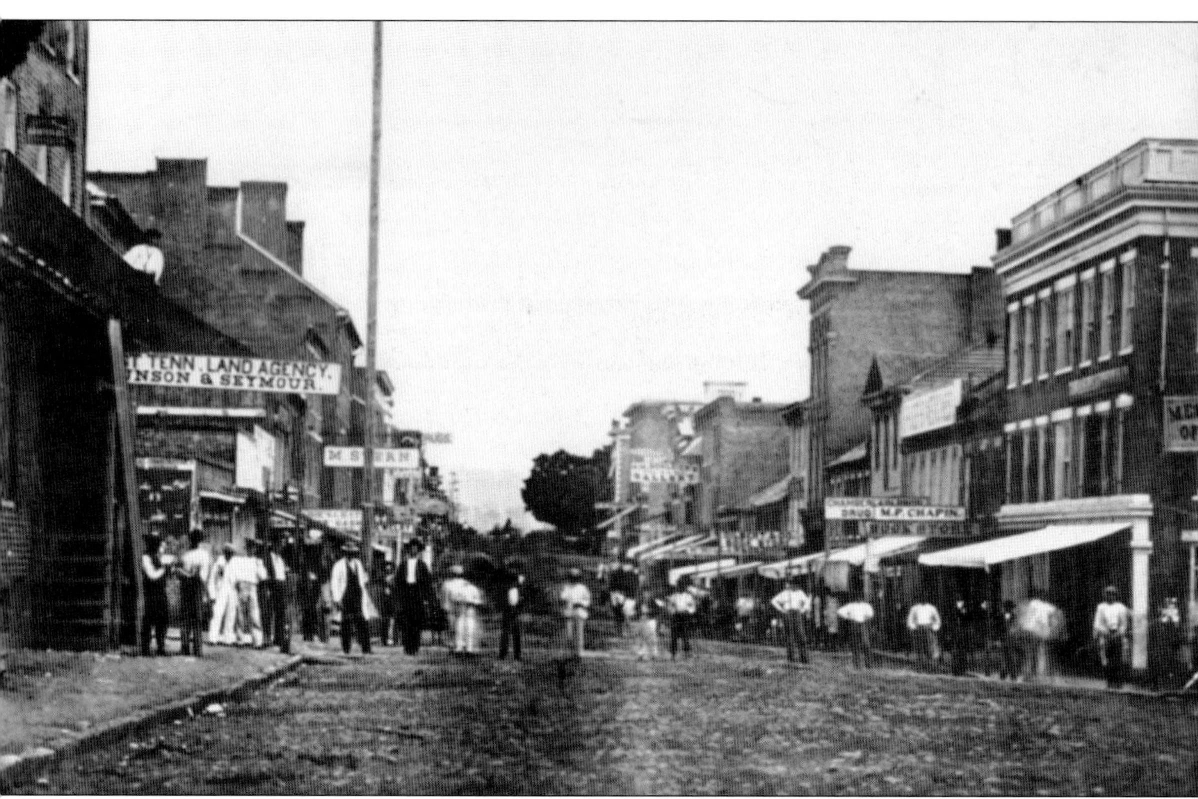

This rare 1869 street scene offers a glimpse of rough-edged postwar Knoxville. On the left in this view, looking north on Gay Street from Main Street, are a sign for M. (Moses) Stern, a Jewish clothier, along with the East Tennessee Land Agency, offering 200 tracts in the Knoxville area. Visible on the right are two bookstores, including that of Capt. M.P. Chapin, a former Union officer, who ran a second-floor shop advertising sheet music, Dickens novels, and chess sets. Prussian-born T.M. Schleier was the resourceful "photographist" who likely took this picture. The *Messenger of Peace* was a religious weekly that aspired to "heal the bleeding wounds of our country." The copse of trees in the distance are in the yard of the Crozier family at Clinch Avenue. The event that prompted a dozen men to stand athwart Gay Street is lost to history.

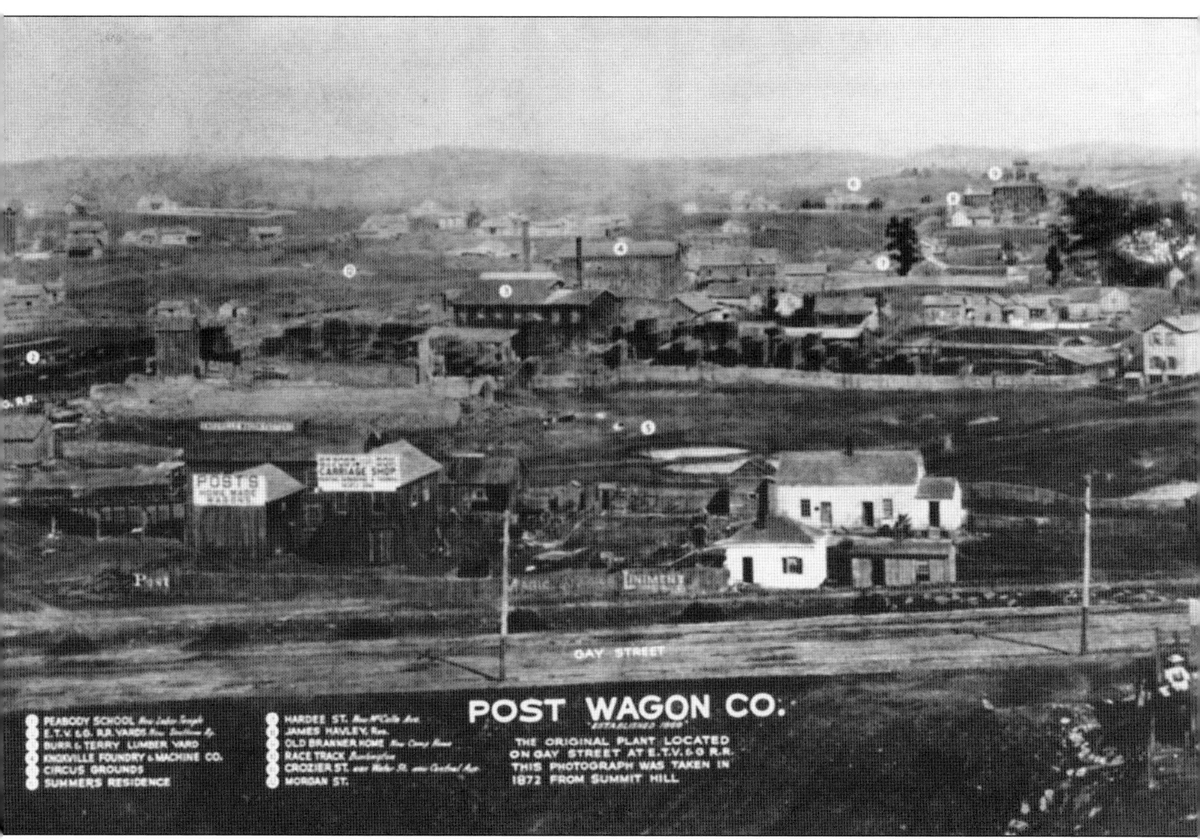

Looking east across the northern end of Gay Street in the 1870s provides an insight into what was happening in the mid- to late 1800s in the area that is known today as the "Old City." The East Tennessee, Virginia & Georgia Railroad was redefining the use of the area, home of the Post Wagon Company, a wagon and buggy manufacturer, in the foreground. Post still exists as a trailer-repair company on Sutherland Avenue, arguably Knoxville's oldest business. Behind it is the Burr and Terry Sawmill. The open land separating those two businesses formed the old Circus Grounds. At upper left is the new Peabody School, the only building in the photograph that still stands today, now serving as the Democratic Party headquarters on Morgan Street. (McClung, Thompson Photograph Collection.)

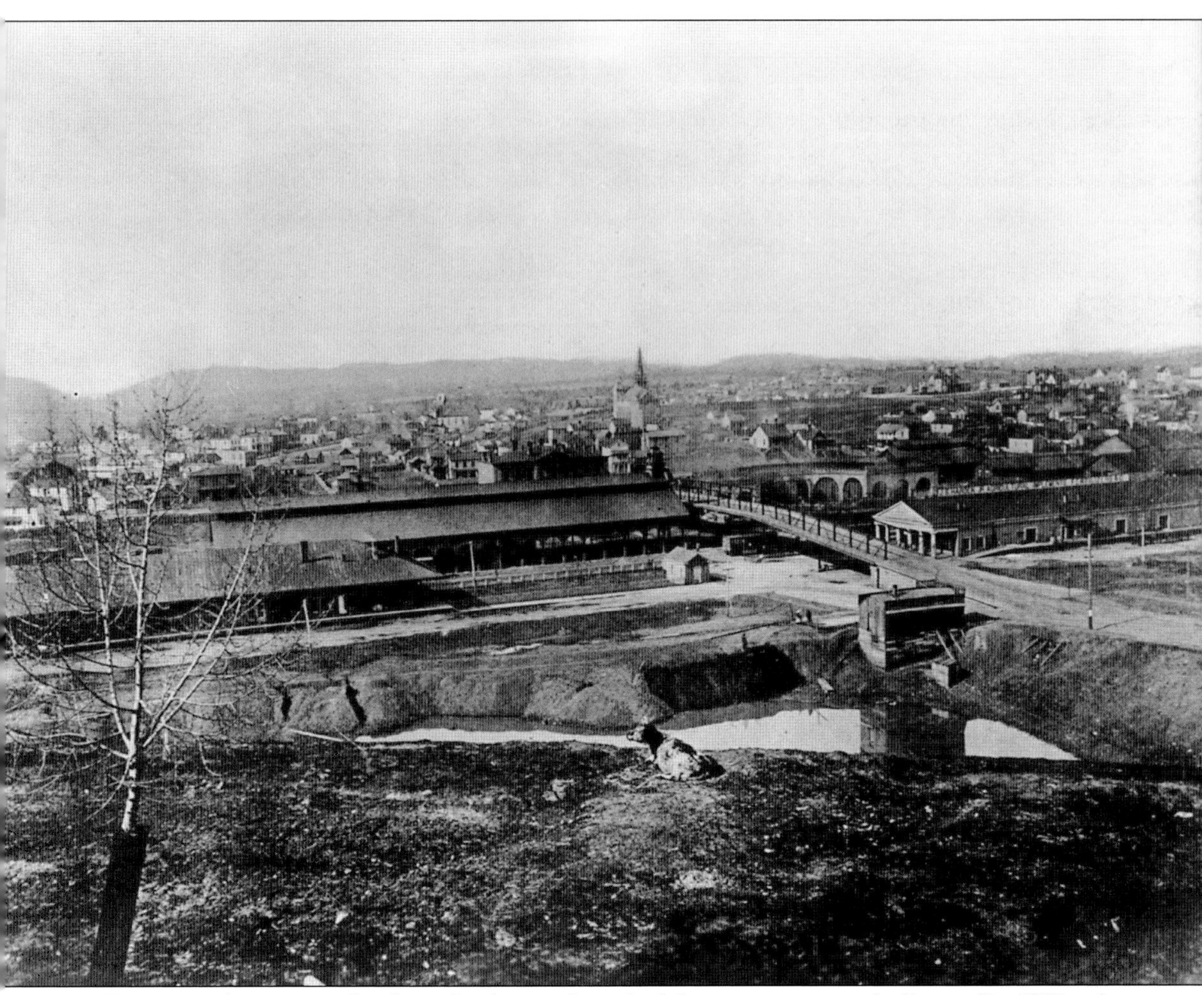

For years, the swampy land on the far north end of downtown was a challenge. By 1872, when this photograph was taken, Flag Pond was a small remnant of its former self, but it attracted at least one cow, giving the area a rural feeling—despite the East Tennessee, Virginia & Georgia Railroad station dominating the center of the photograph. The building on the right, just above the pond, is the Peter Ricardi Confectionery, an Italian-owned business on Gay Street. The area was not completely drained and filled to facilitate development on the 100 block of Gay Street until the late 19th century.

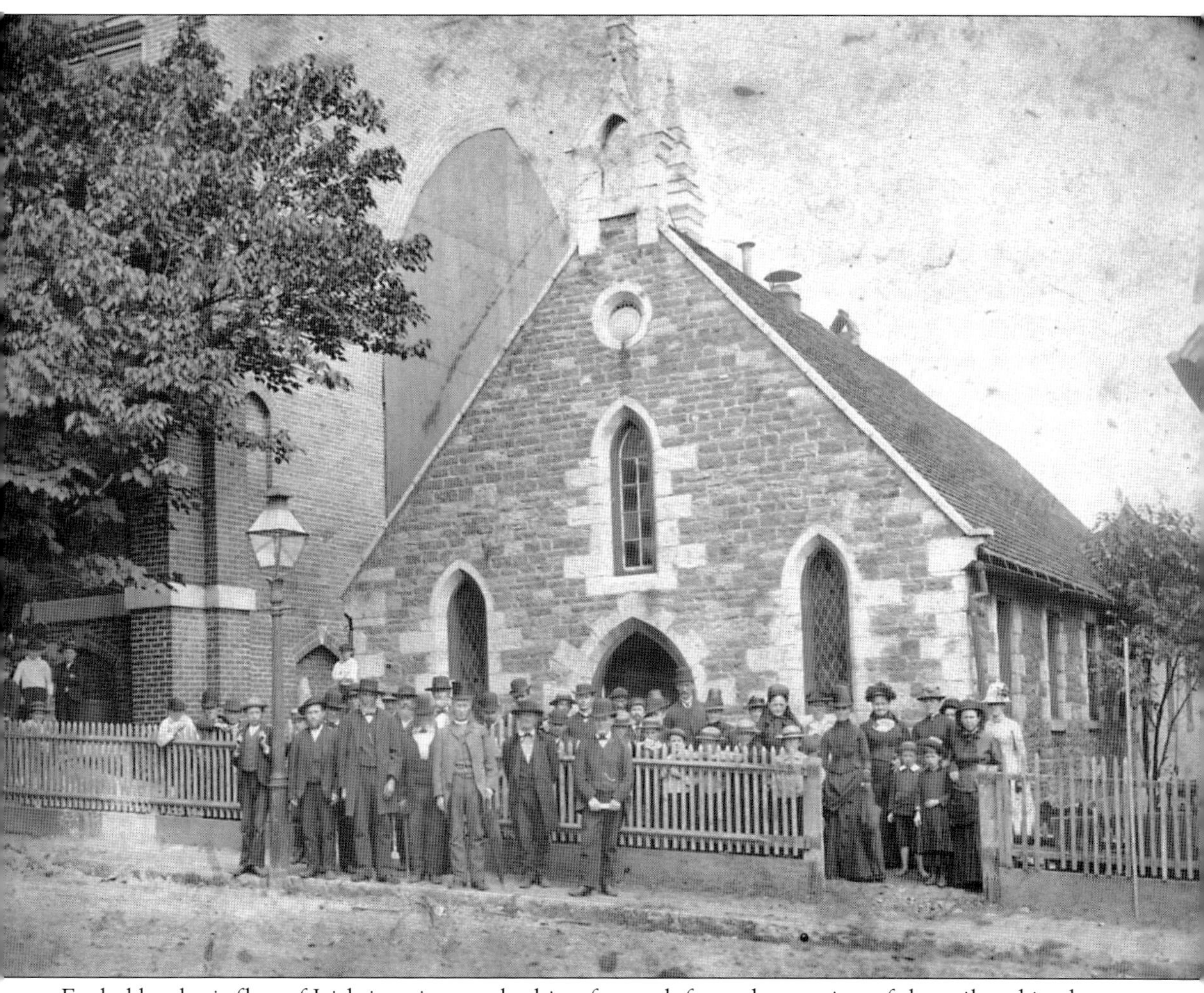

Fueled by the influx of Irish immigrants looking for work from the coming of the railroad in the mid-1850s, Knoxville's Catholic community began to grow. This photograph from 1886 shows a group of parishioners on Walnut Street with the original stone church behind them. To the left, the much larger church that replaced it was new when this photograph was taken. Note the early gas lamp on the street.

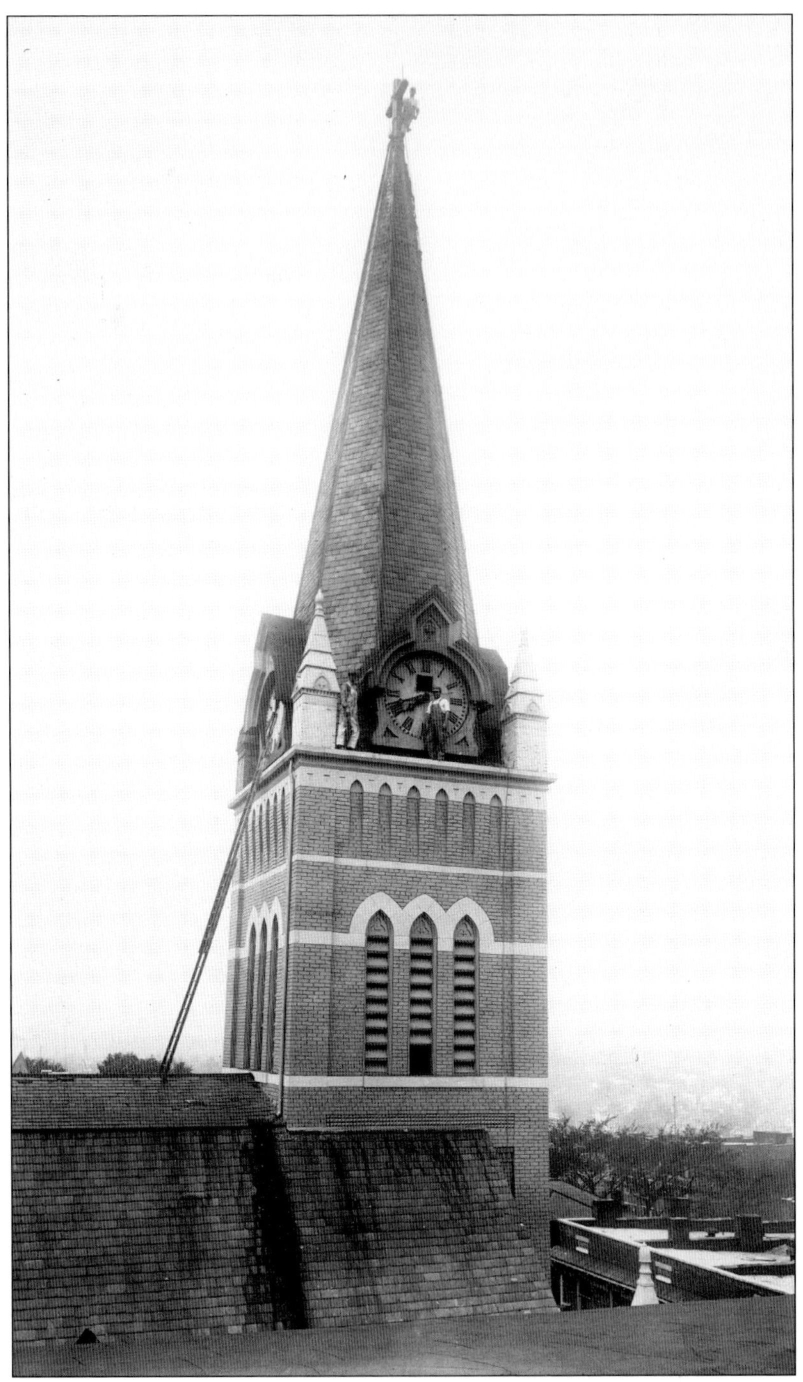

This 1920s photograph of the Immaculate Conception Church tells an interesting downtown story. Designed by Knoxville's Baumann Brothers, the church and steeple faced north across the railroad tracks toward the immigrant community known as Irish Town. Initially, there were no plans for the spire to house a clock, but the city offered to finance a four-sided clock to serve all residents of the town since it would be visible from other downtown points from the first railroad station on Depot Street to Market Square. (McClung, Thompson Photograph Collection.)

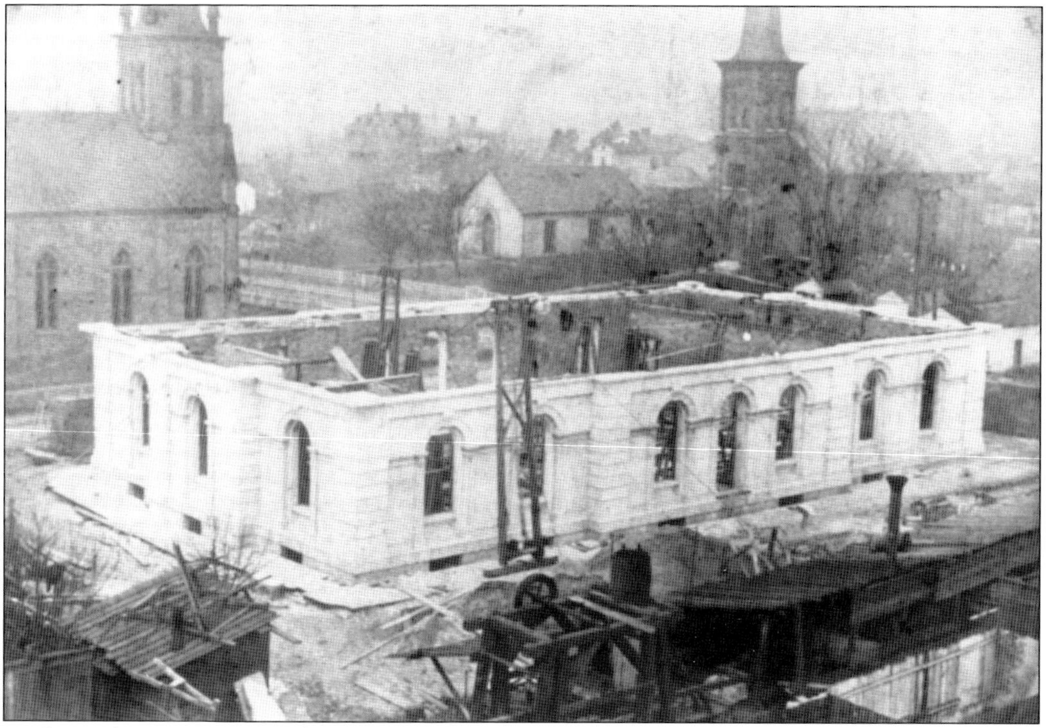

In the early 1870s, Knoxville was growing at such a rate that a new US post office and custom house was planned for the corner of Clinch Avenue and Prince Street (later Market Street). Designed by US Treasury Department architect Alfred Mullet, the building was constructed using local Tennessee marble between 1871 and 1874. Here, construction has only reached the first floor. Two early churches are clearly visible in the background: on the left is the First Methodist Episcopal Church, and on the right is the Second Presbyterian Church. (McClung, Small Photograph Collection.)

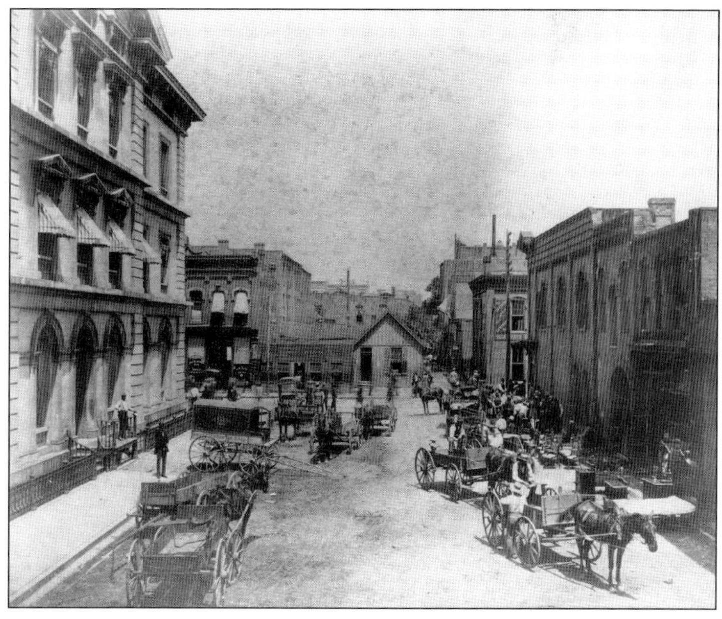

Until a new wing was added on the custom house in 1910, a plaza existed between the building and the Fouche Block on Gay Street. In this photograph looking north toward an alley in the background, at least one mail carriage sits outside the entrance to the post office. On the right, a group of merchants with empty wagons is engaged in what might be a public auction or sale, given the array of chairs, cabinets, and beds on display. (McClung, Thompson Photograph Collection.)

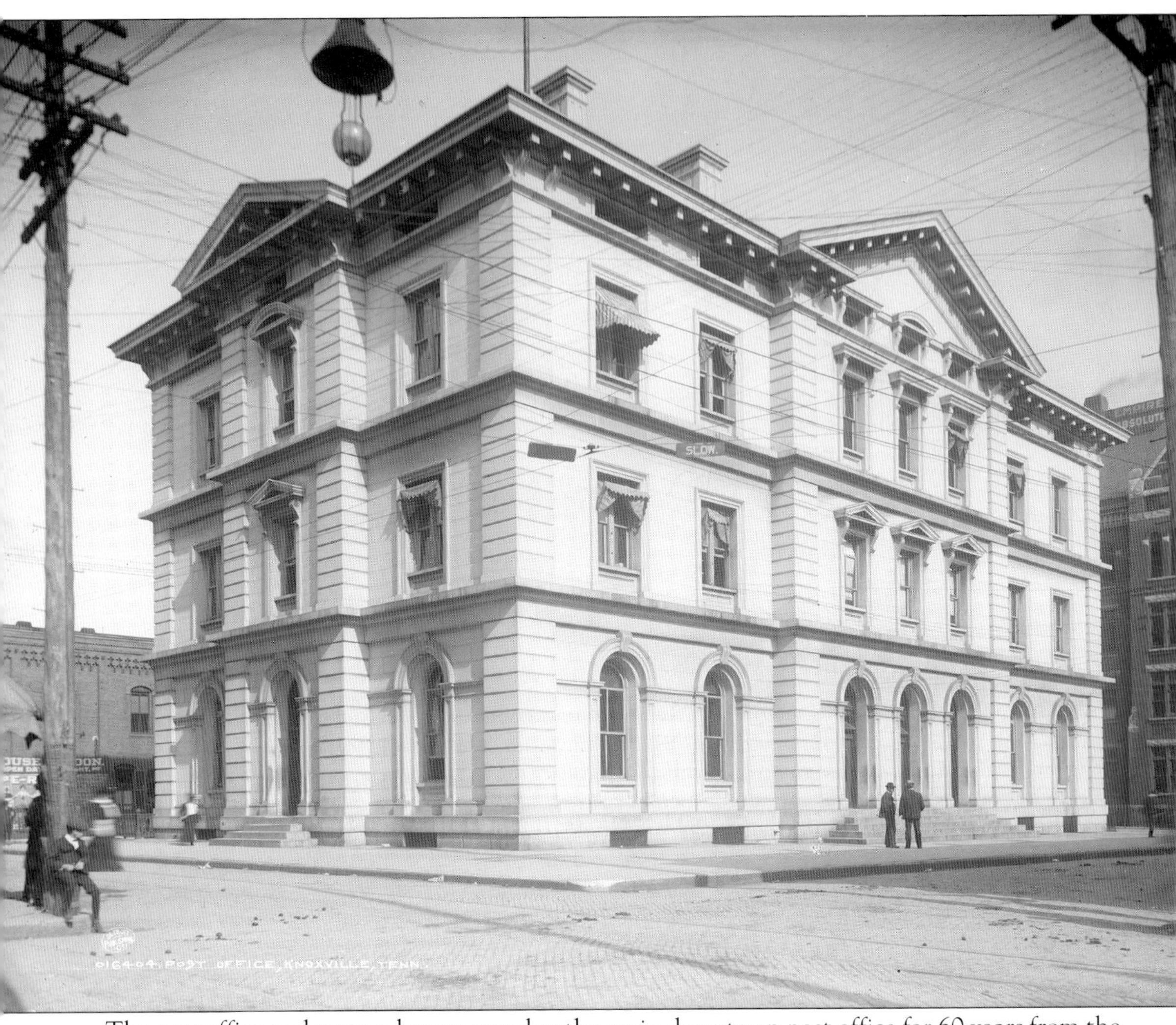

The post office and custom house served as the main downtown post office for 60 years from the time of its completion in 1874 until 1934, when operations moved to a new building on Main Street at Walnut Street. Mail delivery service in Knoxville started around 1883; until then, Knoxville residents had to visit the general post office here on Market Street to get their mail. For a time, an office existed to regulate local commerce, and the custom house name persisted. A federal courtroom occupied the third floor. One of the most infamous cases was that of outlaw Harvey Logan, also known as "Kid Curry," one of Butch Cassidy's "Wild Bunch." Curry was arrested in a downtown saloon in 1901 and spent 18 months in the county jail before his dramatic escape.

Three

Boom Town

Following the Civil War, Knoxville slowly began to recapture its pre-war momentum. Between 1870 and 1900, the city and its opportunities drew newcomers from all over the western world. By 1900, over 30,000 people lived within walking distance of downtown, with all of the amenities needed for daily sustenance and opportunities for comfort and entertainment just down the sidewalk.

By the mid-1880s, Knoxvillians may have felt that the city had finally grown up. A new county courthouse rose on Main Street, the city established an official fire department, and a much grander Lawson McGhee Library crowned a run of cultural improvements that began in 1872 when Staub's Opera House began attracting vaudeville shows, lectures, concerts, music festivals, and occasionally operas.

By the time Knoxville was a century old, it was a modern urban city. Flickering gas lamps were yielding to electric streetlamps, which brightened its streets and avenues. Still, gunfights on Gay Street and in the Central Street "Bowery" interrupted the city's fashionable prosperity.

Knoxville was a boom town. Fueled by the local iron, lumber, furniture, coal, textile, and marble industries (Knoxville justly earned its nickname, the Marble City) and enabled by railroad connections that served other markets, downtown now had a signature post office and custom house, a new courthouse, a new train station, and even the Woman's Building, hosting galleries, studios, and an auditorium. Shoppers were well served by inviting stores such as Newcomers and George's Department Stores. Arnstein's lured shoppers from across the region, as Kern's emporium tempted them with its ice cream parlor, soda fountains, and German-inspired candy.

The arrival of the electric streetcar in 1890 enabled everyone who could afford a token to get around the city, offering a chance to escape the city's smog with a ride to Chilhowee Park. For many, the completion of a new Market House in 1897, nestled back-to back with City Hall, would come to exemplify downtown's sights, sounds, and smells for the next 60 years.

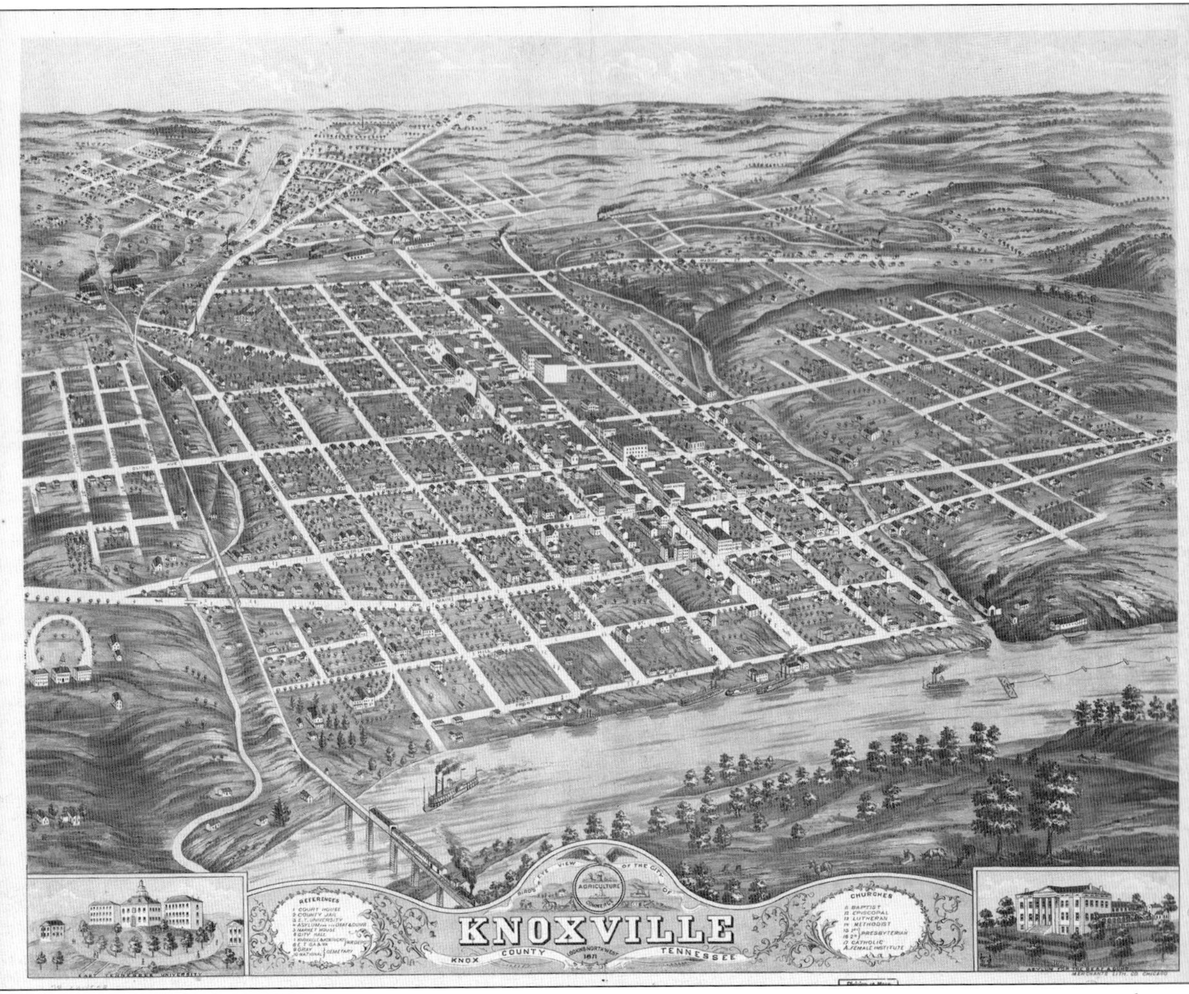

This bird's-eye view of Knoxville from 1871, published by Merchants Lithographic Company of Chicago, shows the city moving beyond the Civil War era and about to enter a period of growth. The town is beginning to expand eastward and also to the west where East Tennessee University (now the University of Tennessee), just off the map, is highlighted by an illustration at bottom left. At bottom right, another illustration depicts the Asylum of the Deaf and Dumb, later the Tennessee School for the Deaf, as one of Knoxville's most prominent buildings, which still stands today as part of Lincoln Memorial University. Knoxville had not yet replaced the bridge lost in the flood of 1867, and Knoxvillians had to rely on ferry service to get across the river here. The first Market House and the first City Hall are visible on Market Square just above the center of the map. (Library of Congress.)

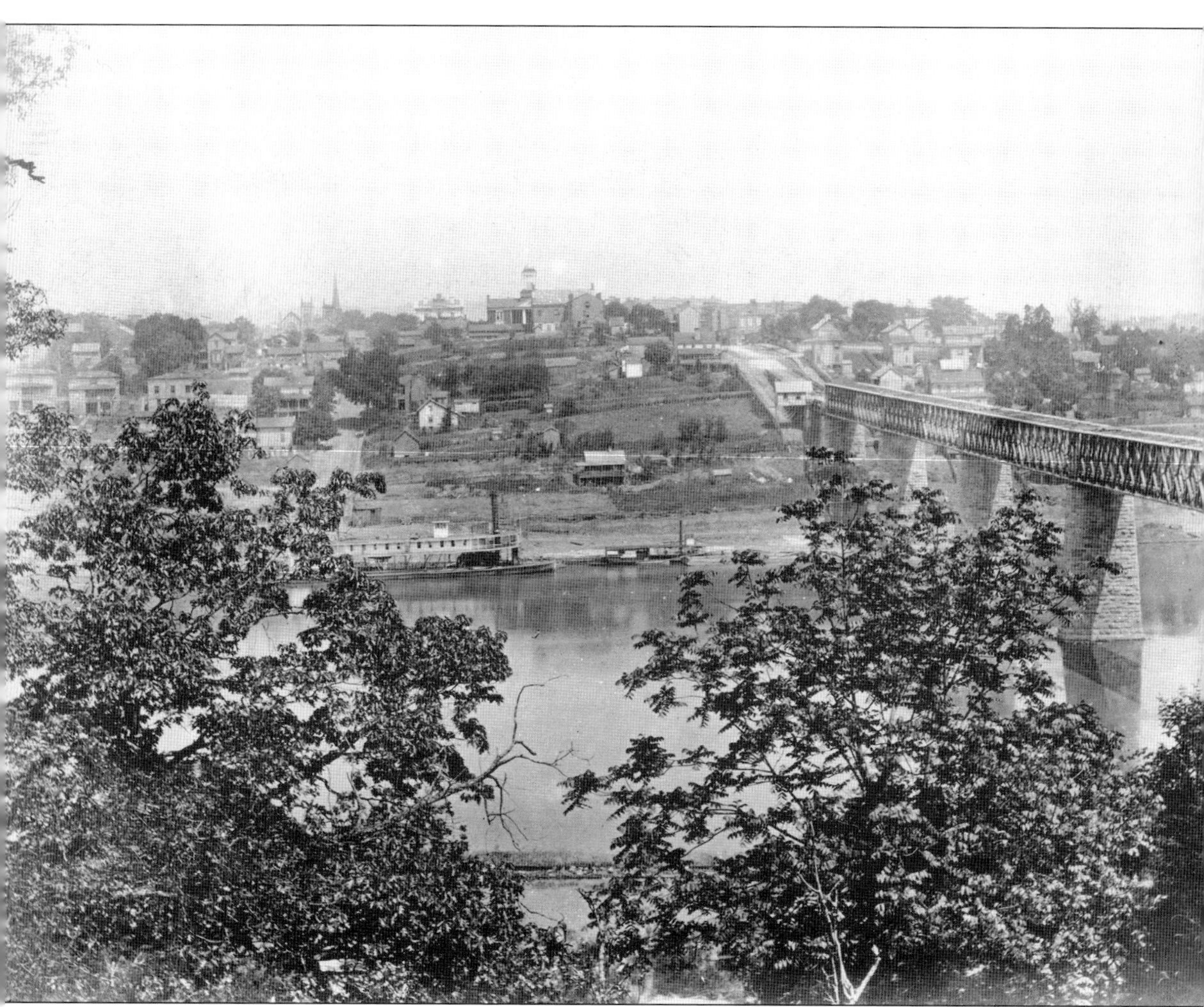

This photograph, taken from the southern heights near Fort Dickerson, shows a reviving city. At right is the third permanent bridge across the Tennessee River not long after it had been constructed about 1880. This bridge replaced an earlier bridge that was destroyed by strong winds in 1875, and an even earlier one that washed away in the flood of 1867. In the days long before effective sanitation, refuse was often dumped directly in the river through a hatch in the middle of the bridge. The riverfront appears to be largely undeveloped, likely due to frequent flooding. Boats docked either at First Creek or Prince Street (now Market Street) when it led down directly to the riverfront where the long steamboat in this photograph appears to be moored.

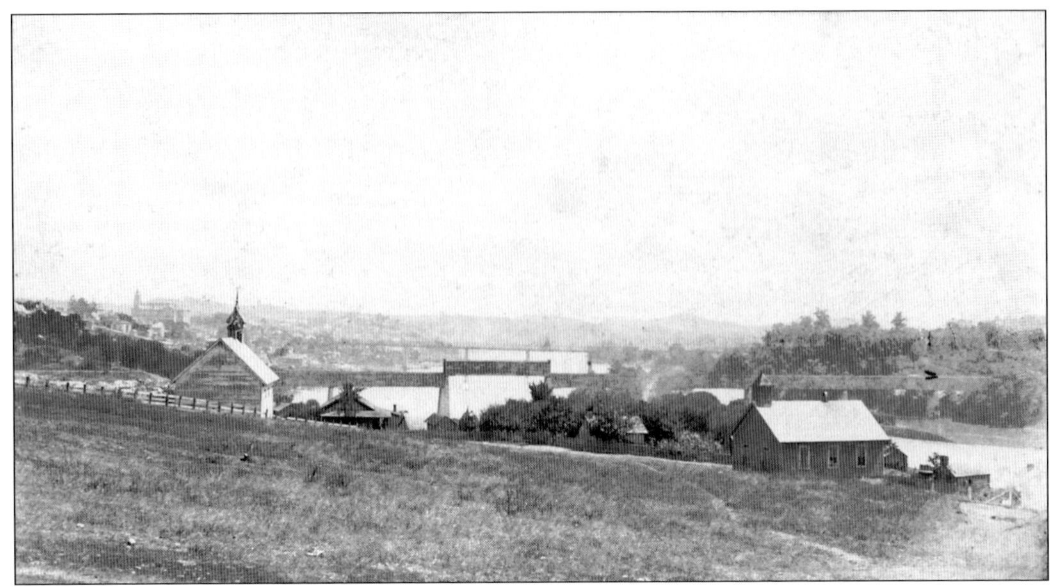

The city is viewed along the Tennessee River when approached from the west, near the University of Tennessee campus, around 1880. The building in the foreground, likely a church, would have been on Clifton Street, just one street away from Circle Park when it was still a residential area. Across the river, the Knoxville and Augusta Railroad bridge led to points south, especially Maryville.

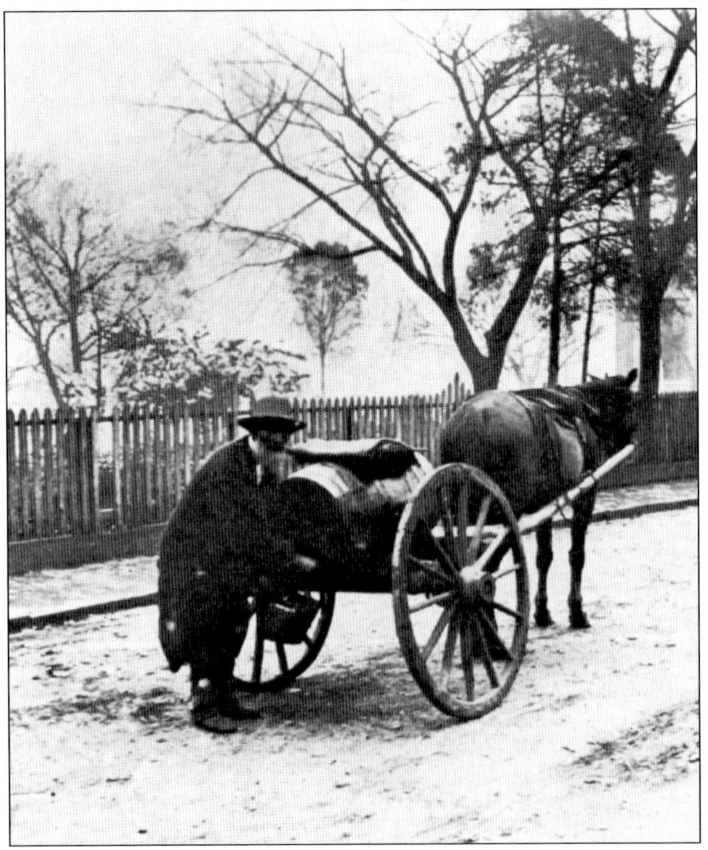

Richard "Uncle Dick" Payne (c. 1812–1891) operated "Knoxville's Original Water Works" long before the city provided its residents with running water. For almost 40 years, he used a mule-drawn, two-wheeled cart fitted with a large barrel to distribute fresh water. For Knoxvillians who lacked a well or a spring, Payne was the city's primary source of clean water, so remarkable he was described in *Harper's Weekly* in 1858. (Knoxville History Project.)

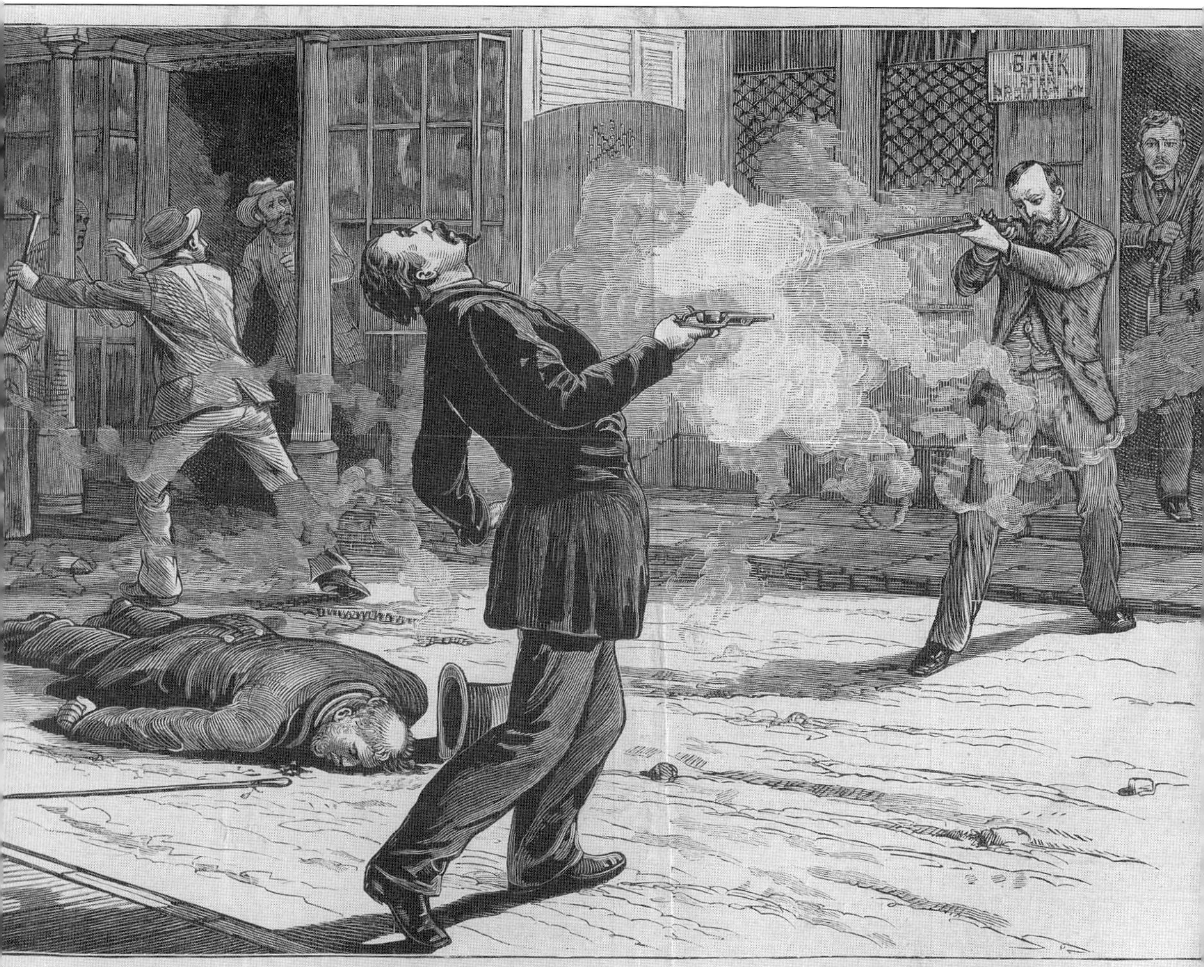

In an era when gunfights were fairly common, one notorious shootout on Gay Street in 1882 surpassed them all. Businessman and land speculator Joseph Mabry, who co-founded Market Square in 1854, had a long-running feud with banker Thomas O'Conner. In October 1882, Mabry approached the Mechanics Bank Building on Gay Street and was shot down by O'Conner. At the same time, Mabry's son Joseph Jr. fired at O'Conner. All three were killed, and several bystanders were wounded. This 1882 drawing is from the *Illustrated Police News*. Mark Twain included an account of the bizarre incident in his 1883 book *Life on the Mississippi*. O'Conner's bank building, though much enlarged, is still there at 612 South Gay Street. (Library of Congress.)

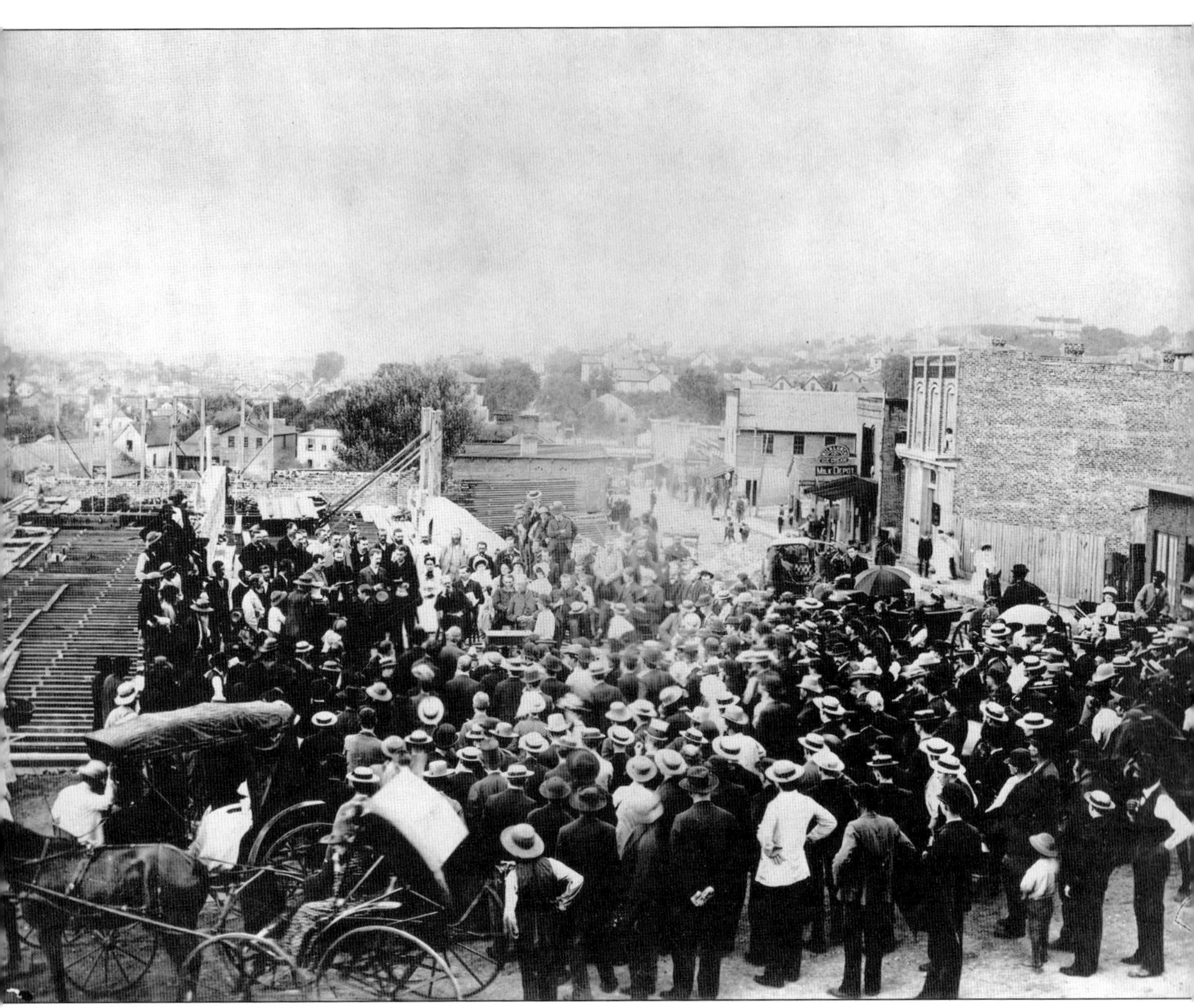

The laying of the cornerstone of the first Lawson McGhee Library occurred in July 1885. Located on Gay Street at Vine Avenue, the three-story building opened its doors to the public in October 1886. The building was dedicated in memory of May Lawson McGhee Williams, the daughter of Knoxville industrialist Charles McClung McGhee. She had died giving birth in New York two years before. The Lawson McGhee Library, now in its fourth incarnation on West Church Avenue, became the first durable public library in Tennessee. Today, the original Gay Street building is known as the Rebori Building after Fiorenzo Rebori, an Italian immigrant who sold fruit and peanuts in a lean-to building alongside the library. After the library was damaged by a fire, Rebori purchased the building in 1915.

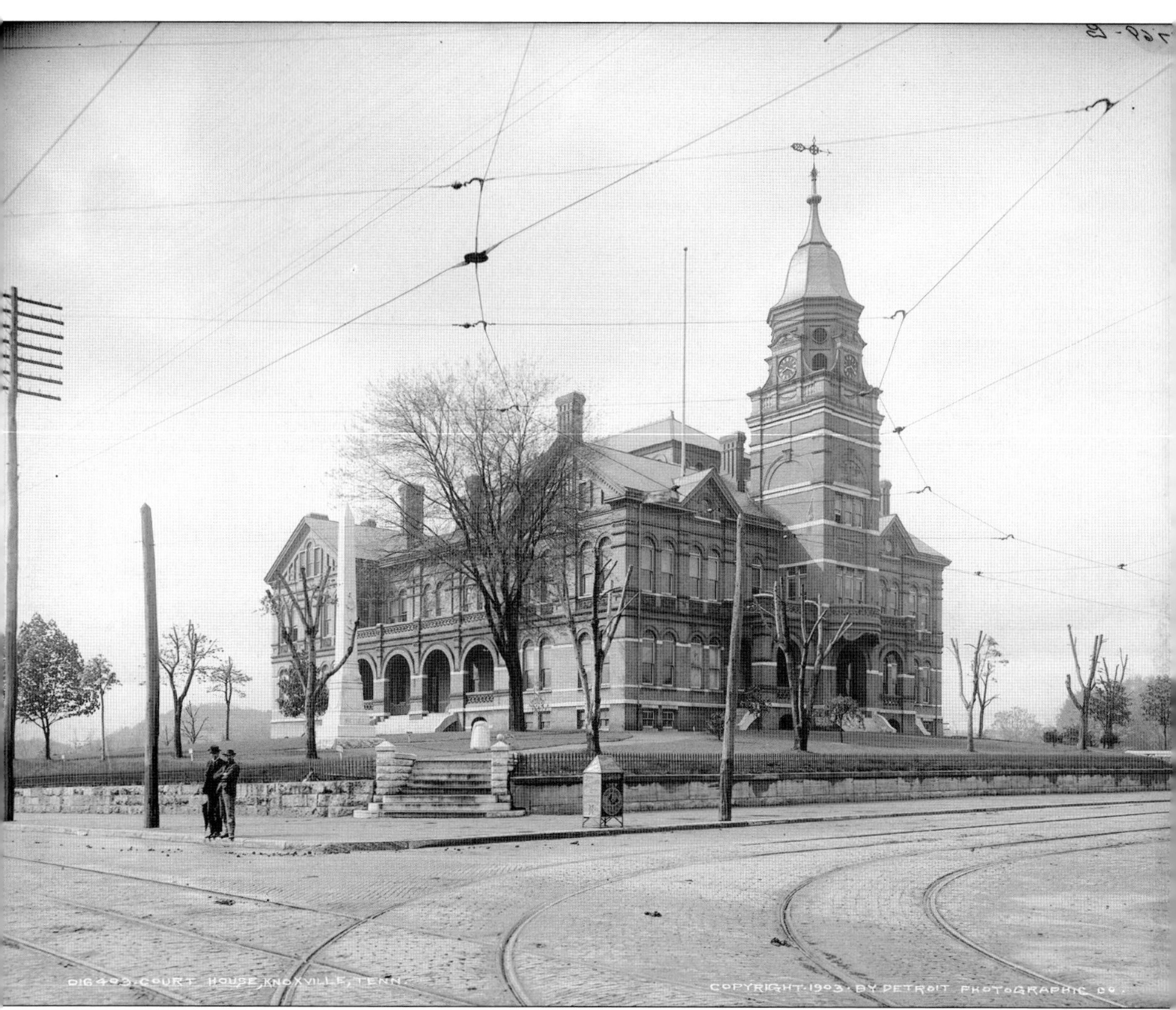

The fourth Knox County Courthouse to be built on Main Street is shown here around 1900. The central part of the building was designed by Palliser and Palliser and completed by Christopher Stephenson and David Getaz, Knoxville architects who came from England and France, respectively. The building is mostly intact but enlarged with wings that have obscured the arched cloister on the eastern side. The white obelisk at left marks the burial place of Tennessee's first governor, John Sevier (1745–1815), reinterred here in 1889, seventy-four years after his death and hasty burial in the Alabama wilderness. (Library of Congress.)

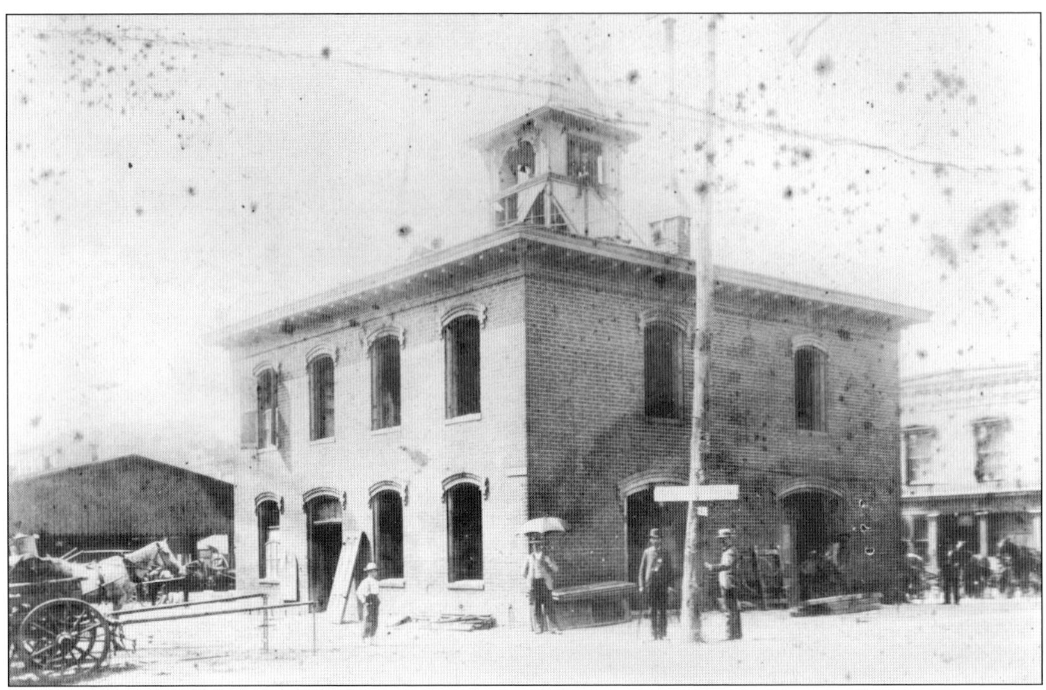

Throughout the city's earliest days, city officials kept offices at the courthouse and in other buildings. By the 1850s, officials sought a dedicated location, but it was not until after the Civil War that a solution was found. The first City Hall, built on the north end of Market Square in 1868, contained council rooms, offices for law enforcement, and a garage for a fire engine.

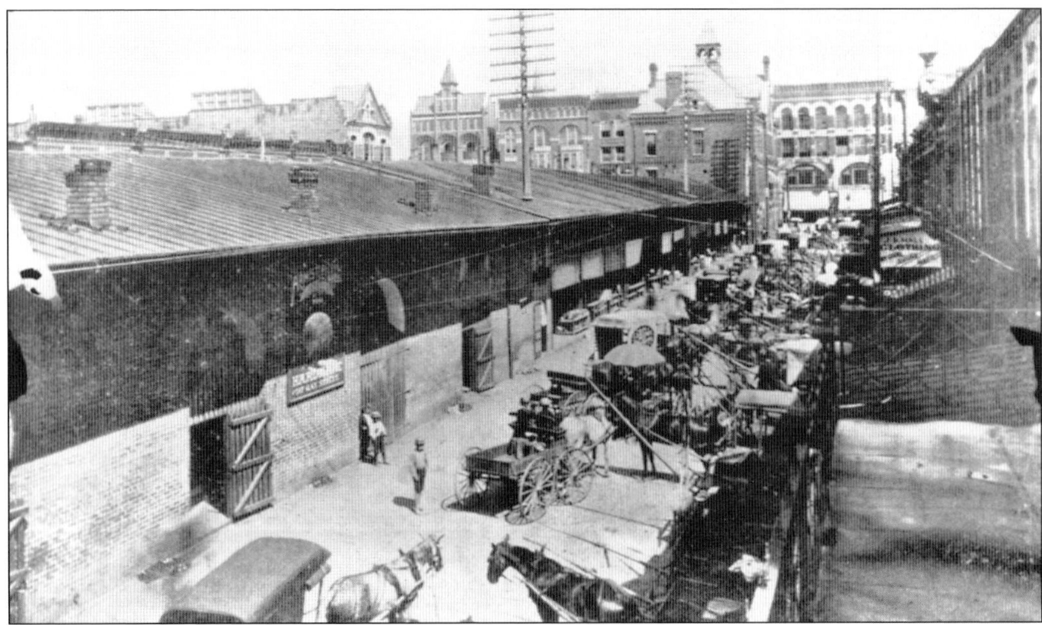

Several years after the Civil War, the first Market House expanded to connect from the southern end of Market Square to an enlarged City Hall, as seen in the background of this photograph taken from the southeastern corner. In this scene from around 1889, farmers park their mule-drawn wagons along the eastern alley.

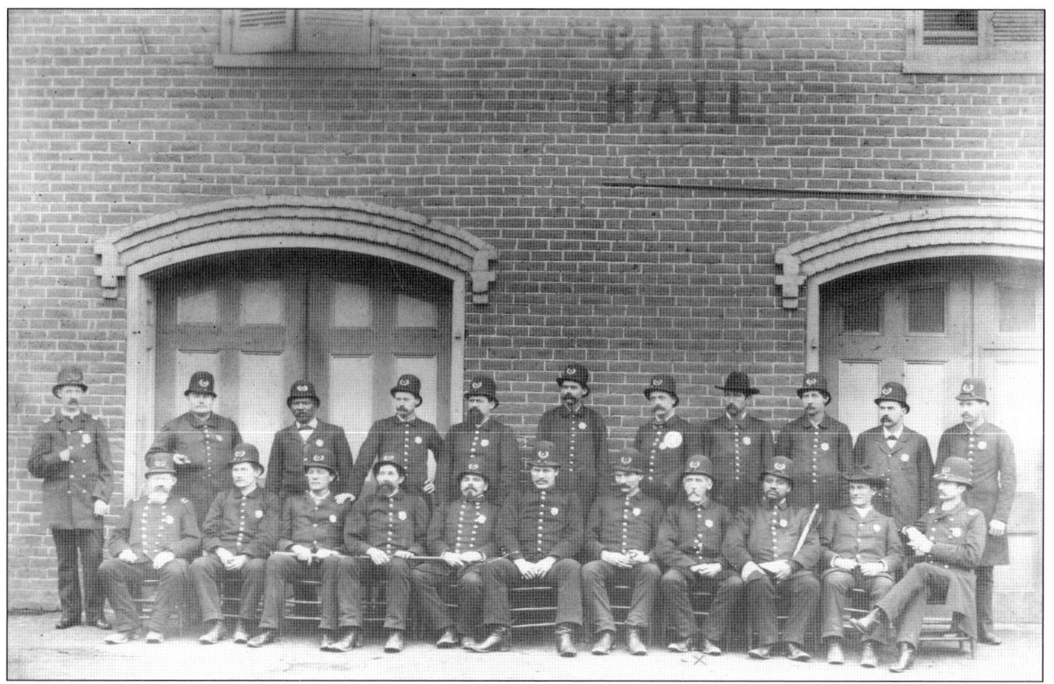

By around 1877, when this group photograph was taken, the town's modest police force was headquartered in City Hall. Featured are two African American police officers: James Mason (second row, third from left) and Hugh B. Draper (first row, third from right). Few cities in America had Black officers before the 1900s.

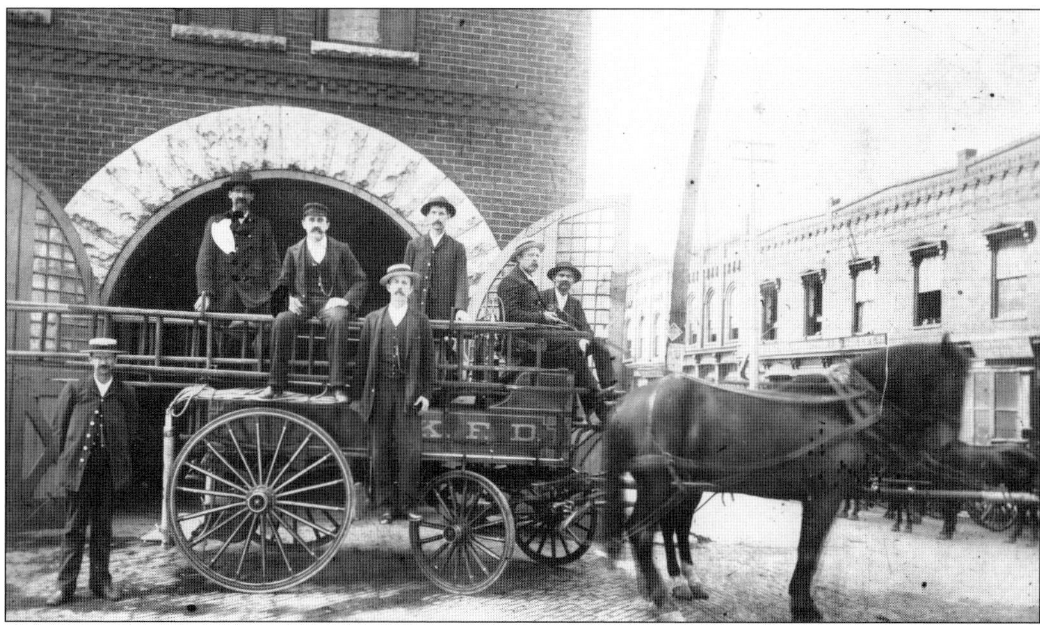

For years, the fire department was headquartered in the northern end of City Hall on Market Square facing Wall Avenue. Here, around 1898, is the city fire department's first ladder wagon. Standing at the back of the wagon is fire chief Col. William Cross. In 1903, the fire department moved to a dedicated building on Commerce Avenue.

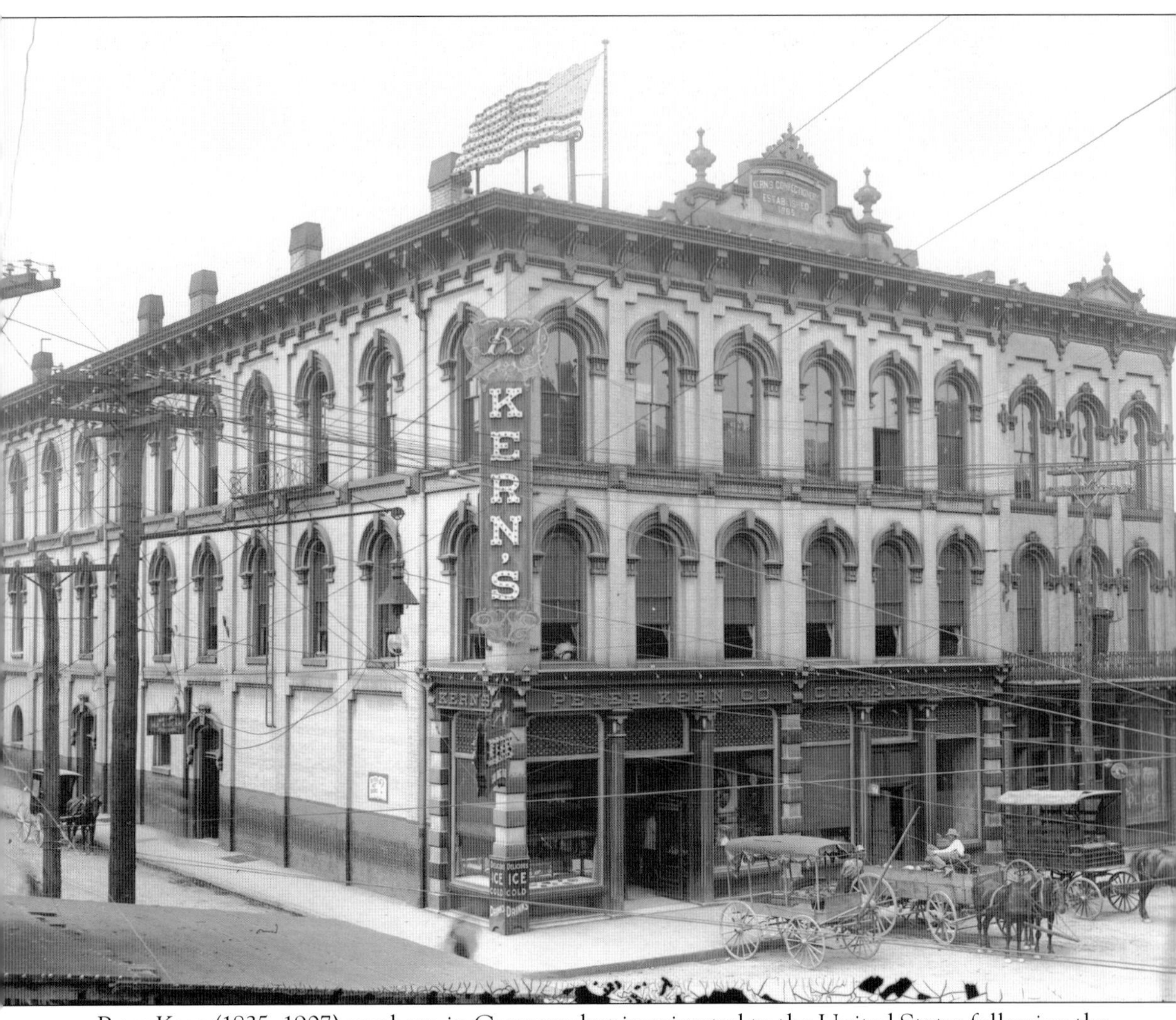

Peter Kern (1835–1907) was born in Germany but immigrated to the United States following the catastrophic revolutions of 1848 in Europe. Stranded in Knoxville during the Civil War, Kern discovered a knack for baking. His business was so successful that in 1876 he built what is still the grandest building on Market Square. Its designer was Joseph Baumann, arguably Knoxville's first professional architect. The ground floor contained a soda fountain and candy shop, the second floor an ice cream saloon, reportedly one of the most elegant in the city, and the third floor an Odd Fellows Hall that sometimes hosted public concerts. The bakery was in the back. Kern served as alderman in 1885 and became mayor of Knoxville for one year in 1890.

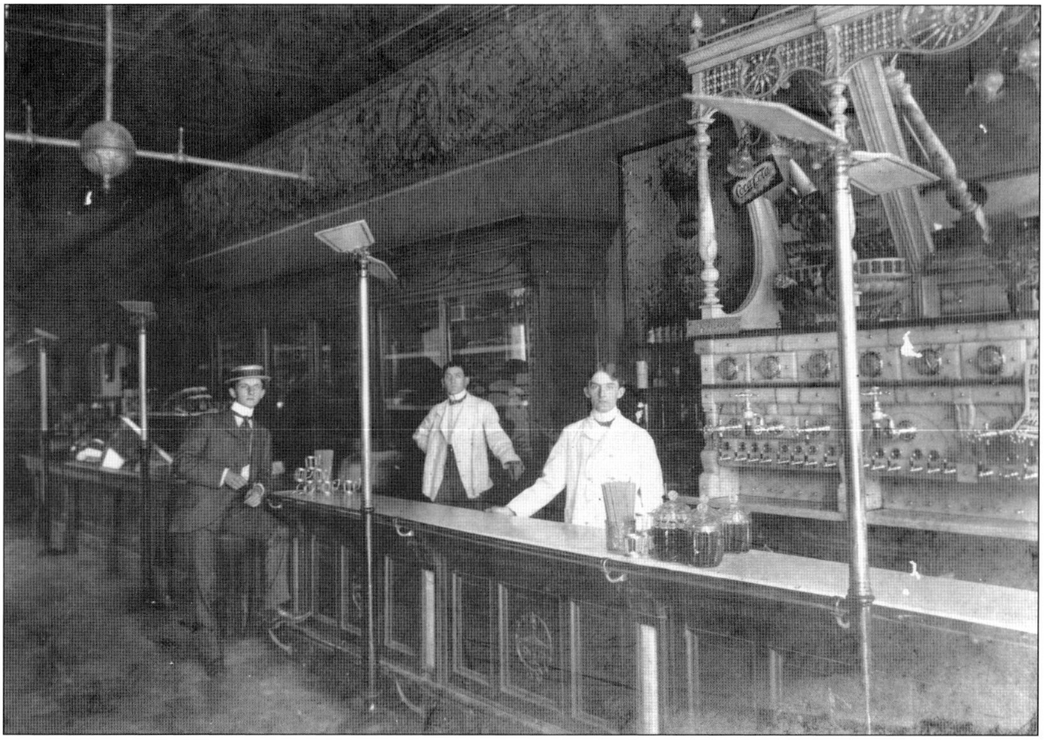

Kern's ice cream parlor and soda fountain was open until late in the evening, and was where many Knoxvillians first tasted what would become a new sensation, Coca-Cola (sign at upper right). Through its festive advertising, Kern's influenced early celebrations of Christmas in the city. Fireworks were also sold here; setting them off around Christmastime was popular in the late 1800s.

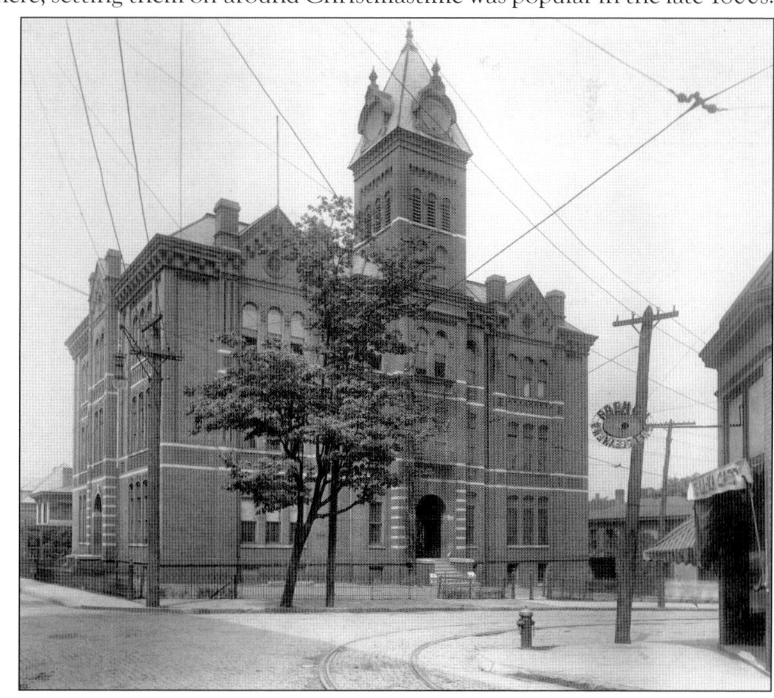

The Girls High School on the northwest corner of Union Avenue and Walnut Street was built in 1886 and had evolved into Knoxville High School by the early 20th century. Future Hollywood director Clarence Brown attended here. In 1910, the school moved to a new building on Fifth Avenue. This building subsequently hosted Boyd Junior High School before it burned down in 1924.

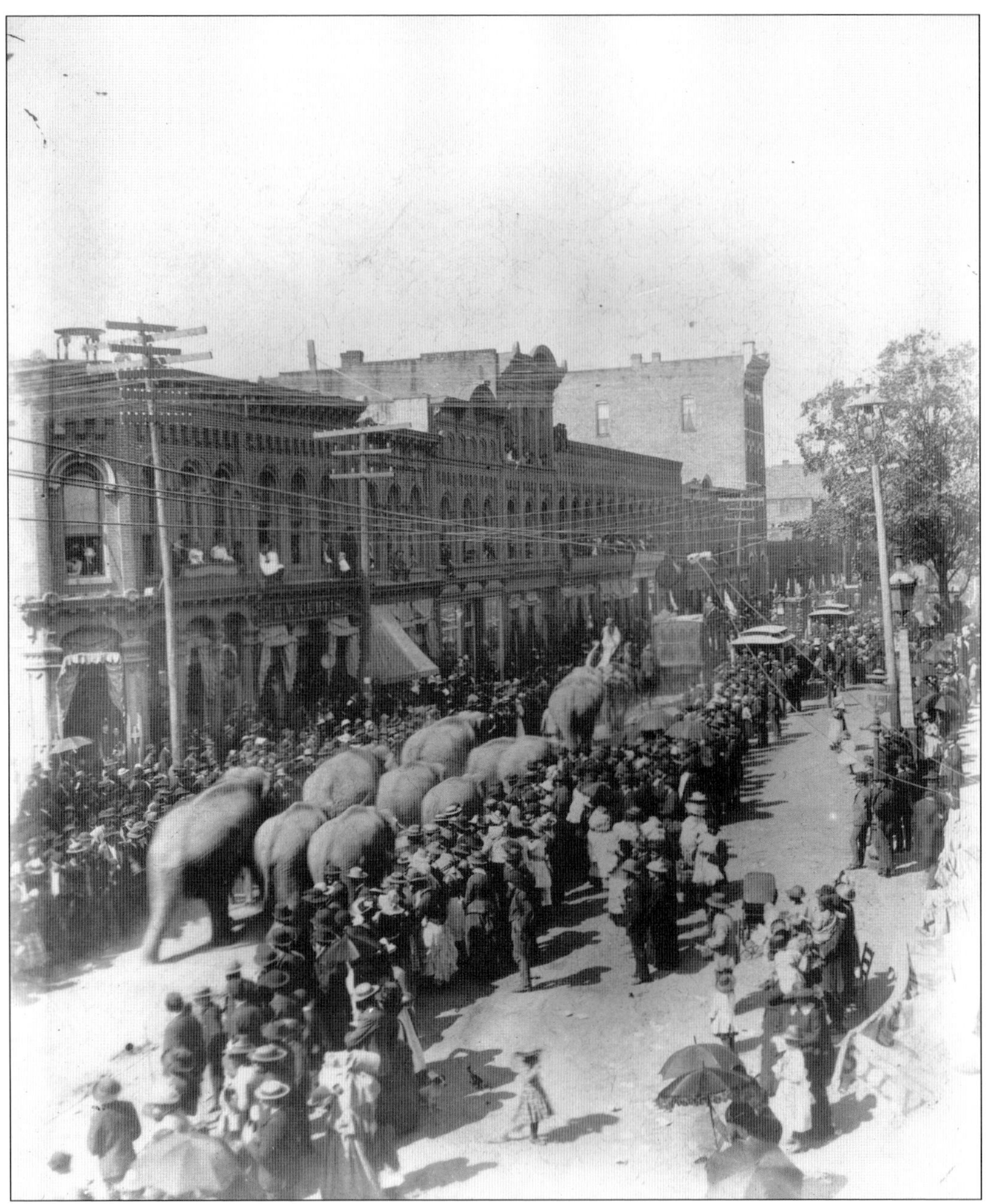

Immense anticipation circulated around Knoxville ahead of the famous P.T. Barnum Circus planned for the city in October 1886. Purpose-built billboards, erected weeks earlier, promoted the spectacle billed as the "Greatest Show on Earth." Thousands flooded into town by train and horse cart from surrounding counties and even Chattanooga. On arrival, many found downtown stables full and were turned away by hotel proprietors, leading many to sleep under the stars near the circus grounds on Asylum Street. In this photograph, elephants bring up the rear behind carriages during the Great Free Street Parade heading north along Gay Street at Clinch Avenue as crowds line the sidewalks and watch from almost every balcony and window.

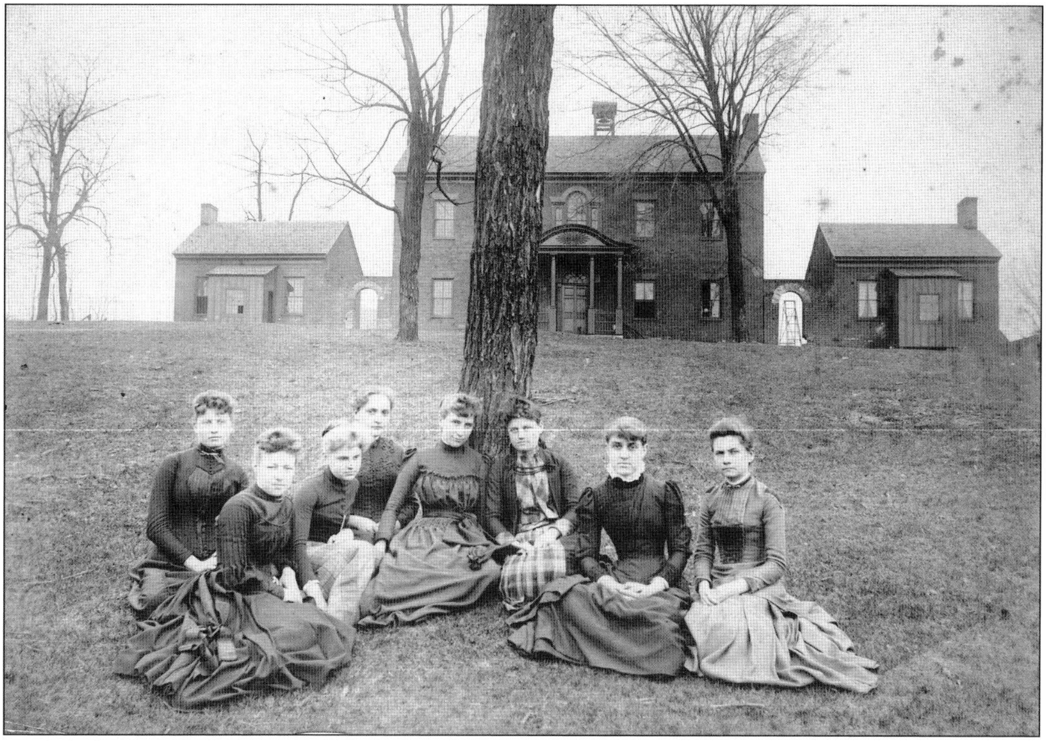

Founded in 1827, the Knoxville Female Academy was an important institution in the education of young women. The school flourished in the 1880s under the direction of Lizzie Crozier French, the city's leading activist for social reform. Overlooking the Tennessee River, the academy was on the corner of Henley Street and Cumberland Avenue, near where Church Street United Methodist Church stands today.

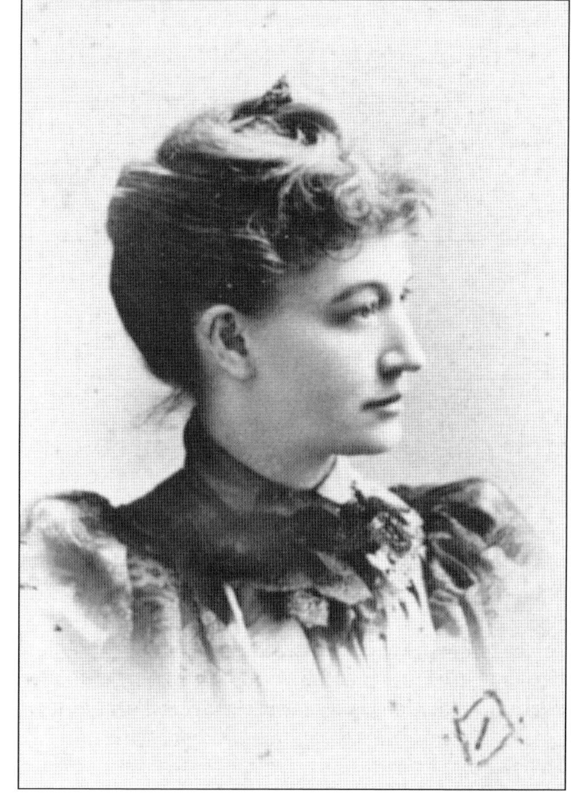

Lizzie Crozier French (1851–1926), a formidable public speaker, published *A Manual of Elocution* while leading the Knoxville Female Academy. She also worked tirelessly to further women's causes and later served as the leader of the local suffrage movement, inspiring others, likely including those in the Tennessee legislature who gave women the right to vote with the passage of the 19th Amendment in 1920.

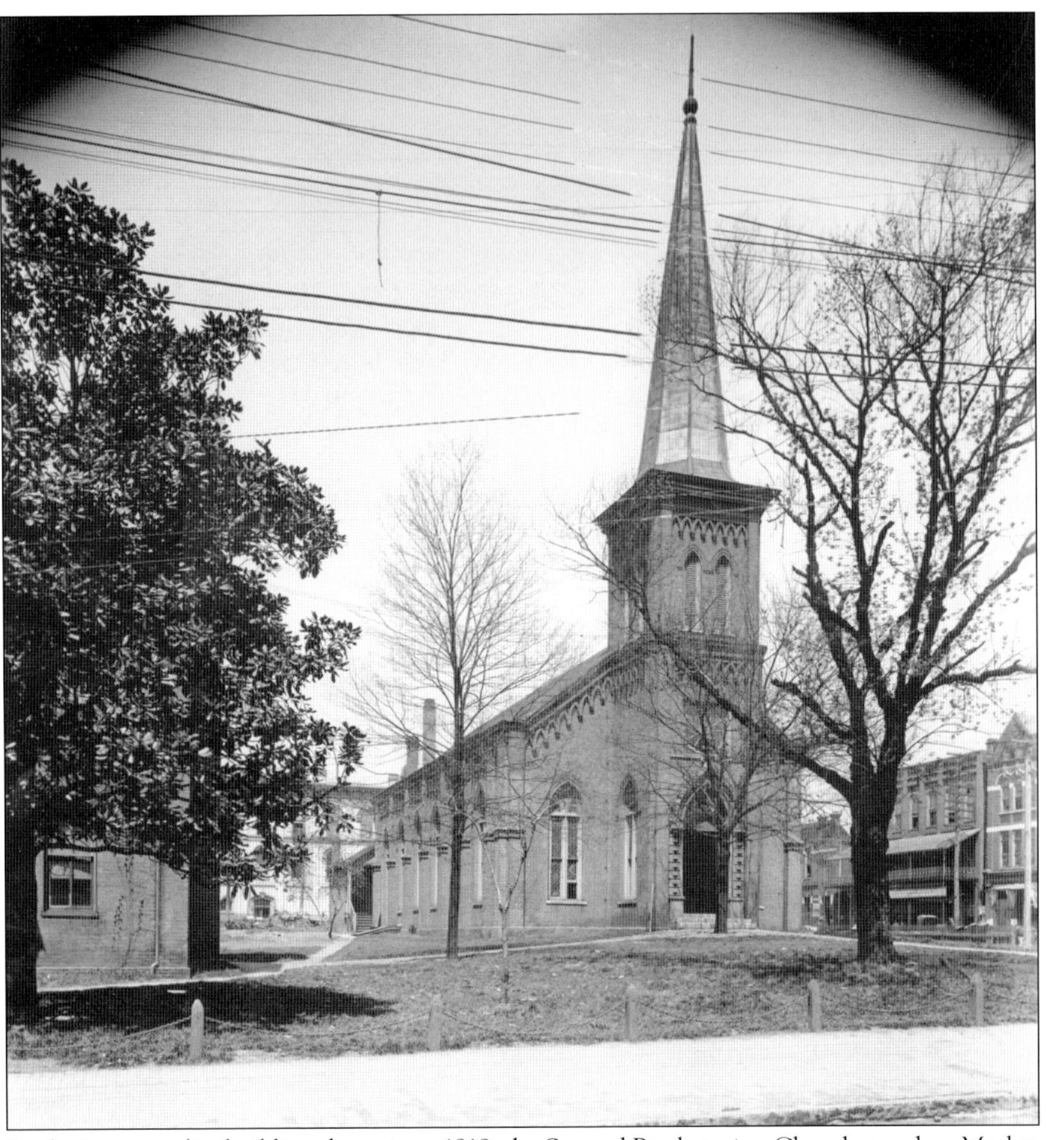

Replacing an earlier building there since 1818, the Second Presbyterian Church stood on Market Street between Clinch and Union Avenues from 1860 until about 1905. Its congregation moved to Walnut Street and later to Kingston Pike. Behind the church, near Market Square, was the graveyard where Gen. William Sanders was secretly buried in 1863. Those graves have since been relocated. This site is now occupied by Home Federal Bank and the Arnstein Building.

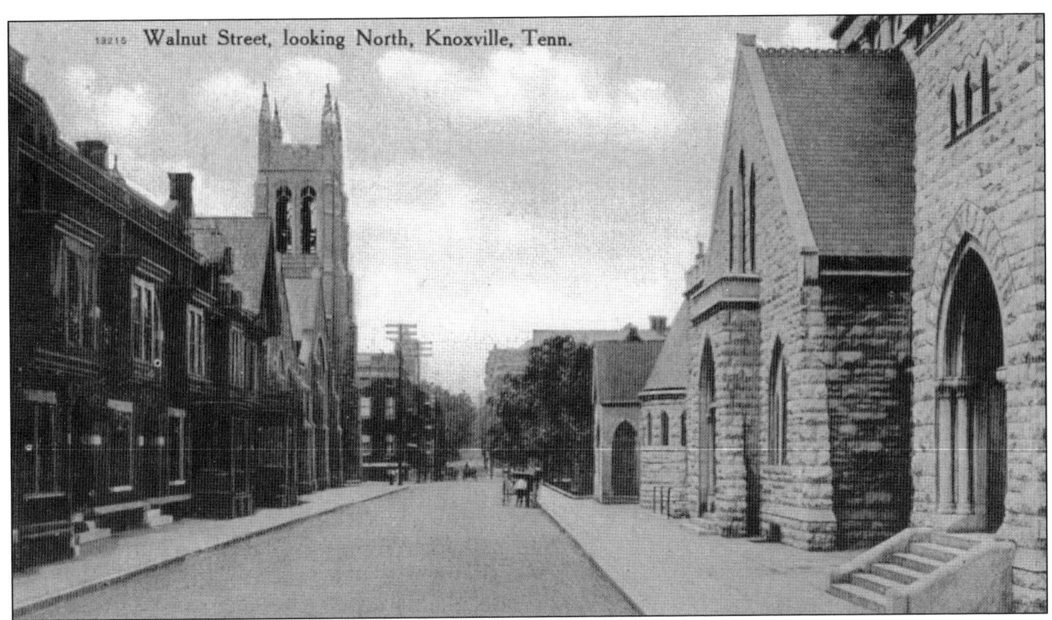

In the postcard above, looking north on mainly residential Walnut Street, St. John's Episcopal Church is on the right. Ohio architect J.W. Yost designed this structure, built in 1892 to replace an earlier church. Still standing, it is now officially St. John's Cathedral. Farther down the street on the left is Second Presbyterian Church in its second location, where it stood until it was demolished in the 1960s. The Lawson McGhee Library is now on that spot. Below, First Methodist Episcopal Church, later known simply as First Methodist, built this church at the southeast corner of Clinch Avenue and Locust Street in 1894. First Methodist was one of two Methodist churches downtown after a north-south schism related to the Civil War. Although this edifice appears to be built to last for centuries, it was torn down in 1966, when the congregation moved to Kingston Pike.

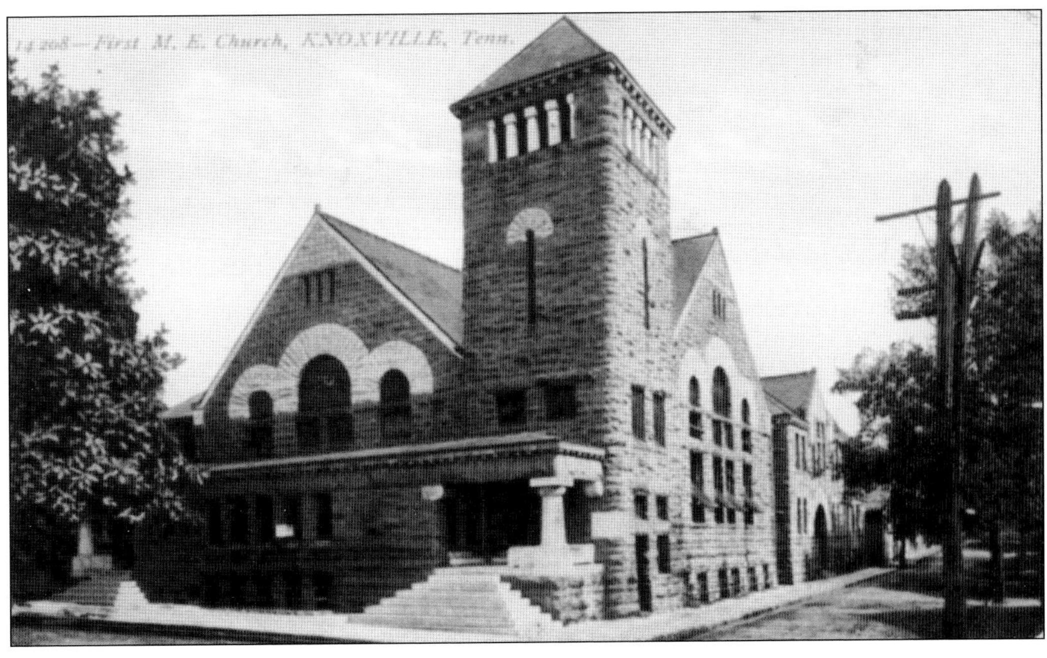

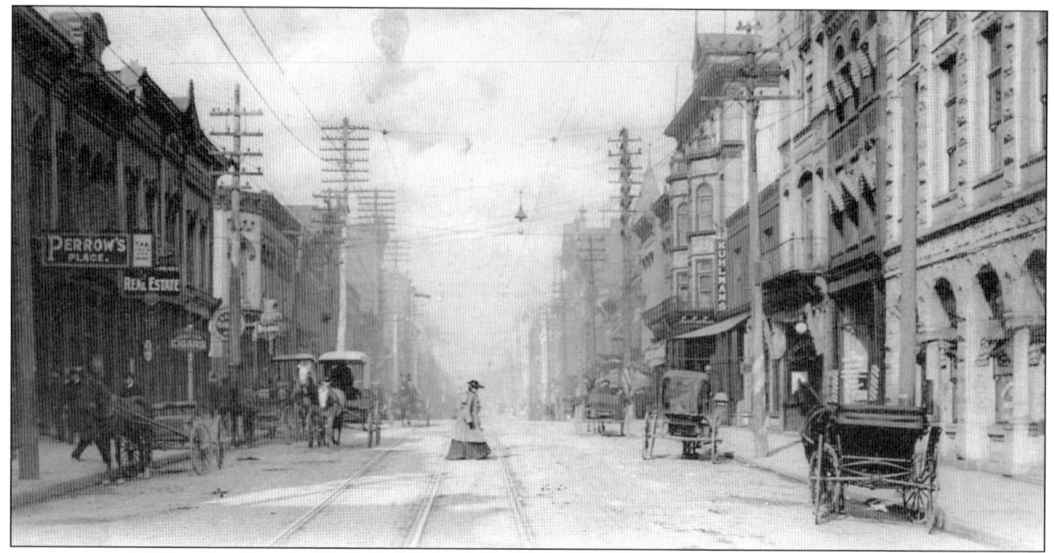

Gay Street looks rather sooty in this postcard from around 1905. The woman jaywalking across the street may be headed to Kuhlman's drugstore on the corner of Gay Street and Clinch Avenue. The Hotel Imperial is just beyond. By this time, horse carts were vying for space with streetcars on downtown streets, as evidenced by the streetcar tracks. Gay Street would soon get even busier with the introduction of the automobile.

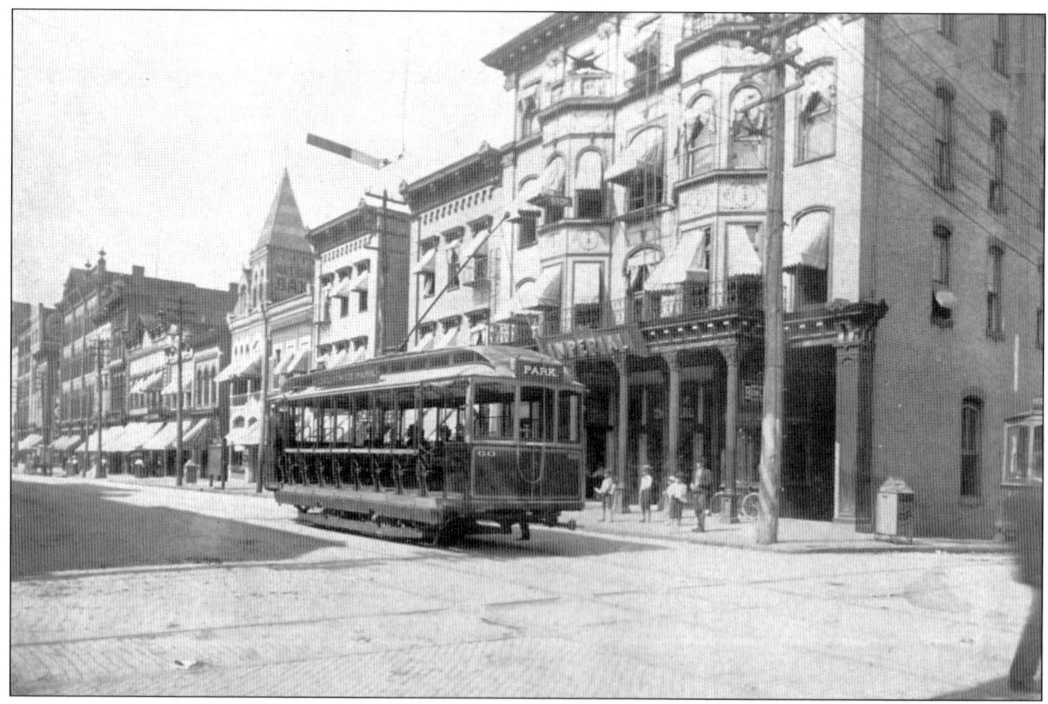

Around the turn of the 20th century, the Chilhowee Park streetcar passes the Hotel Imperial on the northeast corner of Gay Street and Clinch Avenue. Opened in 1894, the Imperial was a remodeled version of an earlier hotel, the Hattie House, and included a barbershop, newsstand, café, and bowling alley. After a lightning fire destroyed the Imperial in 1916, the Farragut Hotel was built in its place, opening in 1919.

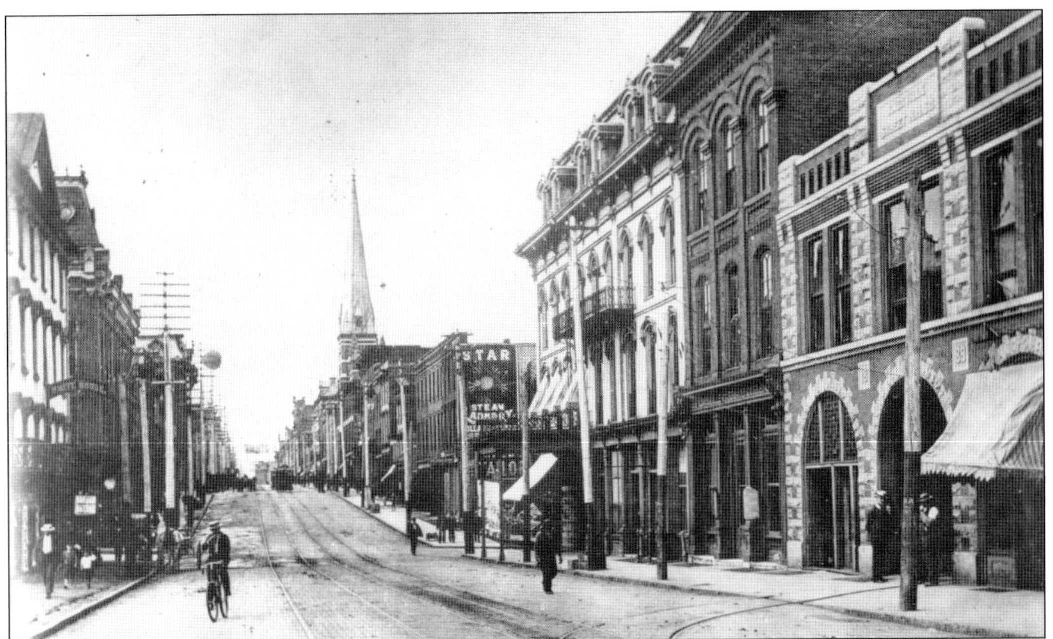

Looking north on Gay Street from Main Street in the late 1890s, on the left, a small sign on the white building reads "The White House," a later name for the Lamar House, where the Bijou Theatre is today. Across the street is Staub's Theatre, and in the foreground is the streetcar depot with tracks leading into it.

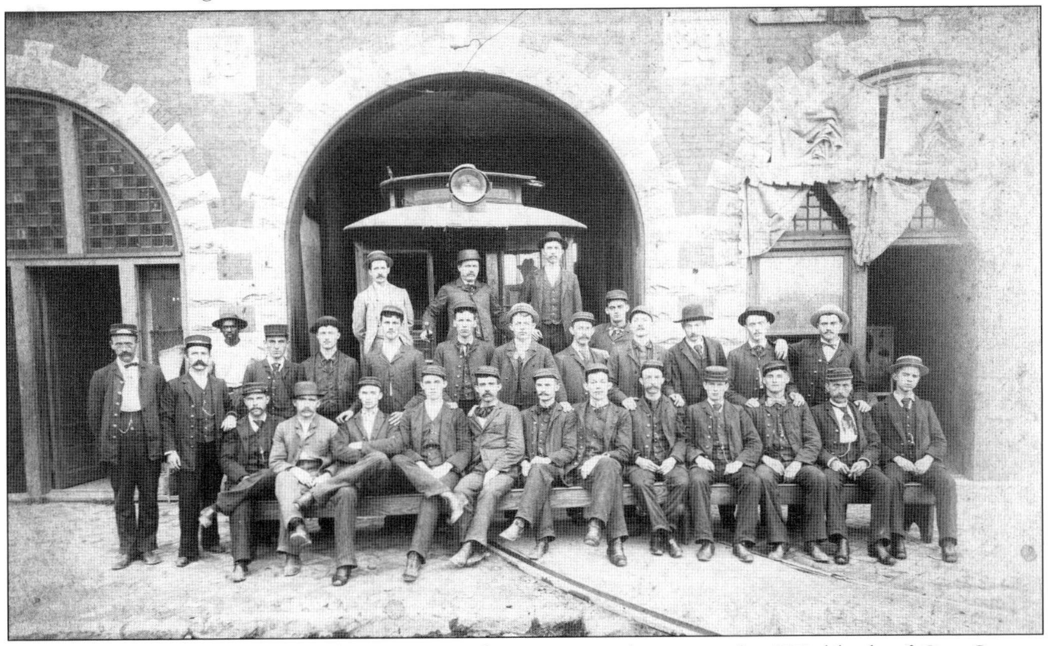

Streetcar conductors and workers pose at the streetcar depot on the 800 block of Gay Street. The building, owned by the Railroad and Light Company, shows the date of 1889. By 1907, it was modified to form the Colonial Hotel. Buildings on the block were demolished, mostly in the 1950s, for a department store that was never built. The Plaza Tower, still the tallest building in East Tennessee, rose here in 1978.

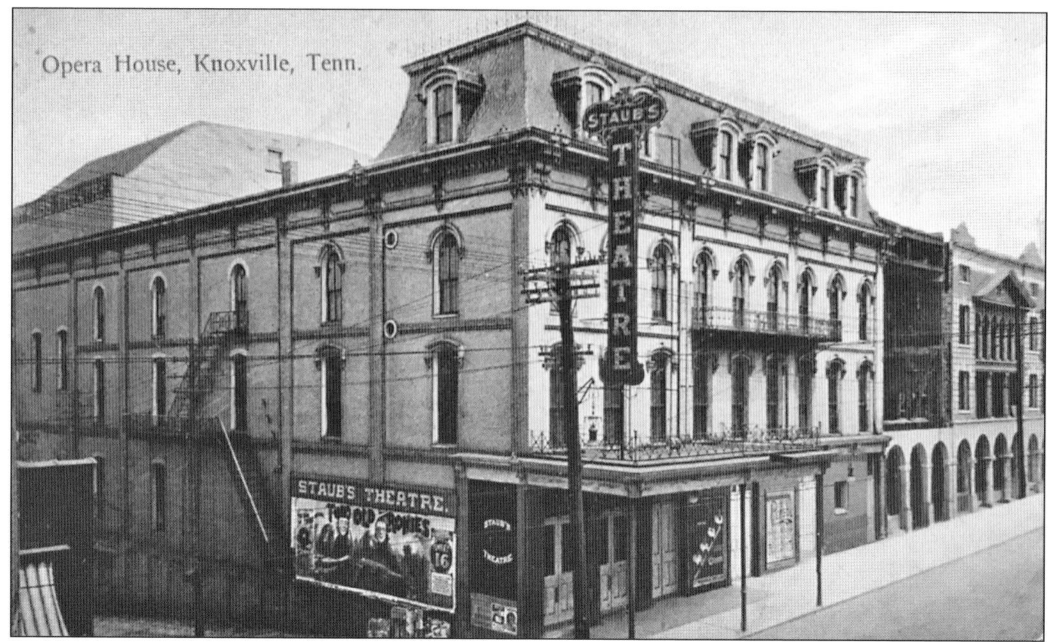

Staub's Theatre, originally Staub's Opera House, was one of the downtown wonders of the Victorian era. Built in 1872, one of the first designs of prolific architect Joseph Baumann, the theater featured a European-style auditorium with multiple balconies and a fresco ceiling. It served audiences for more than 80 years. Builder Peter Staub was a Swiss immigrant and two-time Knoxville mayor. His son Fritz Staub ran it after his father was appointed consul to Switzerland. In 1883, Staub's hosted the first of its groundbreaking annual music festivals featuring French and Italian comic operas. Among the performers who had the view below of the audience from the stage were Ethel Barrymore, W.C. Fields, Lillie Langtry, and Sarah Bernhardt, as well as speaker Frederick Douglass.

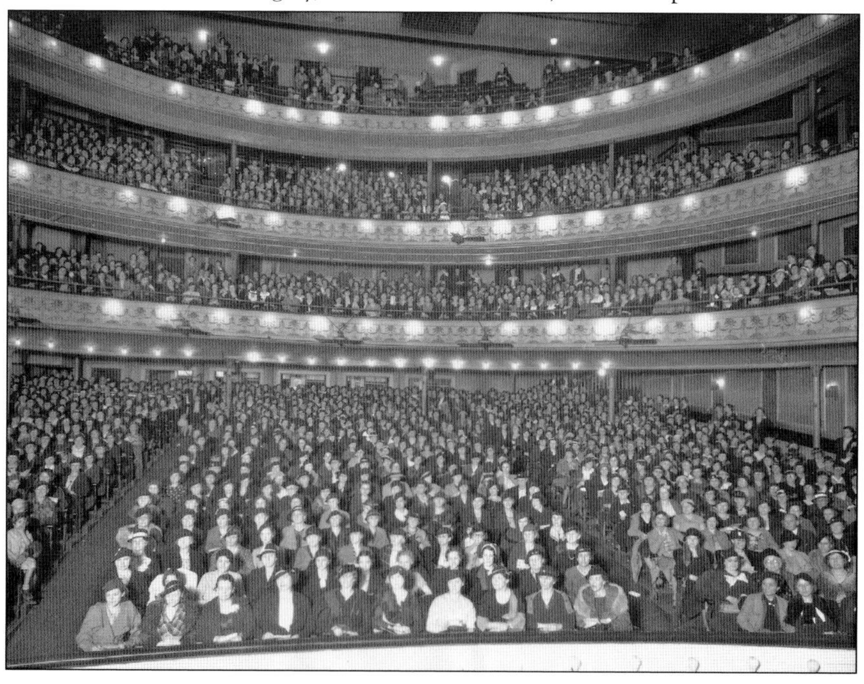

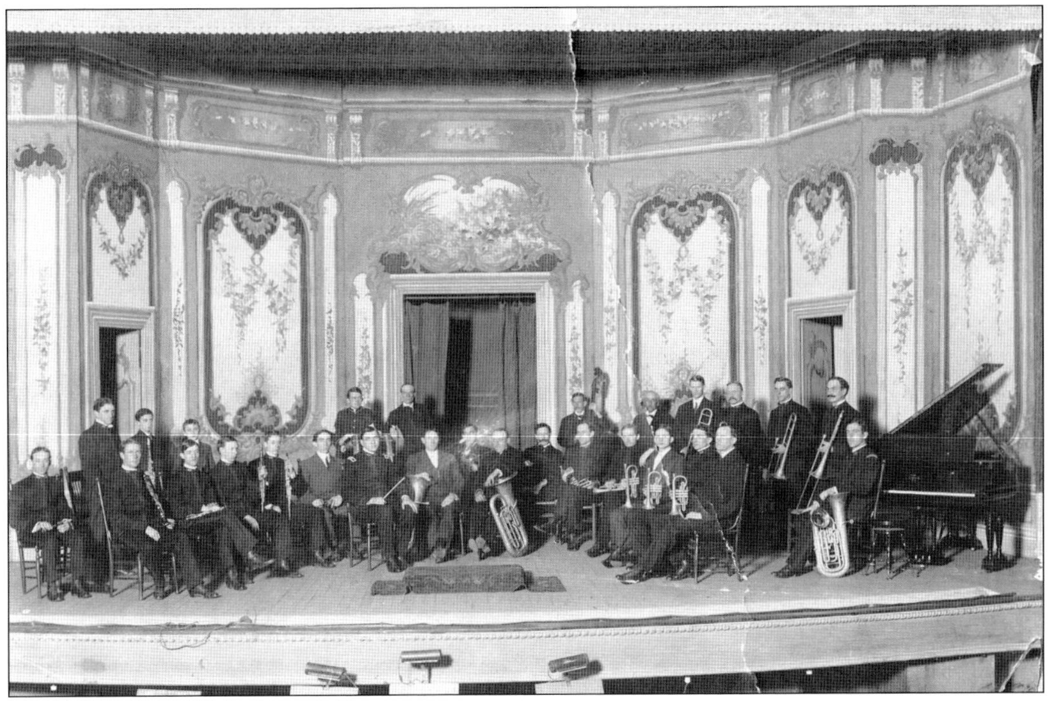

Shown above on stage at Staub's is Crouch's Orchestra, a Knoxville band led by Charles Crouch, a retail florist whose shop was on Gay Street. The program at right promotes a "Grand Wrestling Match" in April 1907 pitting English champ Jim Parr against the "Russian Lion" George Hackenschmidt. According to the *Knoxville Journal & Tribune*, although the match was an anticipated sellout, "ladies will be admitted free with one paid admission."

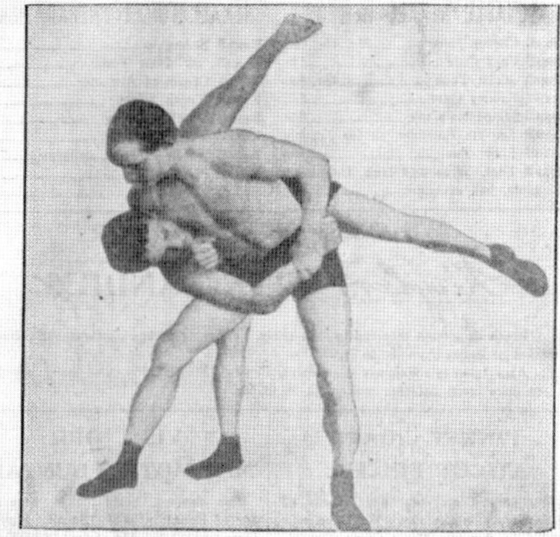

I-X-L BARBER SHOP
DEADERICK BLDG., PRINCE ST.
South Side of Post Office
The Only Hand Vibrator Massage in the City
Clean Linen for Every Customer
HOT, COLD AND SHOWER BATHS
All Work Guaranteed.
R. L. WYLY, - - Proprietor

WHEN YOU HAVE USED THE
FOX VISIBLE TYPEWRITER
YOU WILL HAVE NO OTHER.

GRAND WRESTLING MATCH

Staub's Theatre, Thursday, April 4

This match will be for the middle weight championship of the world, between Jim Parr, the champion English wrestler, and Chas. Hackenschmidt, the Russian Lion. This match will be catch as catch can, best two out of three falls.

Ladies will be admitted free with one paid admission. Prices 50, 75 and $1.00.

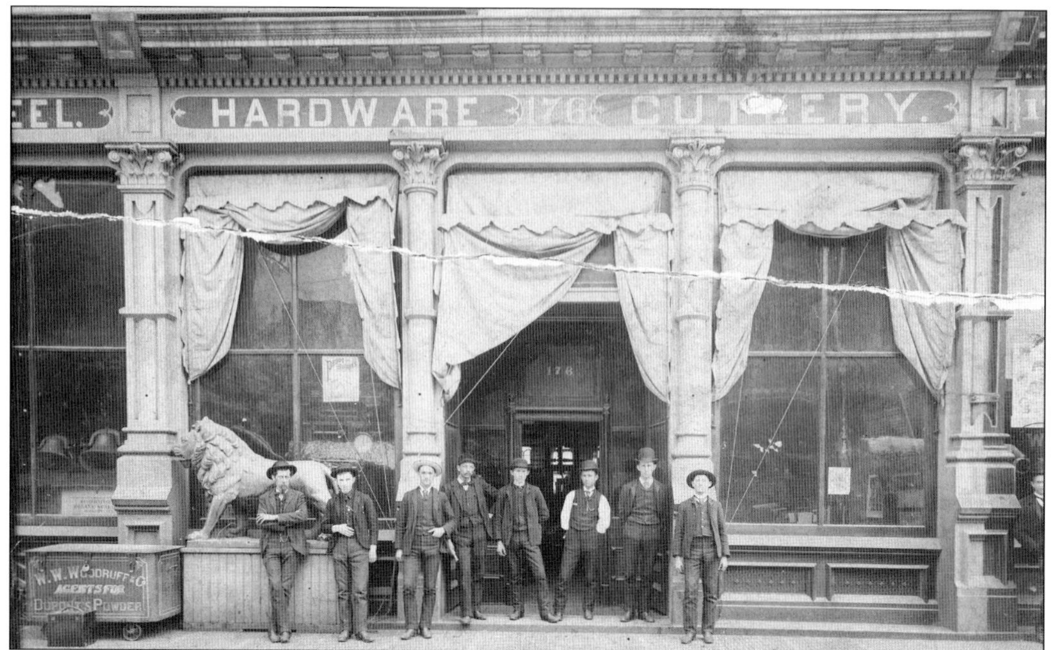

Woodruff & Co., seen here in the 1880s, was founded by Union captain William W. Woodruff just after the Civil War. Built on the east side of Gay Street, it was one of several buildings destroyed in a devastating fire in 1897. The family-owned company thrived here for more than a century, eventually specializing in furniture. The Woodruff name can still be seen on the rebuilt building today. (McClung, Small Photograph Collection.)

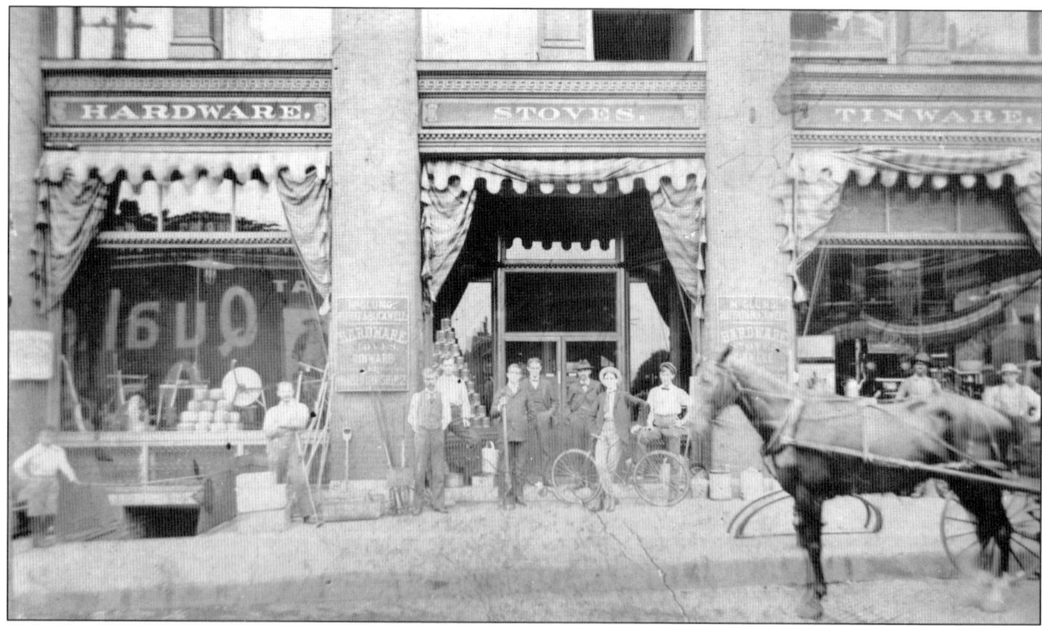

McClung, Buffat & Buckwell was a Gay Street store offering "hardware, stoves and tinware." The McClungs were among Knoxville's founding families; their name had appeared on several businesses for a century by the time of this image in the 1890s. The Buffats were among the French-Swiss immigrants who settled east of the city. (McClung, Knox County Two Centuries Collection.)

Mester, Newcomer & Paulus, business partners from Reading, Pennsylvania, set up shop on Gay Street in 1890. By the early 20th century, the business, known simply as Newcomer's, had become one of downtown's most popular department stores. It proved hugely popular at Christmastime, especially for children, with its Christmas Toyland and a real-life Santa Claus. Today, this same building is occupied by a comparable business, Mast General Store.

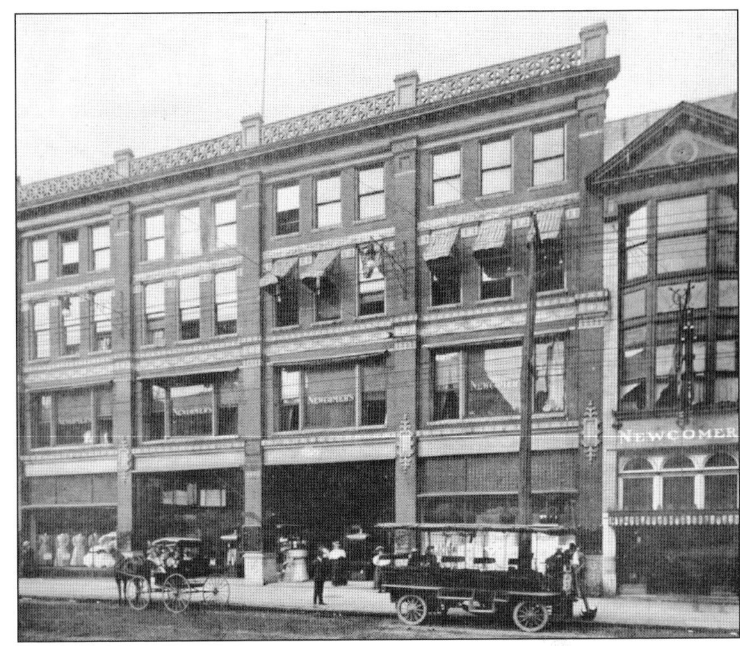

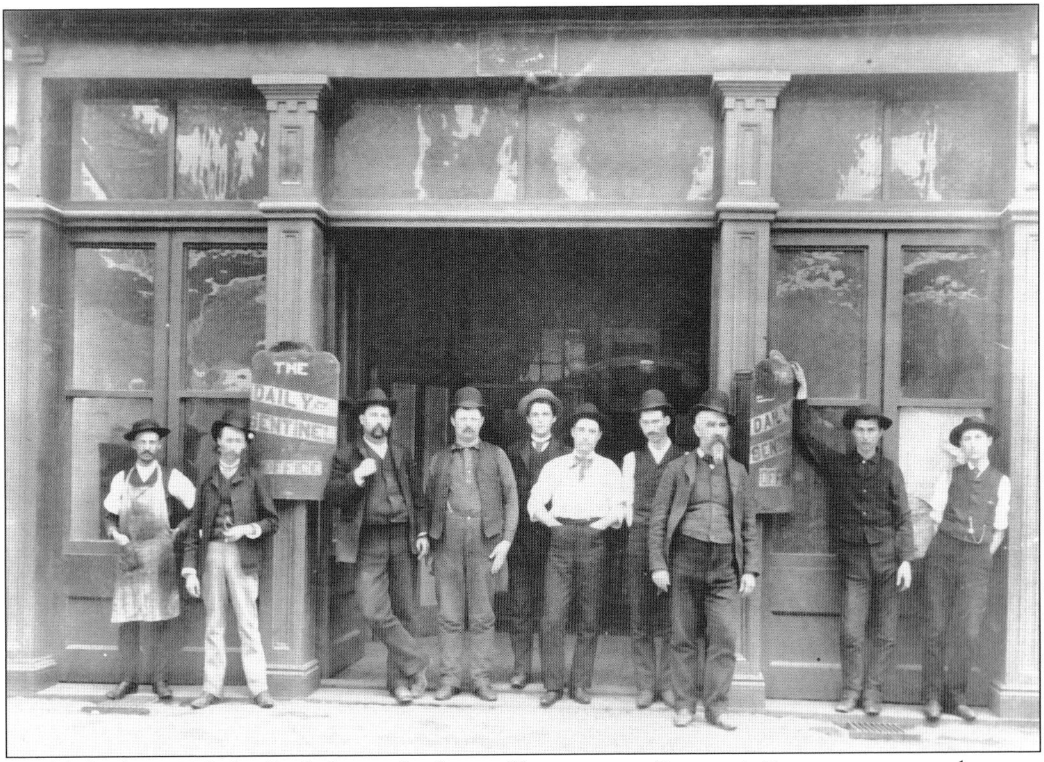

Established in 1886, the *Daily Sentinel*, whose offices were on Reservoir Street, went on to become one of the city's most durable businesses. By 1893, its name changed to the *Knoxville Sentinel*, and it continued that way until 1926, when it merged with the *Knoxville News*, becoming the *Knoxville News-Sentinel*. In this 1889 photograph, the conspicuously casual staff includes, at far left, a typesetter with an ink-stained apron. (McClung, Thompson Photograph Collection.)

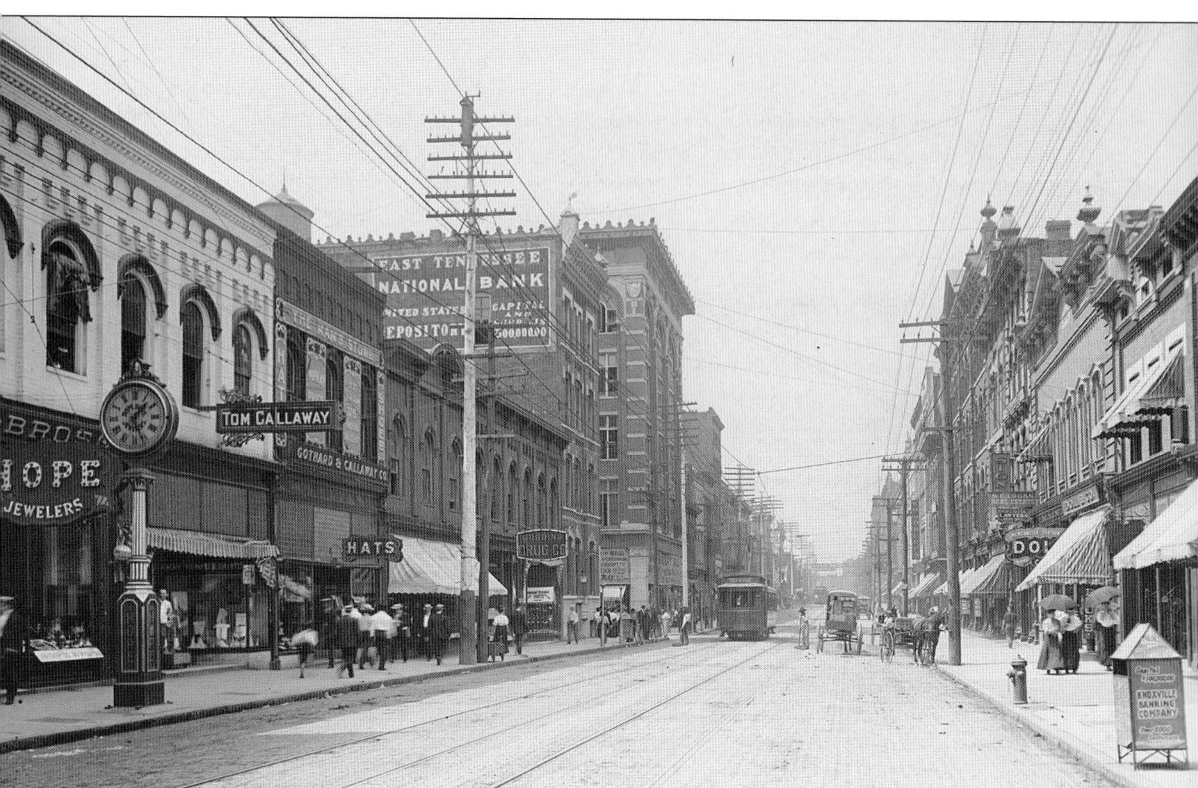

This c. 1905 view of the 500 block of Gay Street shows Hope Brothers Jewelry with its ornate street clock, Gothard and Calloway (the "Man's Store") offering a line of men's clothing including shirts and hats, and at the end of the block is the East Tennessee National Bank with its large painted sign on the side of the building. In front of it is a streetcar serving North Knoxville's Oakwood community. Just beyond is the brand-new Miller's department store. (Library of Congress.)

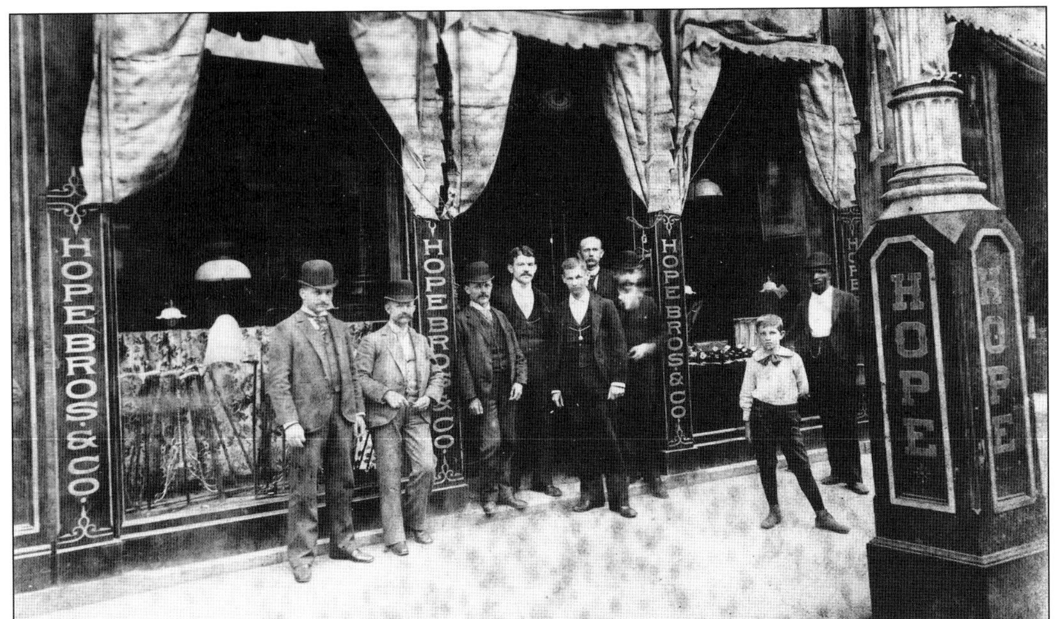

Founded in 1868, Hope Brothers Jewelry was known for its elaborate street clock, first introduced on the sidewalk on the 500 block of Gay Street in 1886. It later moved diagonally across the street to the 400 block, where it was acquired by Kimball's, which moved with the clock to Kingston Pike. In addition to clocks and jewelry, Hope Brothers specialized in sterling silver, cut glass, fine Delft pottery, and Royal Crown Derby China.

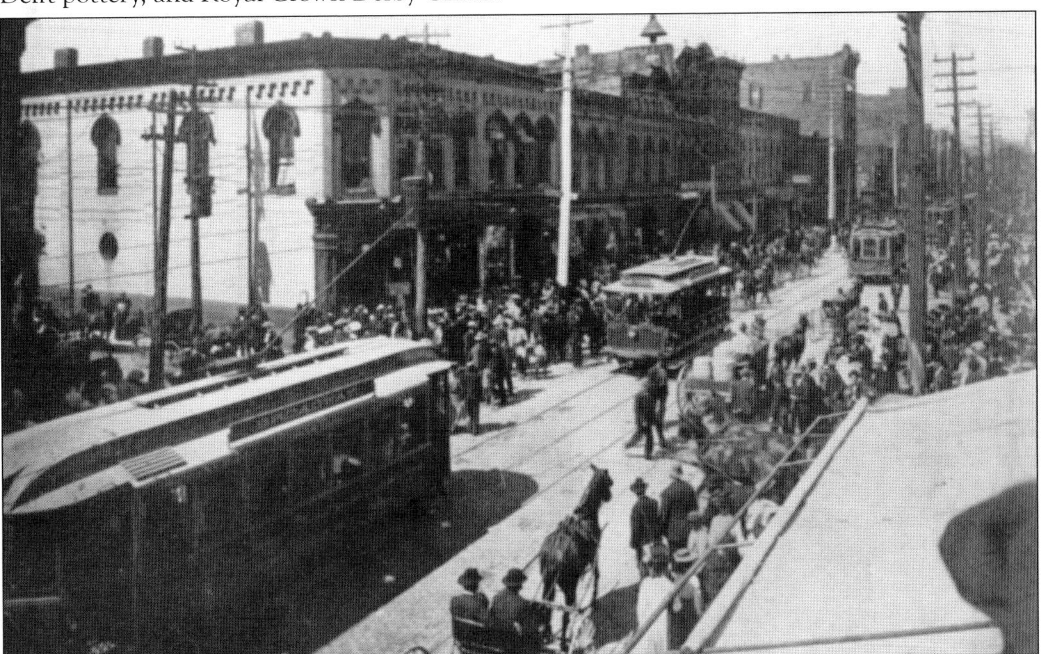

The energy of a booming downtown is captured in this c. 1900 view of the 500 block of Gay Street looking north between Clinch and Union Avenues. There is hardly room for people to move among the crowded sidewalks, horse-drawn carriages, and electric streetcars. None of these buildings still stand.

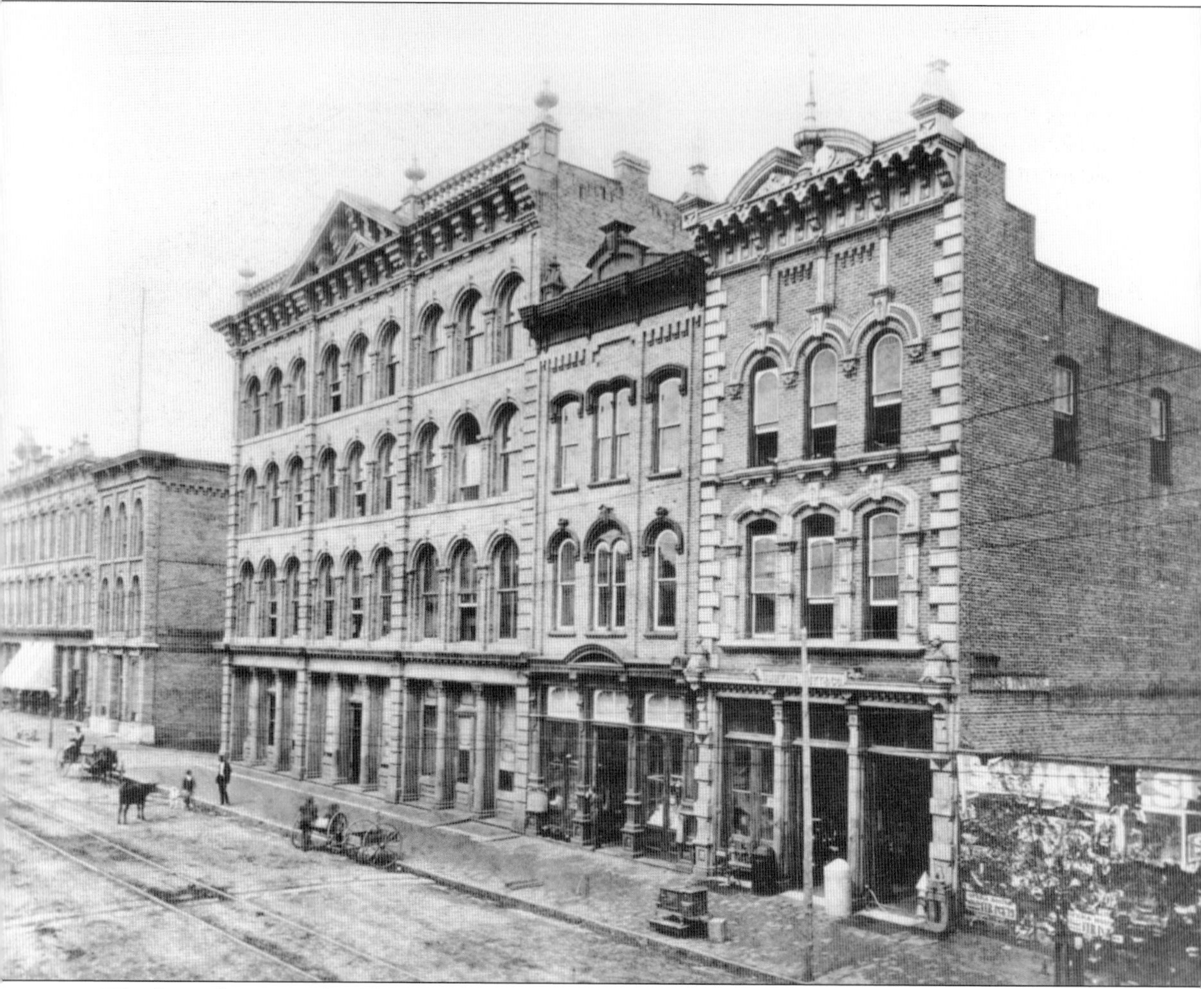

The large four-story building in the center of this c. 1880s photograph is the Cowan, McClung & Company wholesale house on the east side of Gay Street just south of Union Avenue. Built in the 1870s by Frank H. McClung, the firm lasted until 1919. McClung's son Calvin M. McClung (1855–1919) became known for his own firm on Jackson Avenue. His archives became the foundation of the McClung Historical Collection, the source of many of the photographs in this book. The Cowan, McClung & Company building, now radically remodeled and known as the Fidelity Building, is still there, as is a building just beyond it now known as Tailor Lofts. The ornate building at far left was destroyed in the 1897 fire. It is unclear whether the calf in the street was under control or a stray.

Opened in 1873, the East Tennessee National Bank, on the corner of Gay Street and Union Avenue, proved to be one of Knoxville's most durable financial institutions. An early president of the bank was Joseph Jaques, Knoxville's only English-born mayor. One bank officer was R.C. Jackson, a railroad executive, for whom Jackson Avenue is named. Baumann Brothers, early in the history of that prolific firm, took credit for its design.

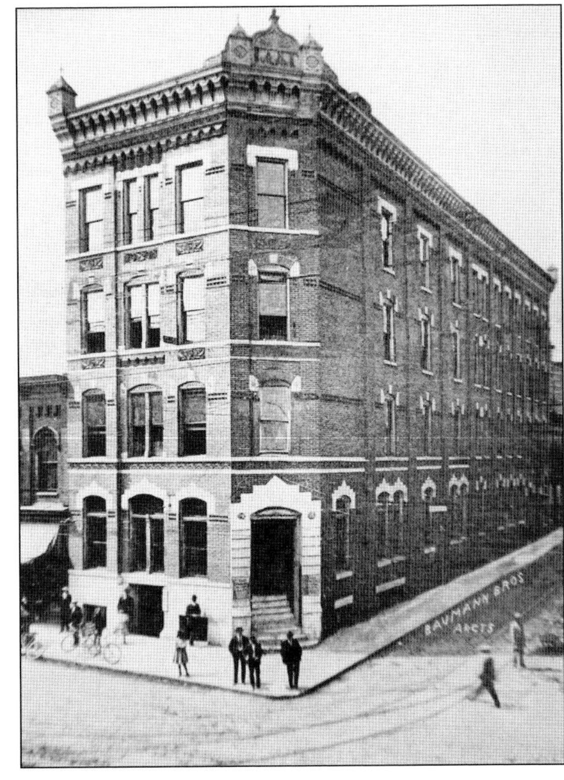

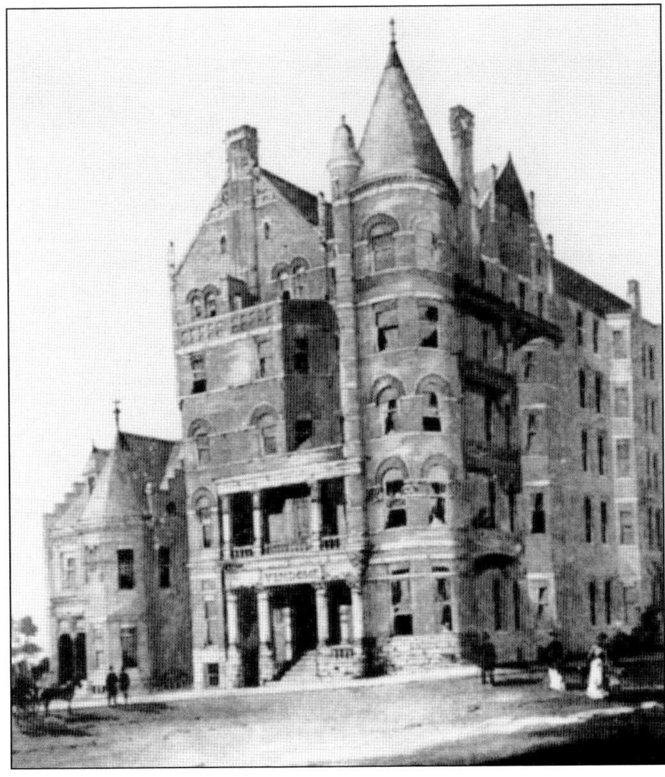

Designed by Ohio architect Leon Beaver, the Vendome was a luxury apartment building that opened in 1890 on Clinch Avenue between Market and Walnut Streets. Its dining room on the fifth floor, presided over by a French chef, was reachable by the city's first elevator. The *Knoxville Journal* reported that its meals were "fit for the gods." The Vendome, of which photographs have proved to be elusive, was torn down in the early 1940s.

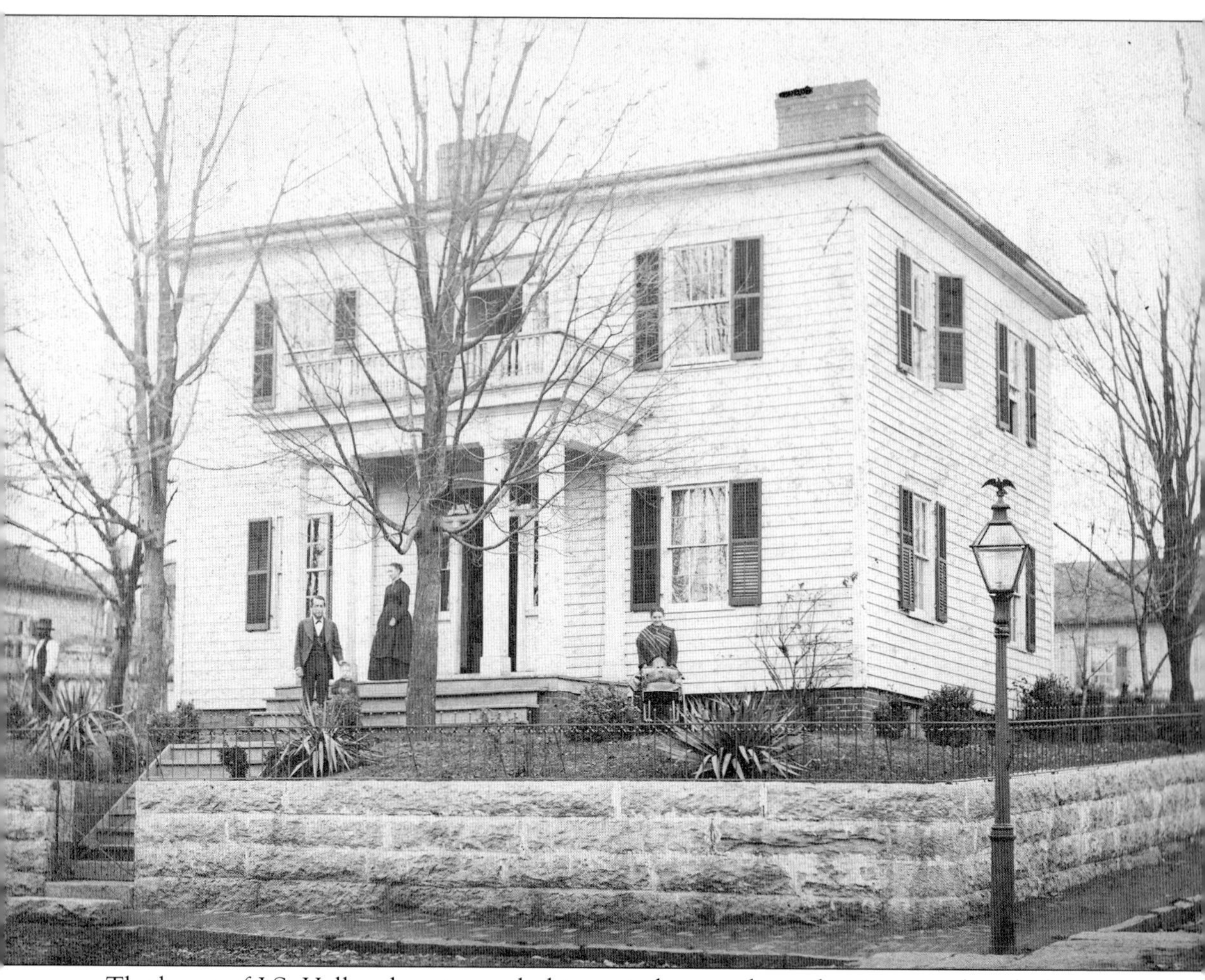

The house of J.S. Hall, a downtown clothing retailer, stood on what is now a largely forgotten street—Oxford Street, northwest of Market Square. Author Frances Hodgson Burnett, who was a Knoxvillian for about a decade after the Civil War, is believed to have lived there briefly in the 1870s. At right is an early gas lamp, seen here in 1872. Gas service first appeared in the 1850s, but electric lights began to take over after 1885.

Main Street proved to be an exclusive residential district. In 1872–1875, businessman Charles J. McClung (1826–1908) built this extravagant Victorian mansion, designed by Nashville architect P.J. Williamson, on the southwest corner of Main and Walnut Streets overlooking the Tennessee River. McClung's business partner, James Cowan, liked it so much that he built one almost identical to it on Cumberland Avenue. McClung's was gone by the 1920s. (McClung, Knox County Two Centuries Collection.)

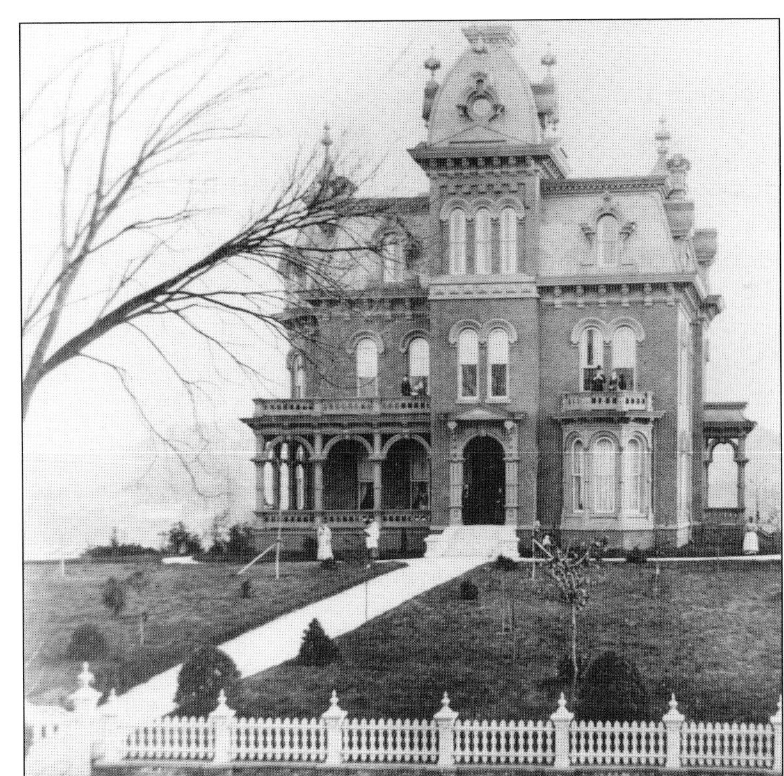

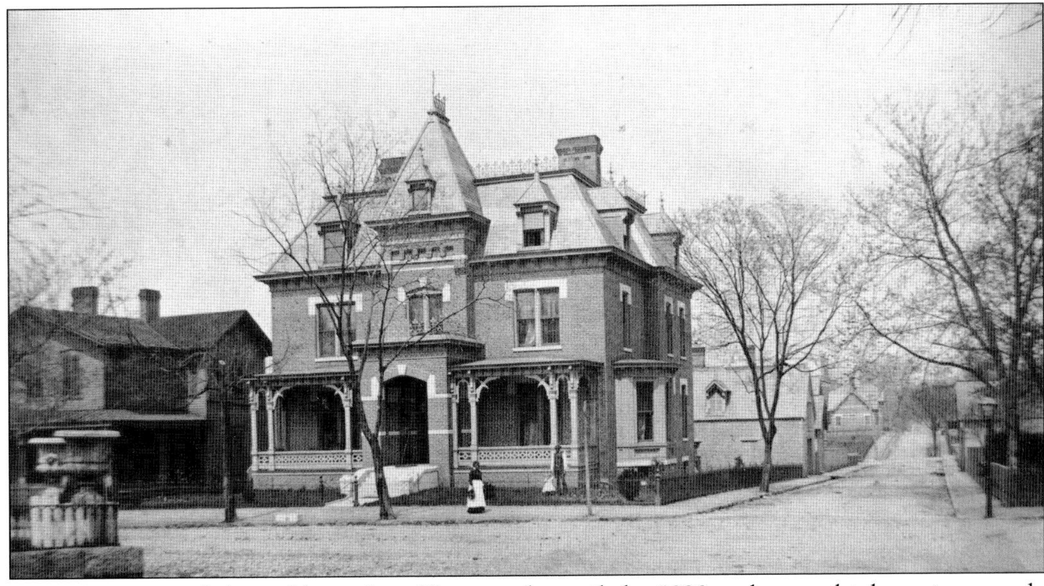

Main Street was fashionable to the affluent only until the 1920s, when multiple projects made it a much more businesslike street. The home of Andrew Jackson Albers (1844–1910), former Union naval pharmacist and wholesale druggist, stood on the northwest corner of Main and Locust Streets. Today, the Medical Arts Building stands on this corner, built around 1930. Albers's business, Albers Drugs, was a major wholesale firm that lasted almost a century after his death. (McClung, Knox County Two Centuries Collection.)

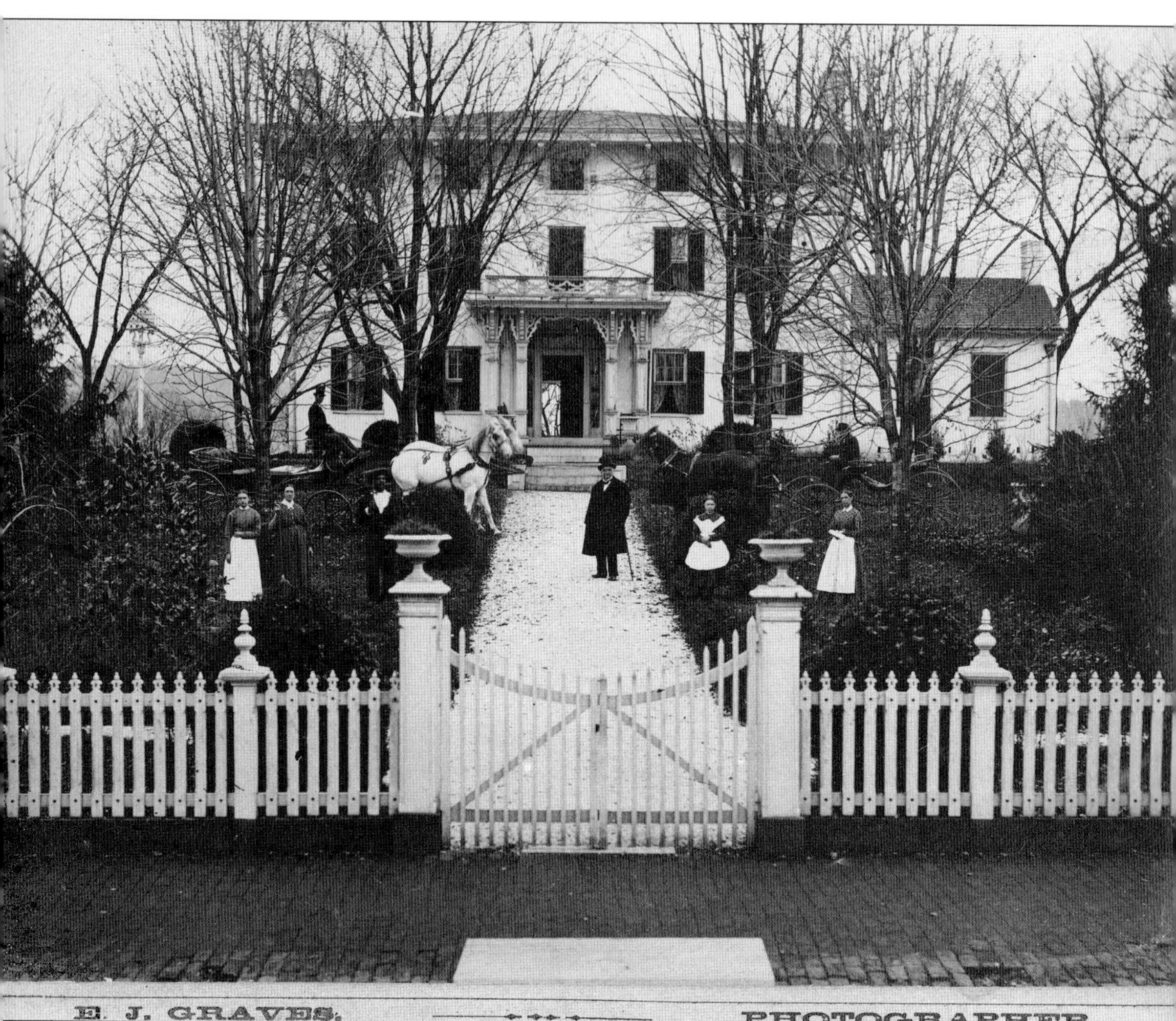

Diagonally opposite the Albers home, on the southeast corner of Main and Locust Streets, stood the Perez Dickinson home. Dickinson himself stands on the path surrounded by what looks like his domestic staff around the 1890s. The Massachusetts-born businessman, an older cousin of poet Emily Dickinson, was one of Knoxville's prosperous merchants and owner of the expansive Island Home estate in south Knoxville. Dickinson was a longtime trustee of the University of Tennessee and began a tradition of celebrating each graduating class here at his home. After Union forces repelled the Confederate siege, this house hosted a gala fete for occupying federal officers, including Gen. Philip Sheridan and Gen. William T. Sherman—who disapproved of the extravagance.

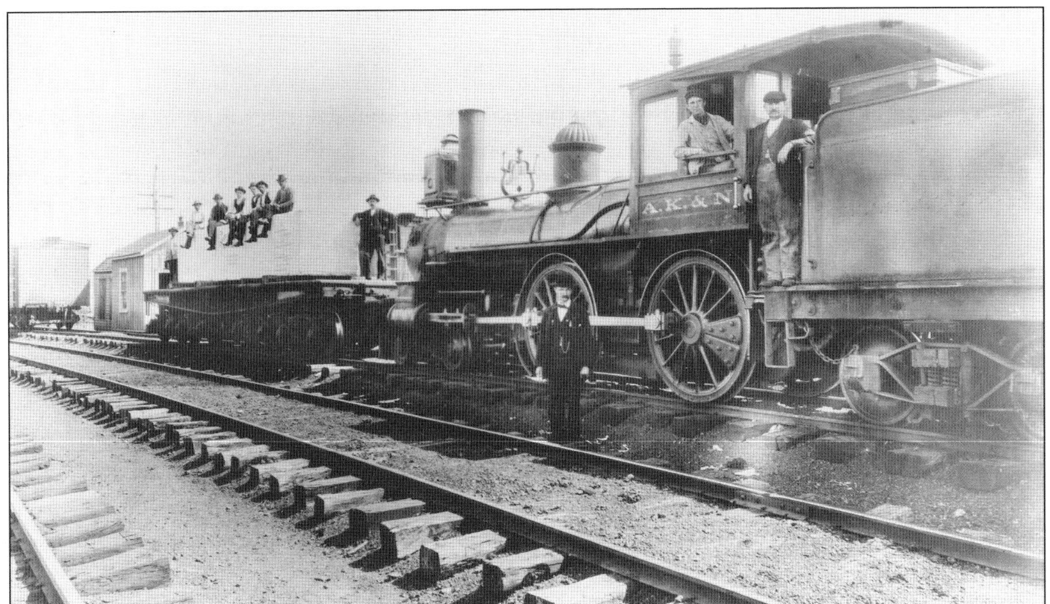

In the late 1800s, Knoxville was known as the Marble City thanks to its abundant marble quarries that provided stone for national markets. In this 1891 photograph, men sit on marble blocks at the short-lived Main Street Station, a modest depot at the western end of Main Street near the University of Tennessee. The lettering on the engine stands for the Atlanta, Knoxville & Northern. This line became part of the Louisville & Nashville (L&N) Railroad in 1902. (McClung, Thompson Photograph Collection.)

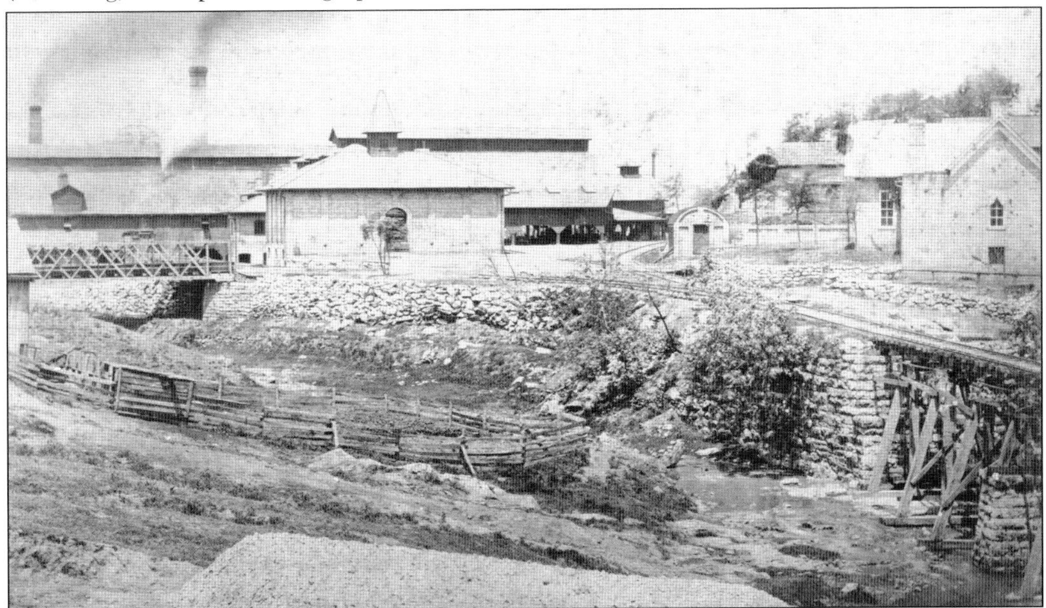

On the northwestern fringe of downtown stood the Knoxville Iron Company, a leading manufacturer established in 1871 that produced nails and railroad spikes for decades. The adjacent community of Mechanicsville is named in honor of its many workers. The company's surviving building was renovated to host the Strohaus, a German beer hall that was one of the popular evening attractions at the 1982 World's Fair. It still stands as the Foundry, a special-events venue.

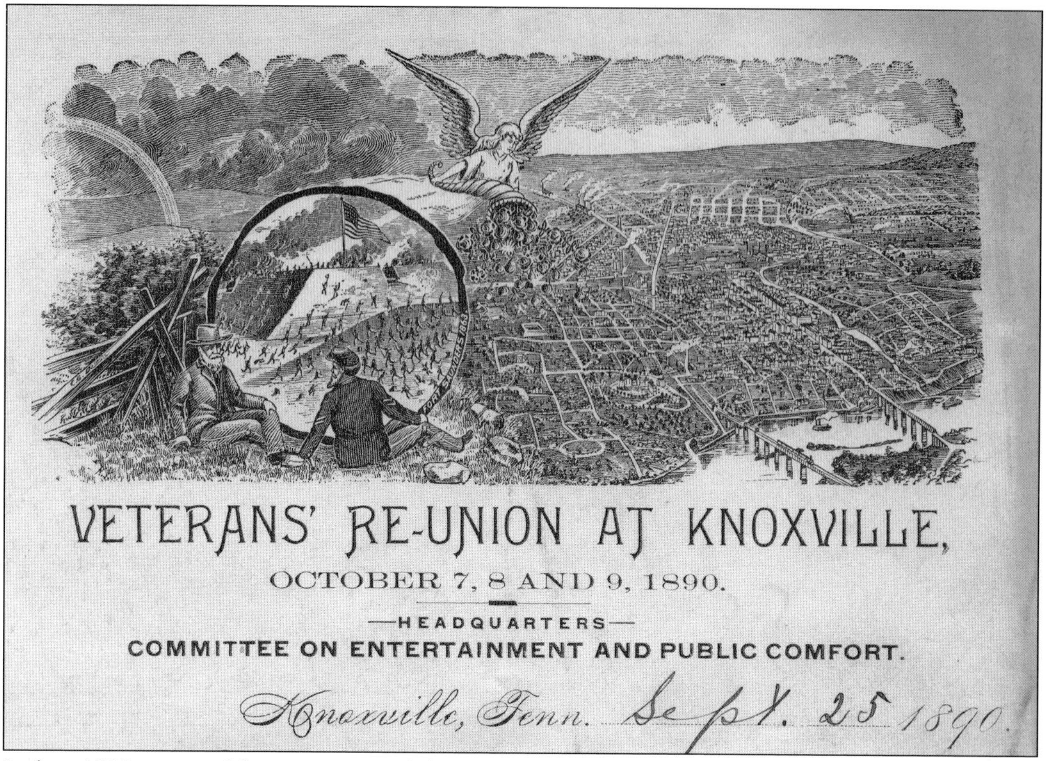

VETERANS' RE-UNION AT KNOXVILLE,

OCTOBER 7, 8 AND 9, 1890.

—HEADQUARTERS—

COMMITTEE ON ENTERTAINMENT AND PUBLIC COMFORT.

Knoxville, Tenn. Sept. 25 1890.

In late 1890, inspired by a reunion of the 17th Michigan Infantry in Grand Rapids, Michigan, earlier the same year, Knoxville hosted its own blue-gray reunion, offering veterans from both sides of the Civil War an opportunity to reflect on past hostilities and celebrate peaceful times. Festivities included parades and receptions and culminated with a grand fireworks display on the ramparts of Fort Sanders, site of the 1863 Battle of Knoxville.

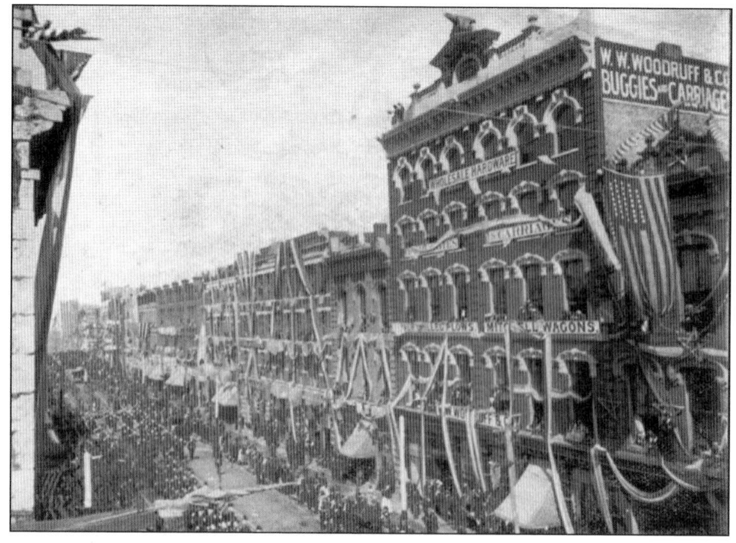

While most events during the reunion took place under a large tent on the remains of Fort Sanders in West Knoxville, many downtown merchants and owners welcomed the arriving veterans with flags and bunting. This photograph of the 400 block of Gay Street shows most prominently Woodruff's huge hardware store. Most of the buildings in this photograph burned down in the fire of 1897.

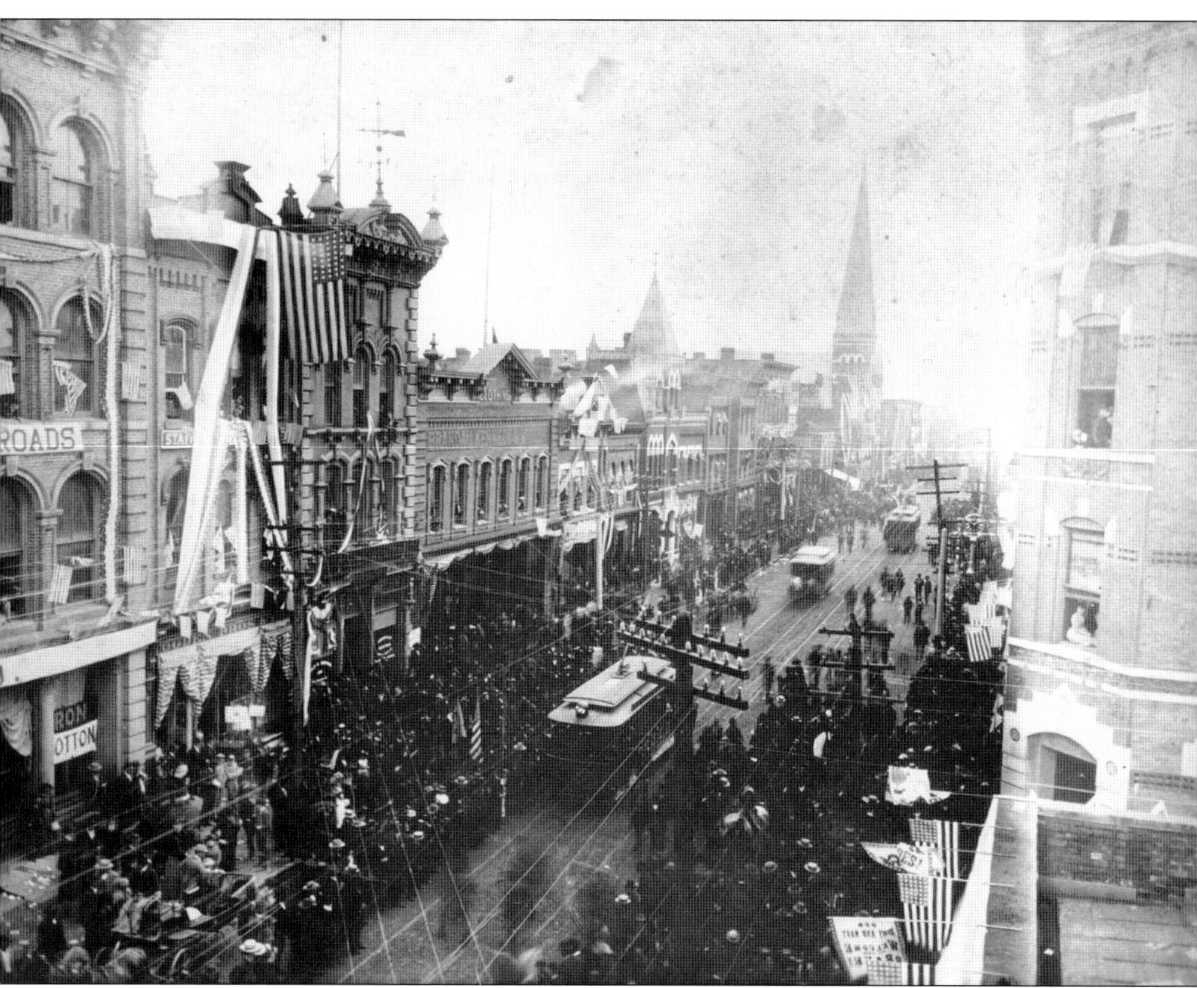

Arriving for the reunion, one old veteran from Nebraska who had lost a leg in the war remarked, "I came expecting to see the same Knoxville of war times, but I did not. There is a large bustling city which has taken the place of old Knoxville. I recognize nothing at all save a few points along the river near the foot of Gay Street. I got off the train at the depot and was lost." This view looking south along Gay Street from the corner of Union Avenue is almost an extension of the previous photograph. Identified as the 1890 reunion, it may actually show a later event.

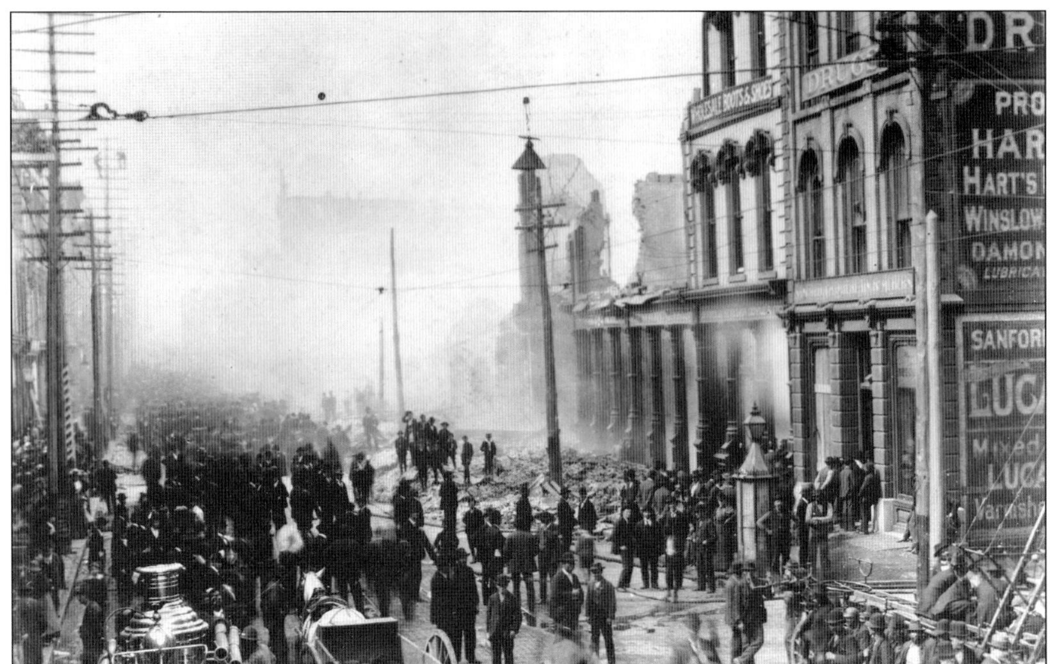

In the early hours of the morning on April 8, 1897, a fire started in the elevator shaft of the Hotel Knox on the 400 block of Gay Street. The first engine to fight the blaze came from the firehall one block away. It soon became evident that it was no ordinary conflagration, and within a short time, the fire had engulfed the buildings between Commerce and Union Avenues. As the inferno raged, the Knoxville Fire Department realized that it was ill-equipped to deal with a blaze of such magnitude and made a distress call to the Chattanooga Fire Department. Fire engines loaded onto railway cars in Chattanooga arrived in Knoxville to help contain and extinguish the blaze. These photographs were taken by 16-year-old James (Jim) Thompson (1880–1976) and are among his first photographs of Knoxville.

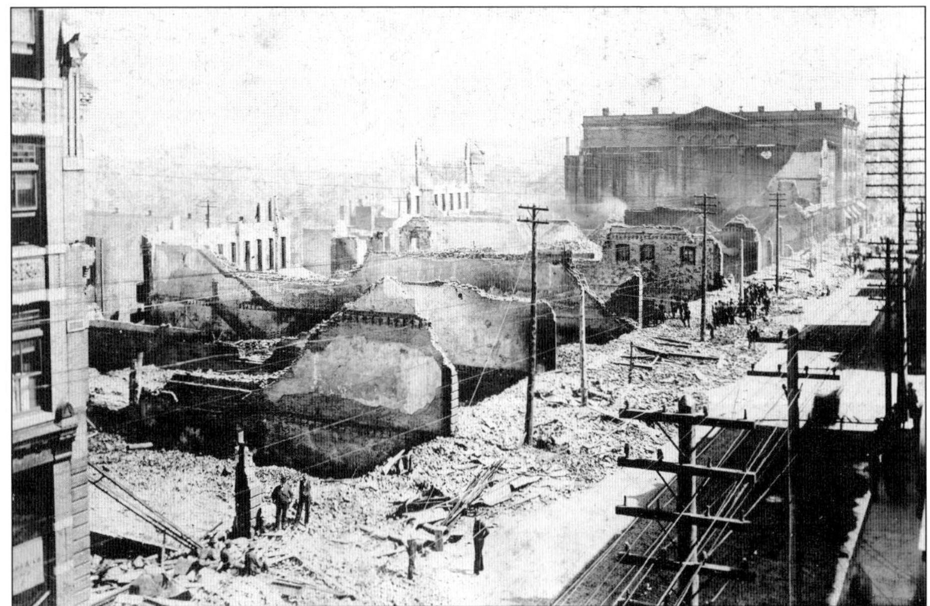

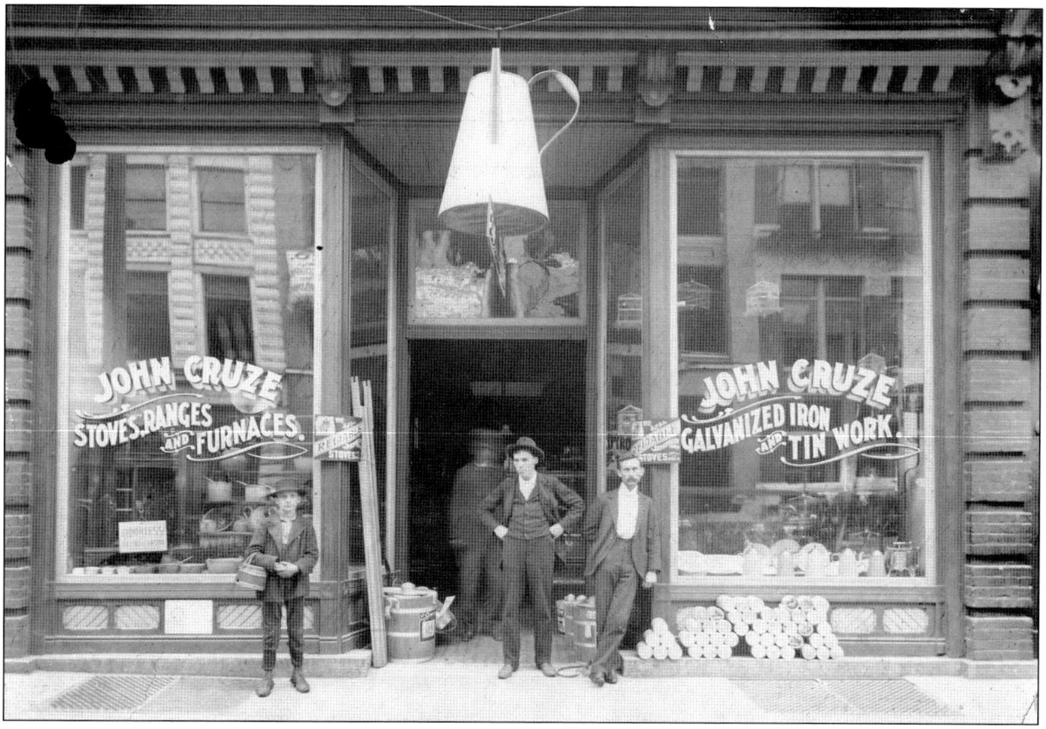

Major Knoxville merchants lost entire buildings and all their stock, including Woodruff's hardware store, Sterchi Brothers furniture and carpet dealer, and Daniel Briscoe and Bros. dry goods. Businesses across Gay Street were also damaged, one of which was John Cruze's, specializing in "stoves, ranges, and furnaces," seen above. The fire spread to buildings on State Street to the east, where the city stables also reported extensive damage. After the dust had settled, the cumulative cost to business owners suggested the term "Million Dollar Fire." In fact, the total cost was far greater than that. At least four people died. Within a year, many business owners who were able to withstand the losses rebounded swiftly, and much of what had been destroyed was rebuilt.

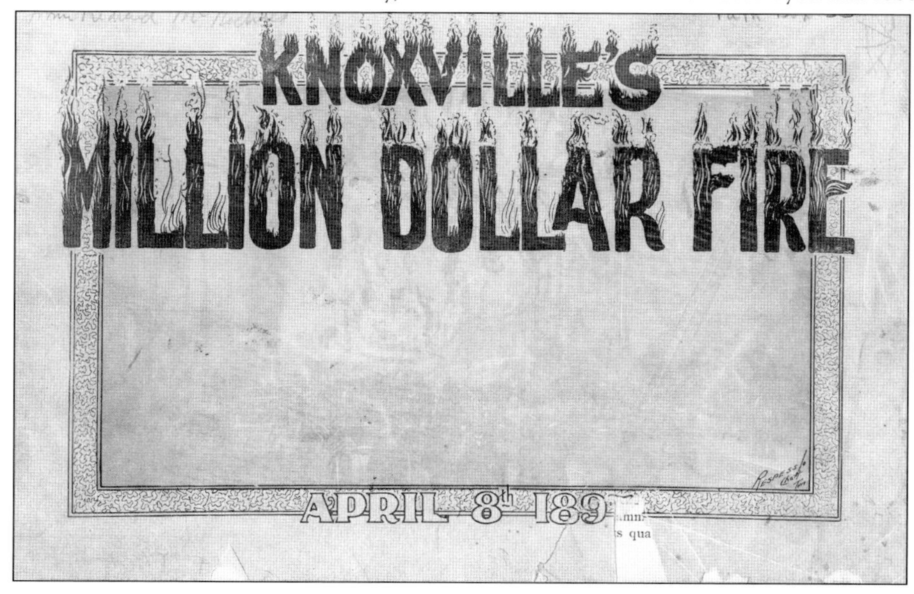

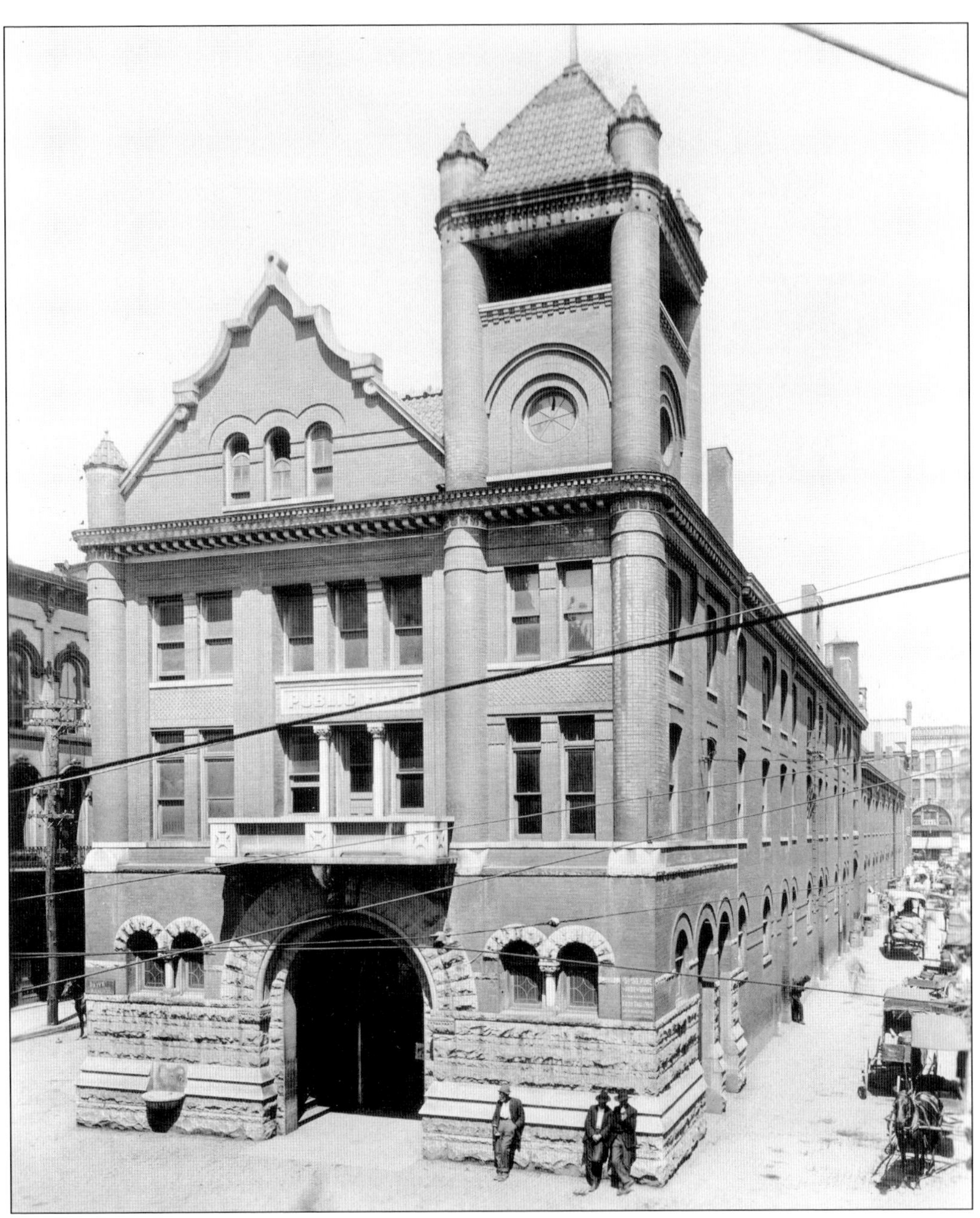

At the close of the 19th century, Market Square received a major facelift. On December 2, 1897, a new Romanesque building lined with Tennessee gray marble was unveiled to a crowd of 6,000. Unusual in shape, the south end of the building facing Union Avenue featured three stories, reduced to two stories in the central section before connecting to the existing City Hall at the north end. An auditorium had seating capacity for 1,000. Some farmers rented stalls inside; others sold from their wagons outside. In his novel *Suttree*, Cormac McCarthy described this building as "the markethouse where brick the color of dried blood rose turreted and cupolaed and crazed into the heat of the day form on form in demented accretion without precedent or counterpart in the annals of architecture." The architects were the local firm Baumann Brothers.

Four

The Progressive Era

As Knoxville moved into the 20th century, it experienced great change. Improvements in transportation affected the number of people coming into the city and how they moved around it. Within a few years, the old and trusted horse and cart had to contend with the novelty of unpredictable automobile drivers as well as streetcar lines.

In 1903, the new Southern Railway station opened and immediately encountered operational problems: architects seriously underestimated its popularity. Knoxville was growing fast, driven by the booming manufacturing and wholesale industries, the latter concentrated along Jackson Avenue, which offered access to the freight yards. A second railway station, the L&N, arrived two years later with its freight yards and associated industry.

Knoxville business boosters began extolling the growing city's greatest strengths through a series of annual *Progressive Knoxville* booklets. They claimed that the city's people and cultural attractions, along with its abundant natural resources (coal, iron, marble, lumber) and proximity to the Tennessee River and expanding railroad connections made for a winning combination.

The Progressive movement brought real improvements as well as the successful Temperance movement, which forced the closure of all downtown's 100-plus saloons in 1907. Many of those saloons immediately closed, while others transitioned to selling soda and confections.

Knoxville staged three cultural expositions in 1910, 1911, and 1913, all held at Chilhowee Park, the last one attracting one million visitors during its two-month run. Beyond their inherent spectacles, the expositions brought thousands of visitors to the city, particularly downtown. The environmental focus of the National Conservation Exposition of 1913 energized several community members who became leaders of the effort to establish Great Smoky Mountains National Park a decade later.

However, before the 1920s began, downtown witnessed one of its darkest days when a Black man was arrested for killing a white woman. The ensuing frenzied riot in August 1919 brought in a brief state of martial law, leaving several dead, many wounded, and downtown businesses ransacked.

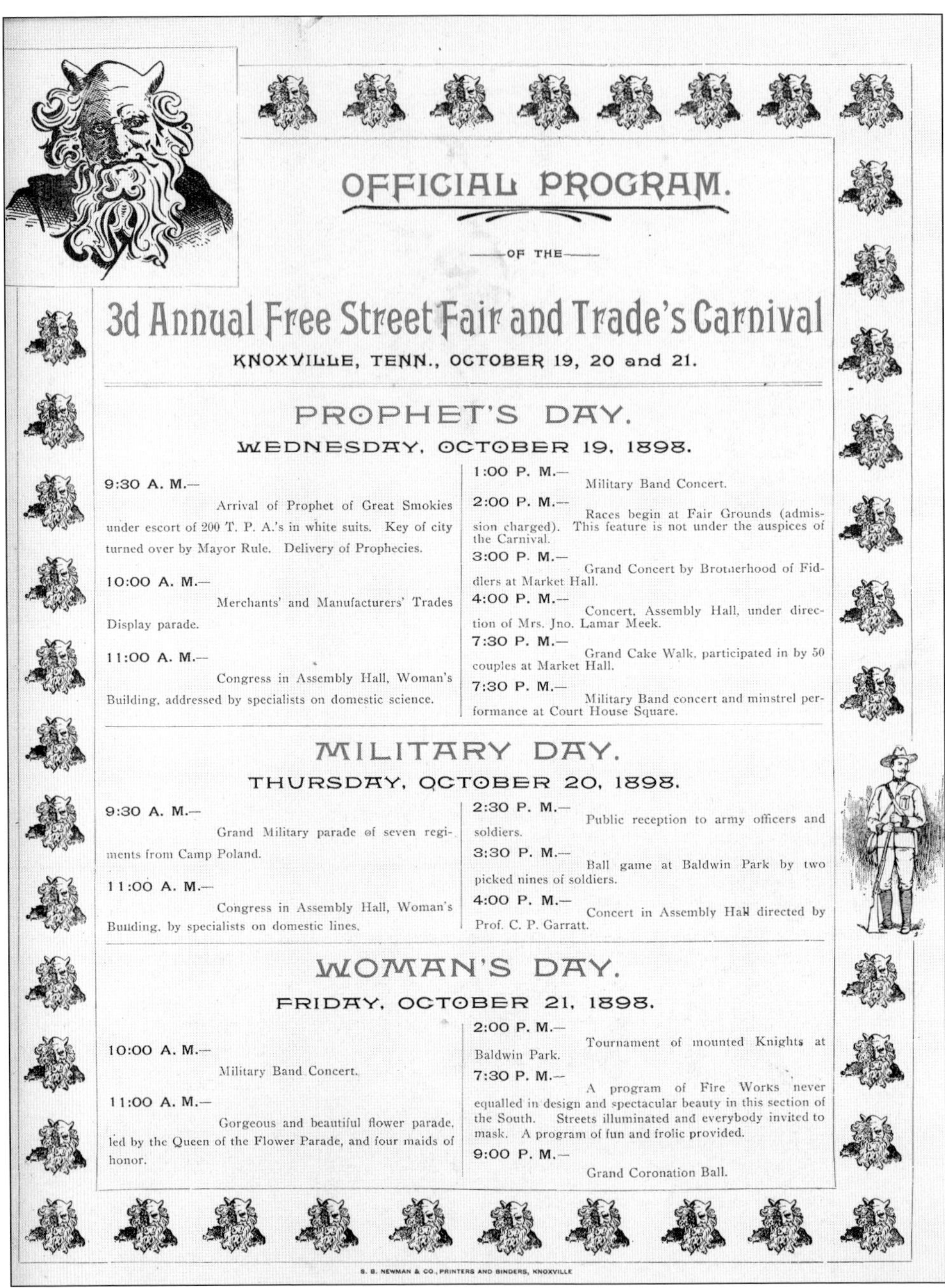

OFFICIAL PROGRAM.

—OF THE—

3d Annual Free Street Fair and Trade's Carnival

KNOXVILLE, TENN., OCTOBER 19, 20 and 21.

PROPHET'S DAY.

WEDNESDAY, OCTOBER 19, 1898.

9:30 A. M.—
Arrival of Prophet of Great Smokies under escort of 200 T. P. A.'s in white suits. Key of city turned over by Mayor Rule. Delivery of Prophecies.

10:00 A. M.—
Merchants' and Manufacturers' Trades Display parade.

11:00 A. M.—
Congress in Assembly Hall, Woman's Building, addressed by specialists on domestic science.

1:00 P. M.—
Military Band Concert.

2:00 P. M.—
Races begin at Fair Grounds (admission charged). This feature is not under the auspices of the Carnival.

3:00 P. M.—
Grand Concert by Brotherhood of Fiddlers at Market Hall.

4:00 P. M.—
Concert, Assembly Hall, under direction of Mrs. Jno. Lamar Meek.

7:30 P. M.—
Grand Cake Walk, participated in by 50 couples at Market Hall.

7:30 P. M.—
Military Band concert and minstrel performance at Court House Square.

MILITARY DAY.

THURSDAY, OCTOBER 20, 1898.

9:30 A. M.—
Grand Military parade of seven regiments from Camp Poland.

11:00 A. M.—
Congress in Assembly Hall, Woman's Building, by specialists on domestic lines.

2:30 P. M.—
Public reception to army officers and soldiers.

3:30 P. M.—
Ball game at Baldwin Park by two picked nines of soldiers.

4:00 P. M.—
Concert in Assembly Hall directed by Prof. C. P. Garratt.

WOMAN'S DAY.

FRIDAY, OCTOBER 21, 1898.

10:00 A. M.—
Military Band Concert.

11:00 A. M.—
Gorgeous and beautiful flower parade, led by the Queen of the Flower Parade, and four maids of honor.

2:00 P. M.—
Tournament of mounted Knights at Baldwin Park.

7:30 P. M.—
A program of Fire Works never equalled in design and spectacular beauty in this section of the South. Streets illuminated and everybody invited to mask. A program of fun and frolic provided.

9:00 P. M.—
Grand Coronation Ball.

S. B. NEWMAN & CO., PRINTERS AND BINDERS, KNOXVILLE

The third annual Knoxville Free Street Fair and Trades Carnival of 1898 was billed as the "Greatest Event in the History of the Marble City." Festivities commenced south of the river, where Mayor William Rule presented a key to the city to the "Prophet of the Smokies," who, according to the official program, "only leaves his mountain home once each year and then to visit his children in the city and bestow blessings on them." The event was a regional draw, with train tickets sold to people up to 200 miles away. The "prophet" was reportedly a local celebrity in disguise. He approached the city across the new Gay Street bridge. A special Woman's Day featured a procession led by the Queen of the Flower Parade and a series of programs at the Woman's Building on Main Street.

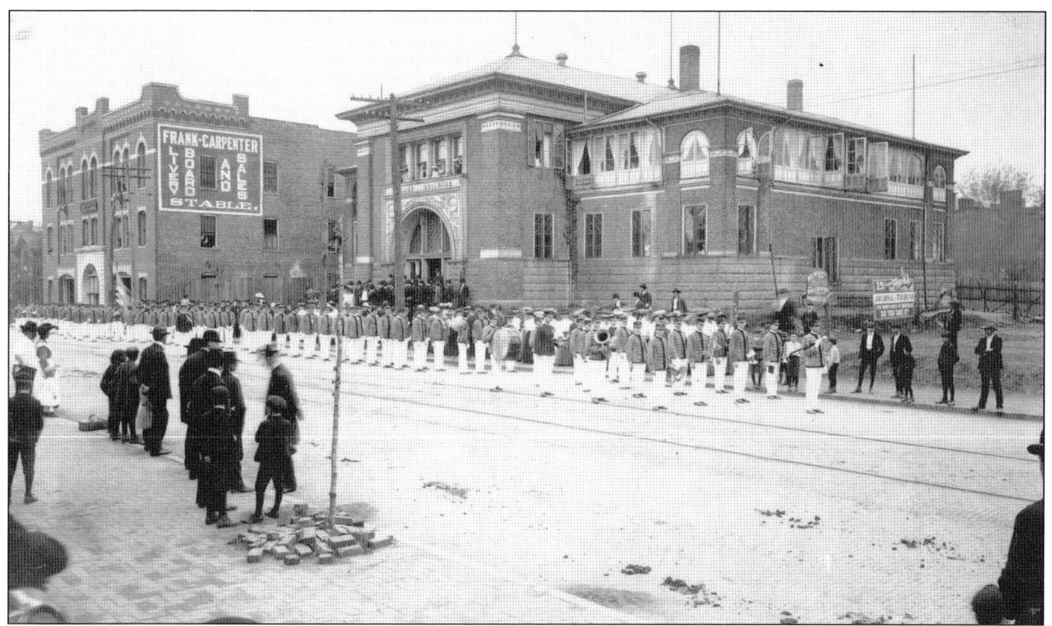

A parade on Main Street honored Dr. Brown Ayres, a distinguished professor of physics from Tulane University who was elected president of the University of Tennessee in 1904. After his death in 1919, the university's striking building on the hill was named Ayres Hall in his honor. The building in the background is the Woman's Building on Main Street, there from 1898 until a Christmas Day fire destroyed it in 1906. (University of Tennessee Libraries.)

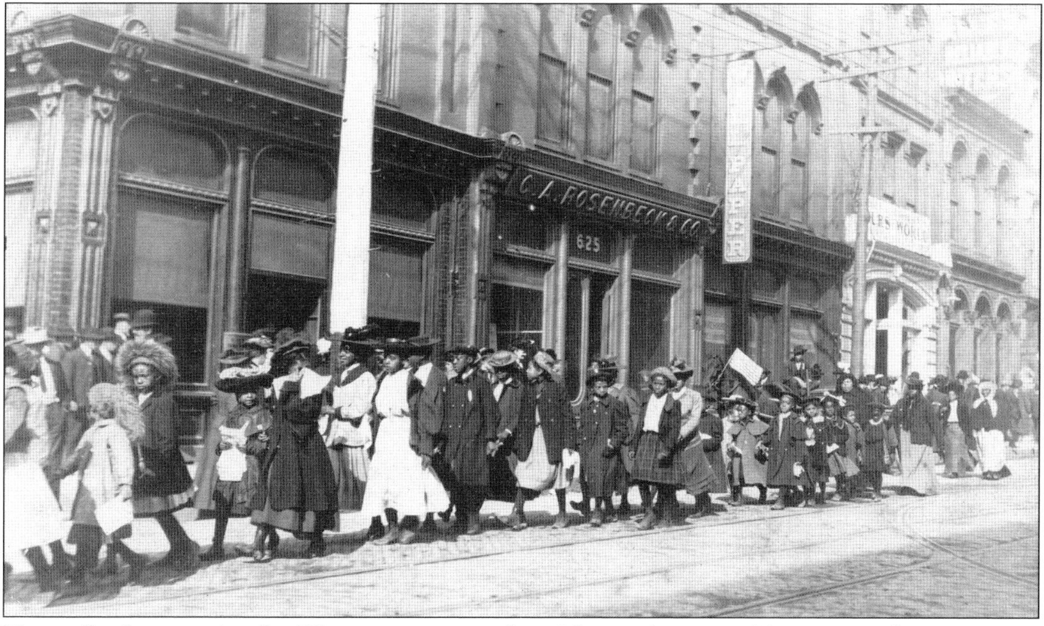

Knoxville photographer Jim Thompson captured an African American Temperance demonstration in support of Prohibition in 1907 as it proceeded south on Gay Street just past Church Avenue. That year, even though not supported by Mayor Samuel Heiskell, Prohibitionists achieved a startling feat: the passage of a local ordinance closing 106 saloons and liquor stores within the city limits. Although beer returned in 1933, liquor by the drink was not re-legalized until 1972.

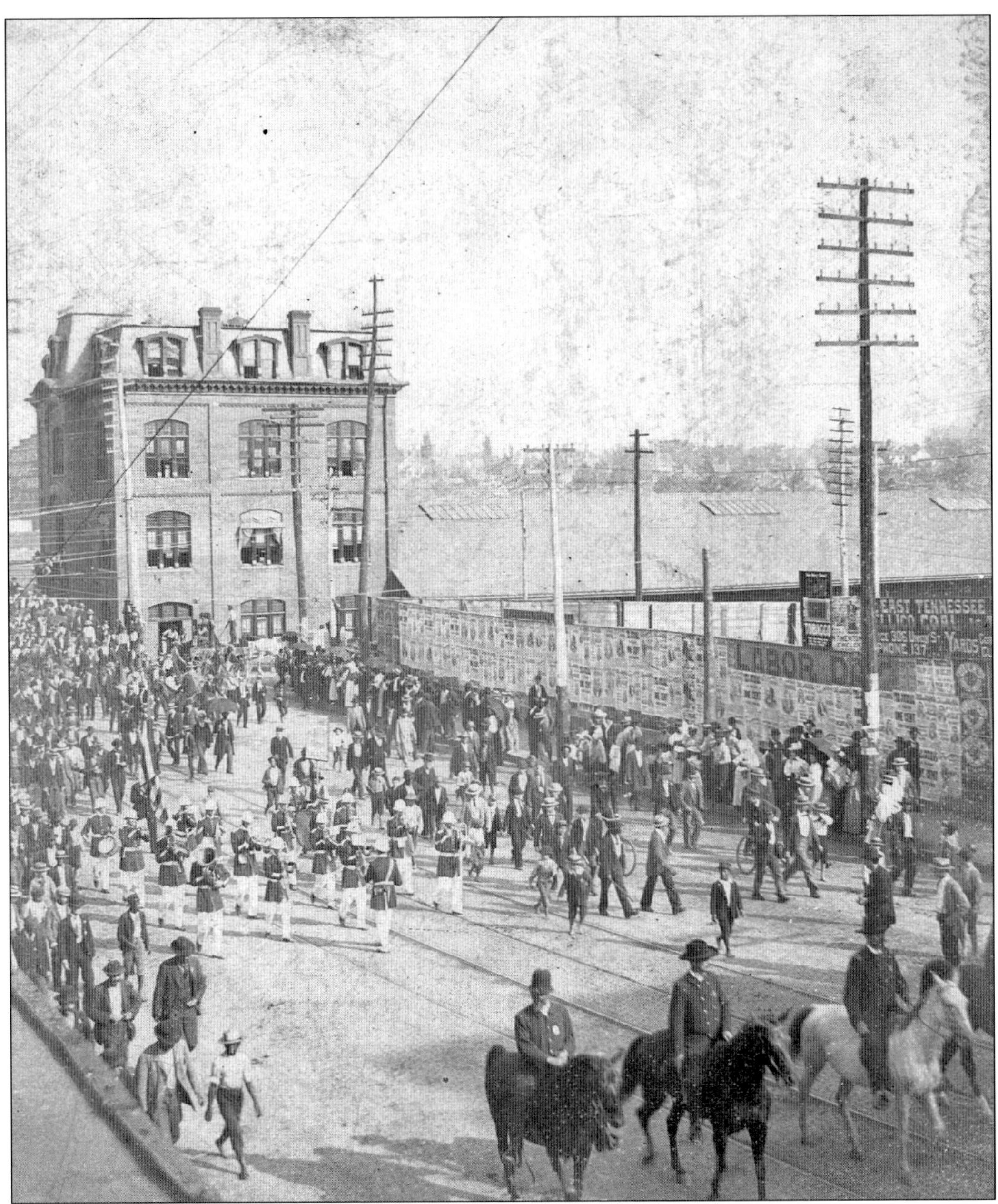

Given the poster on the wall on the right, this undated scene is likely a Labor Day parade around the turn of the 20th century. In that era, numerous workers' unions participated in Labor Day parades, representing tailors, carpenters, plasterers, iron workers, painters, and cigarmakers. As this parade proceeds south on Gay Street past the Knoxville-based East Tennessee, Virginia & Georgia Railroad headquarters building at Jackson Avenue, marchers and spectators include both whites and African Americans. A few attendees are on bicycles. (McClung, Small Photograph Collection.)

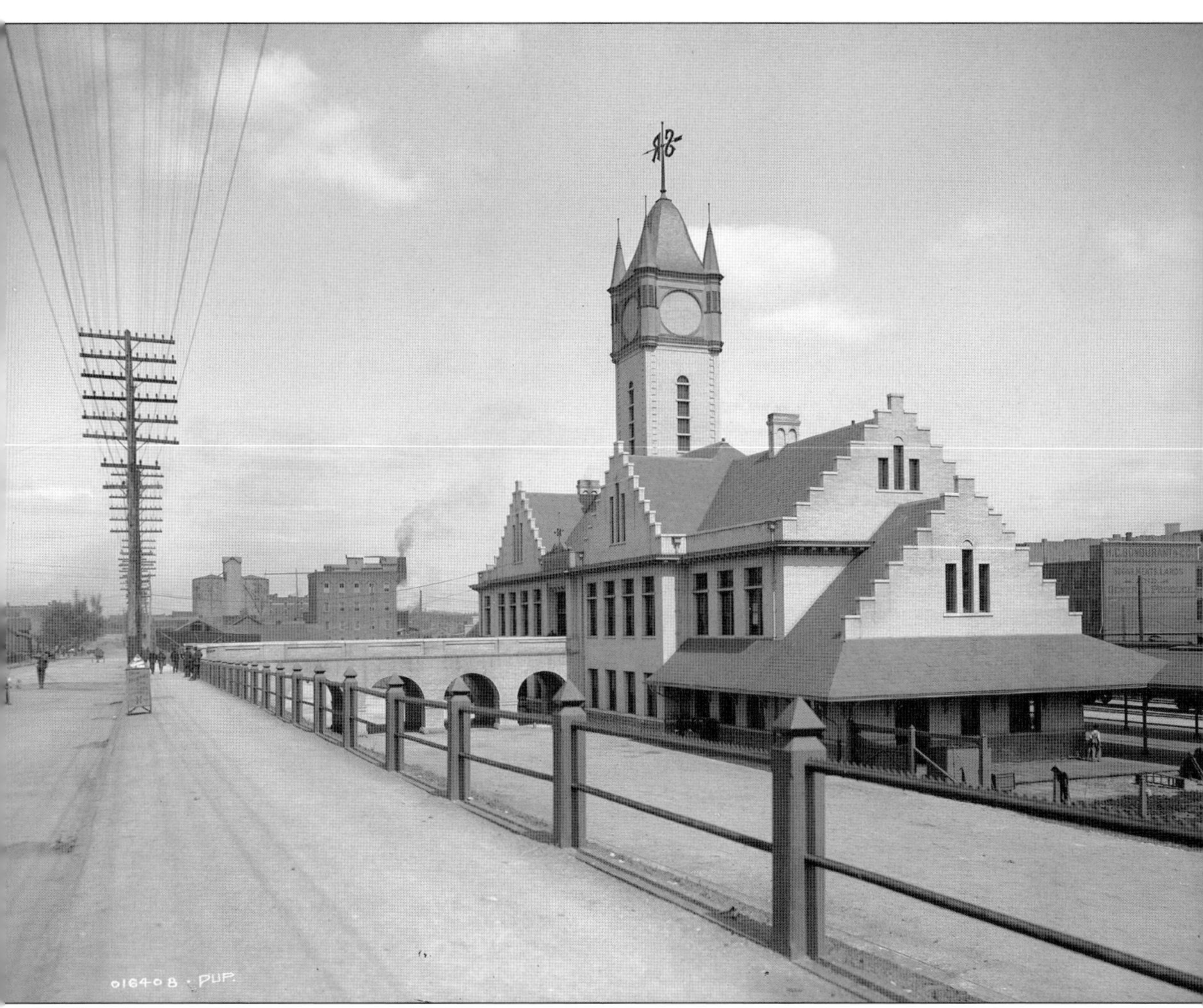

Completed in 1903, the Southern Railway station was designed by architect Frank Pierce Milburn. This oddly sterile image appears to show the station when it was very new, perhaps unfinished, considering the clock lacks hands. In its heyday, the Southern station was open 24 hours, greeting as many as 50 passenger trains a day and serving millions of passengers, among them several US presidents, Buffalo Bill, actress Tallulah Bankhead, Prohibitionist Carrie Nation, and singers Al Jolson and Elvis Presley. The clock tower was removed in 1945. The last regular passenger train departed in 1970. The station building has been used for offices and events since then.

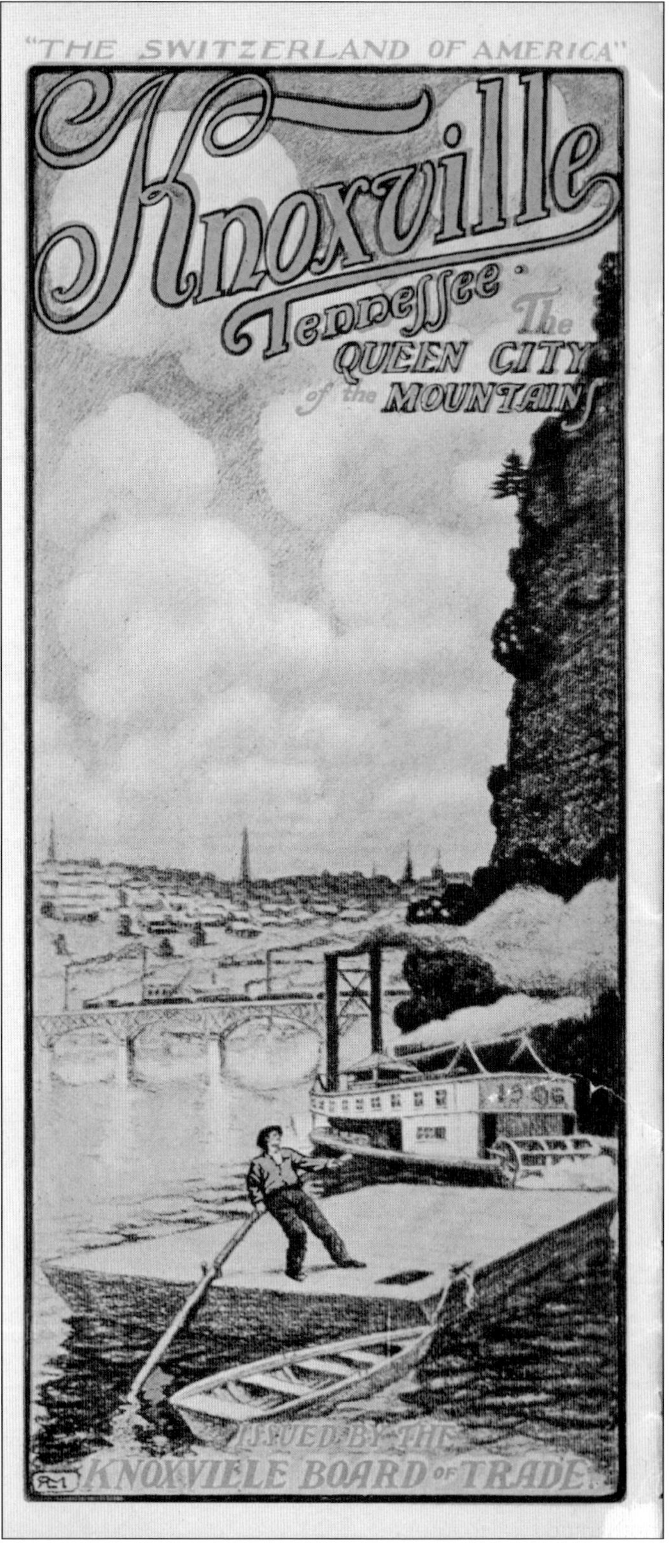

Business leaders with the Knoxville Board of Trade were riding high when this 1906 booster pamphlet described the city as "The Switzerland of the South," and "The Queen City of the Mountains." Downtown was thriving, spurred by a half-century of industrial and wholesale development enabled by both river traffic and railroads, represented by the train crossing the bridge in the distance. (University of Tennessee Libraries.)

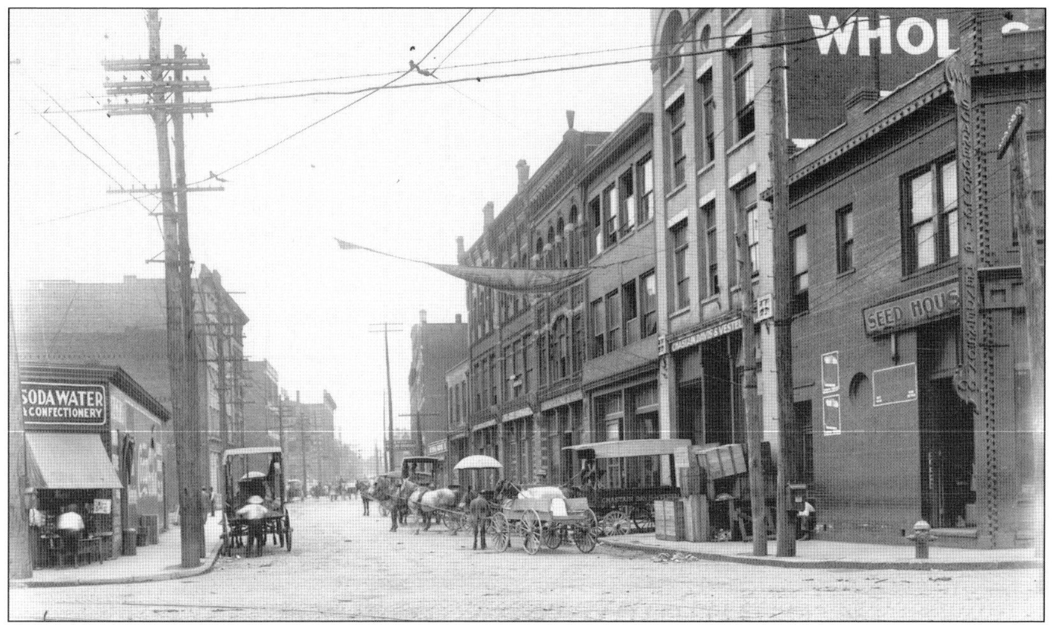

Looking west on Jackson Avenue at Central Street in 1913, this street famous for wholesale businesses hosted mainly garment dealers on the left and grocery suppliers on the right. The "Soda Water" drugstore is where Boyd's Jig & Reel is today. Central Street, famous for its saloons until they were banned in 1907, became quieter in the 20th century.

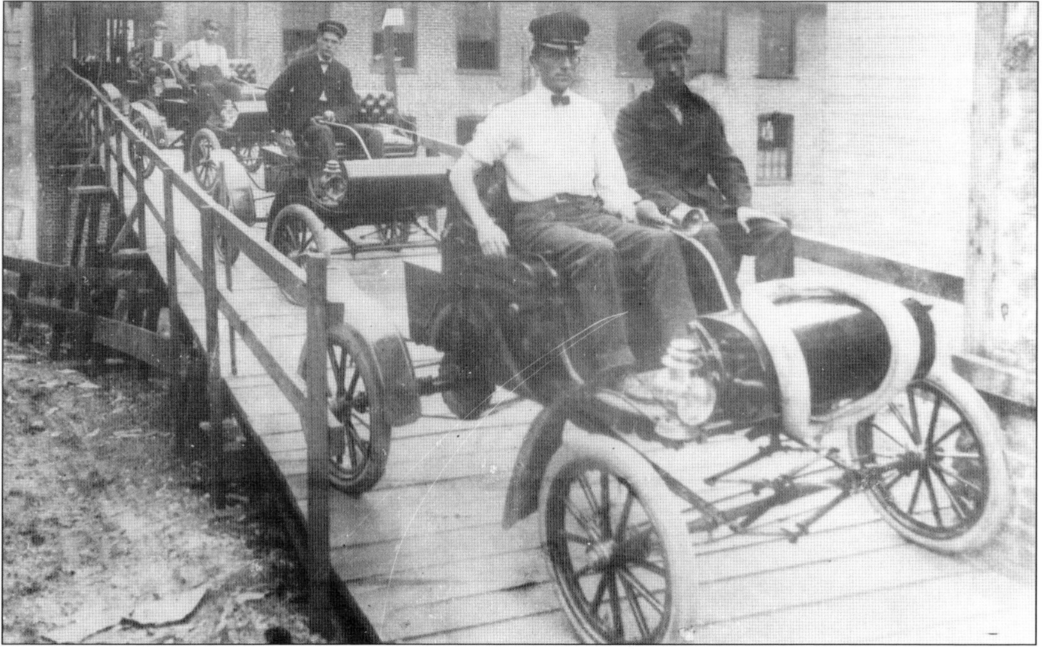
This c. 1903 photograph by Jim Thompson is one of the earliest known images of an automobile in Knoxville. Prominent on the left is Cowan Rodgers (1878–1936), an athlete-turned-inventor who was Knoxville's first car dealer. The car in front appears to be a gasoline-powered Locomobile. Rodgers was also an early advocate of the movement to establish the Great Smoky Mountains National Park. (McClung, Small Photograph Collection.)

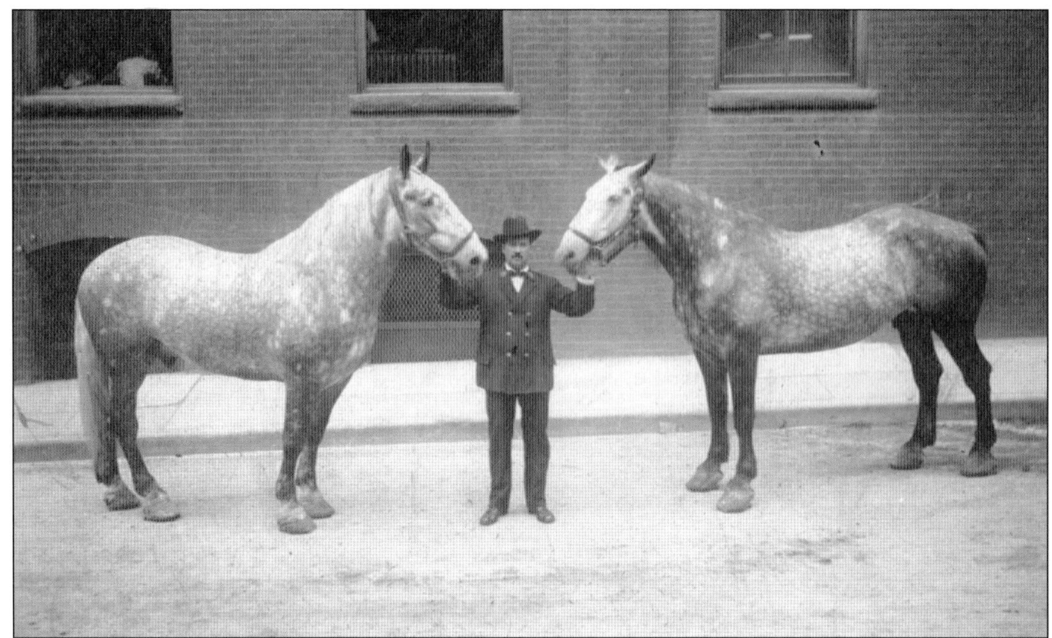

In 1900, the same year that he became chief of the fire department, Sam Boyd (1865–1929) proudly shows two large horses named Ned and George. Boyd served as chief for 29 years before he died of a heart attack while battling a raging fire at the Knoxville Business College on Church Avenue, close to First Presbyterian Church. Boyd is the only Knoxville fire chief who has died in service.

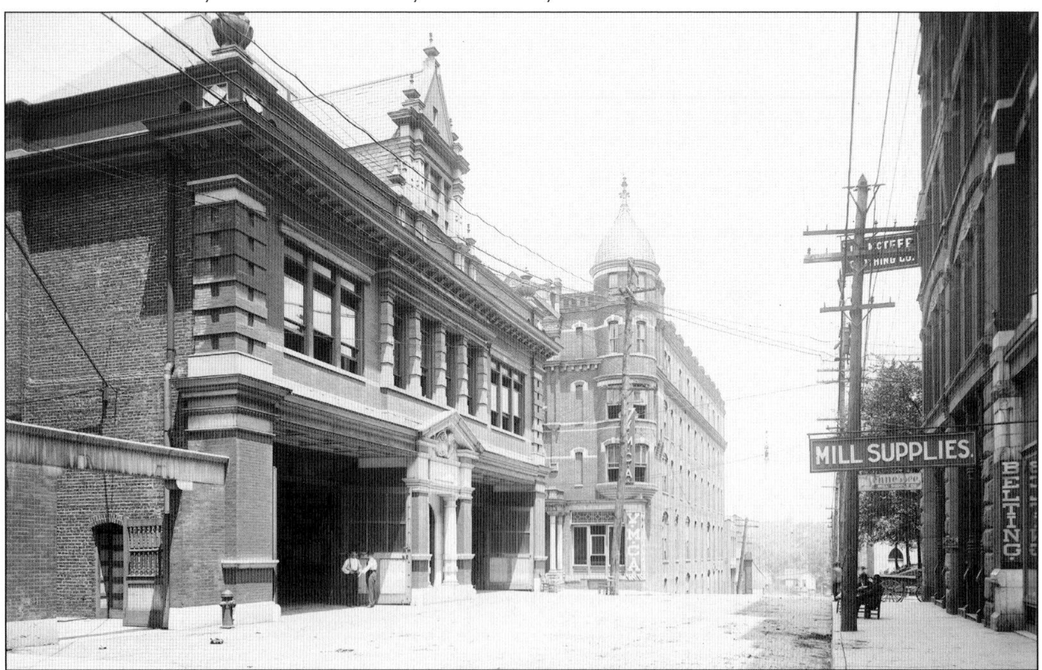

In 1904, the fire department moved from Market Square to Commerce Avenue at State Street. Beyond it is the YMCA building, originally built in 1888 as the Palace Hotel. The old hotel had become an apartment building before it was seriously damaged by a fatal fire in 1975. A campaign to save the fire hall ended in 1977 when it was razed for Summit Hill Drive. (Library of Congress.)

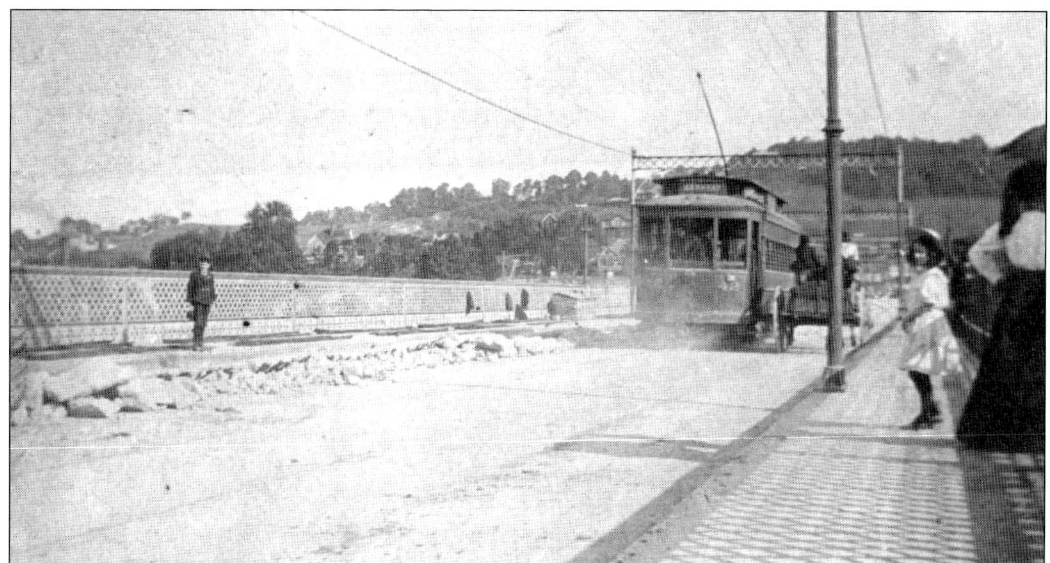

From an unknown photographer, this c. 1915 view of the Gay Street bridge, looking south toward the Fort Stanley heights, shows a streetcar making its way past a line of white debris. Despite the apparent summer-weight clothing of the pedestrians, it may be melting snow. (Knox County Two Centuries Photograph Collection.

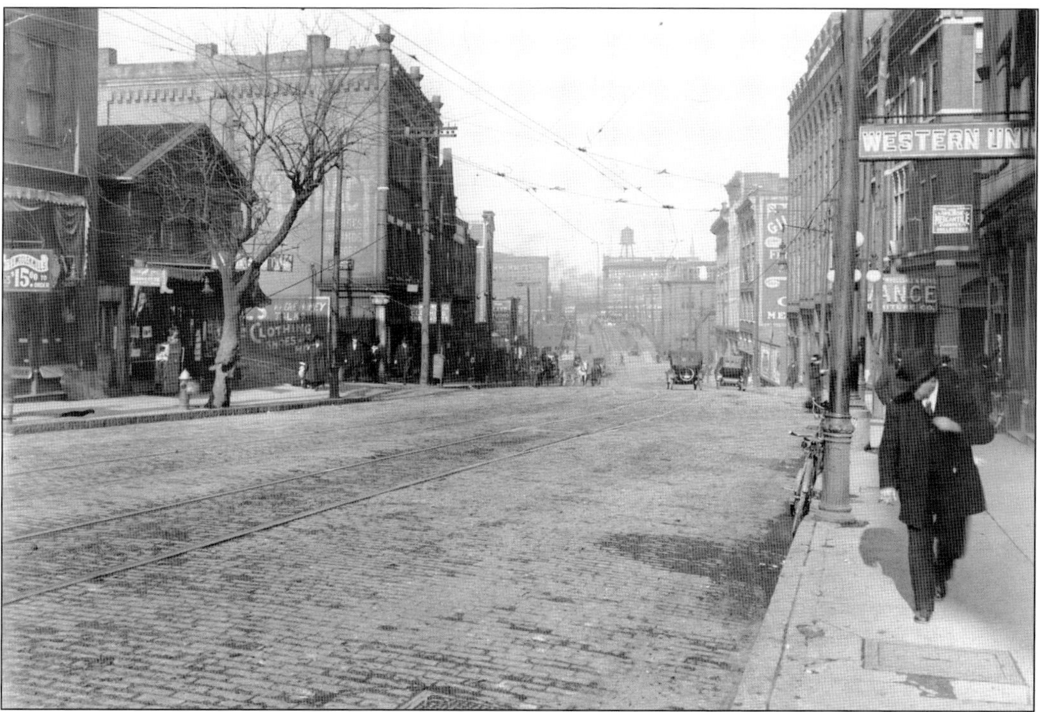

On the left, at Gay Street and Vine Avenue, is Cal Johnson's former Lone Tree Saloon, named for the only tree on Gay Street, which stood in front of it. After Prohibition in 1907, the saloon changed into a shoe repair shop owned by a man named L. Tobe, who tended the tree for years before it finally perished in the 1930s.

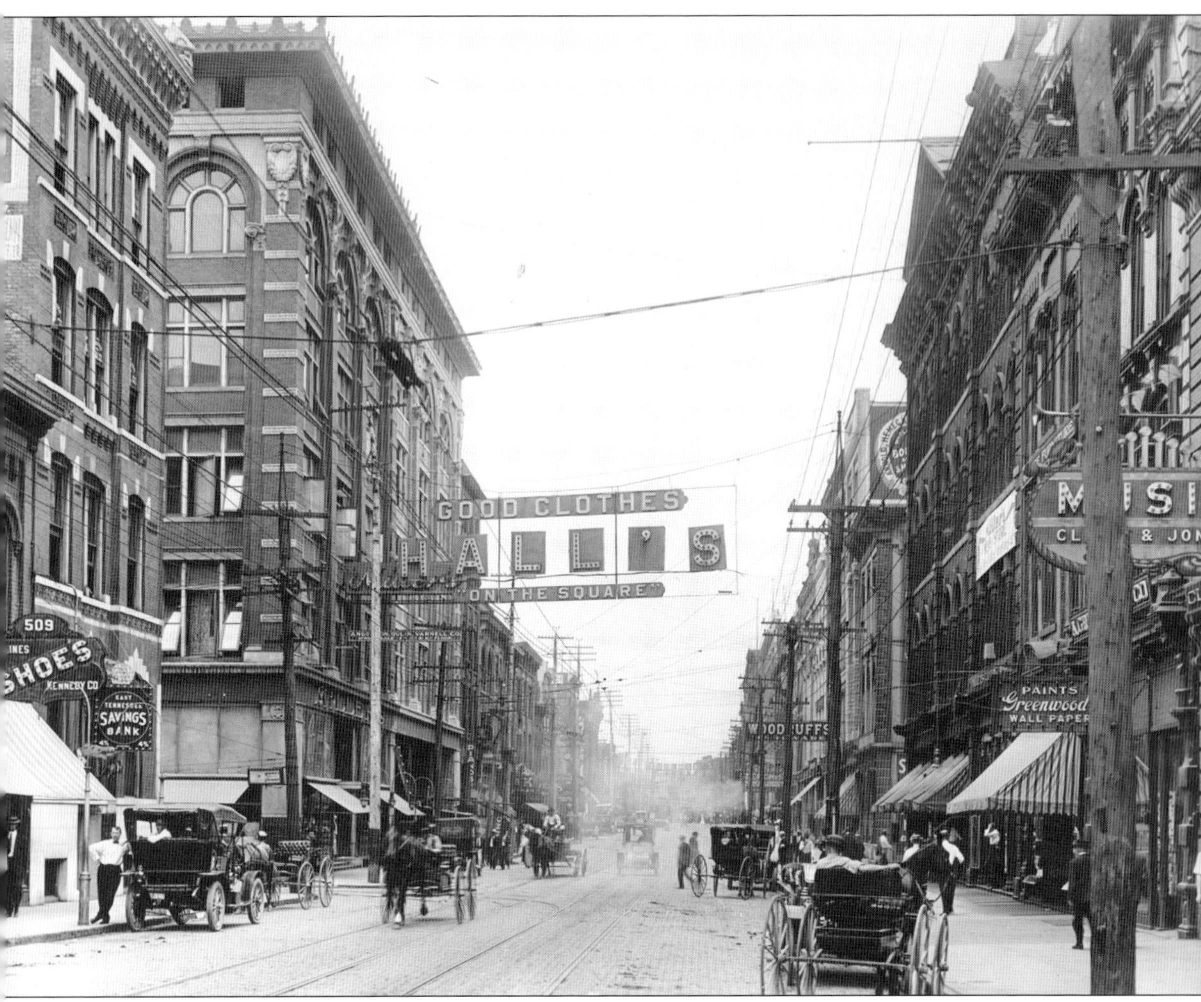

This busy scene shows Gay Street at the intersection of Union Avenue in the early 1900s, in an era when horse carts still outnumbered automobiles. The sign for "Hall's on the Square" suspended over the street highlights the clothing store's location on Market Square. East Tennessee Savings Bank and Miller's department store are on the left. The Clark & Jones music store can be seen on the right. In addition to selling musical instruments (it was Knoxville's prestigious Steinway piano dealer), the store sold gramophones and sheet music and also served as an outlet for tickets to performances at Staub's Theatre and elsewhere.

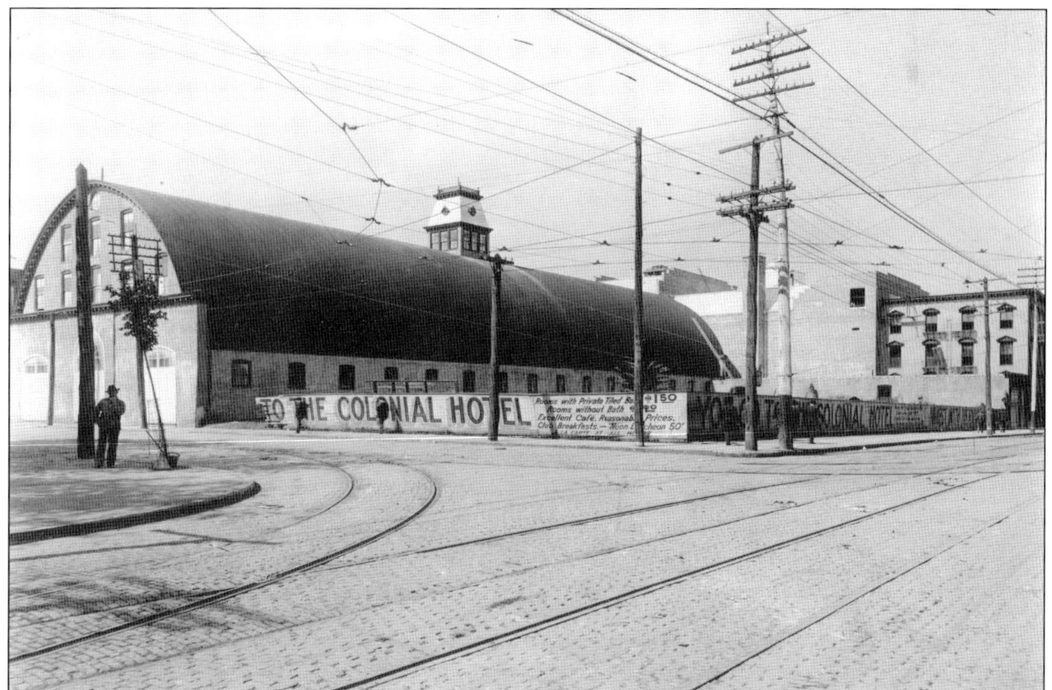

Likely taken around 1909, this photograph captures construction of the Bijou Theatre (at far right), which is almost complete at the rear of the Lamar House. The Quonset hut–shaped building on the corner of Gay and Main Streets was first used as a civic auditorium and as a roller-skating rink, and then adapted for a streetcar barn. It was demolished in 1952 after the end of streetcar service. (Library of Congress.)

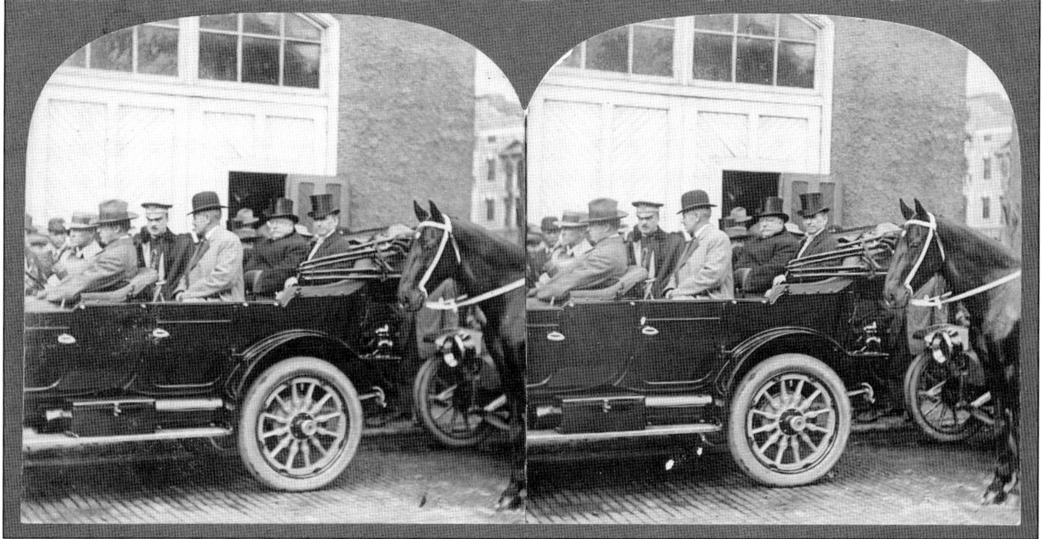

In these stereoscopic images, President Taft arrives to address a biracial crowd at Knoxville's short-lived auditorium on Main Street as part of his 1911 visit. The president first attended a reception at the Atkin Hotel before visiting the Appalachian Exposition at Chilhowee Park. Back downtown, the presidential party paraded along Gay Street, festooned with flags and bunting, to the auditorium, where Taft spoke for an hour.

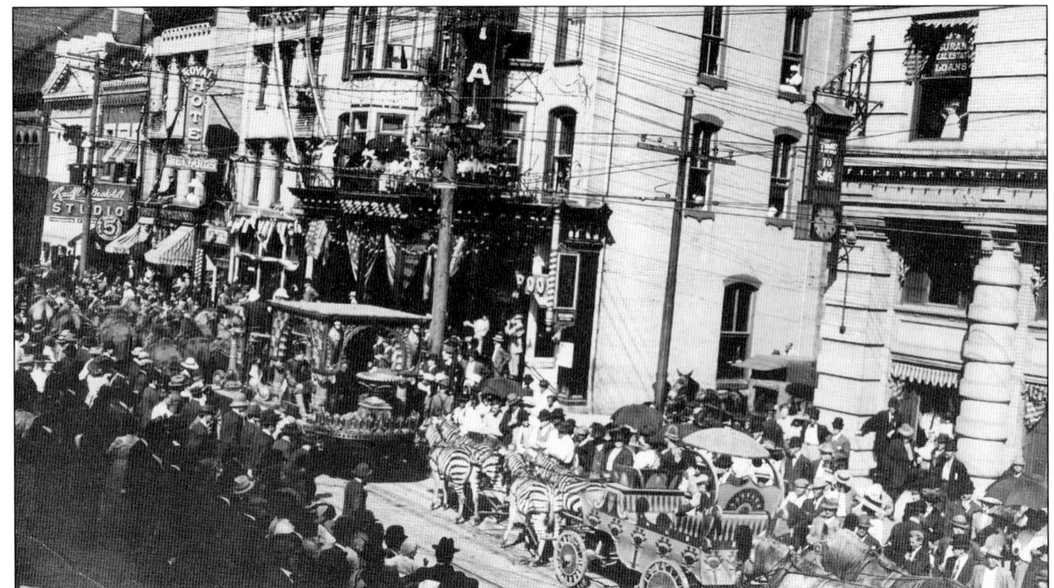

In 1910, a team of zebras pulls a chariot in front of the Imperial Hotel on Gay Street at Clinch Avenue, where guests on the hotel balcony have a spectacular view. Note the hotel's barber pole and advertisement of a pool room. When they came to town, many circuses paraded their animals from the railway station through downtown and on to the circus grounds.

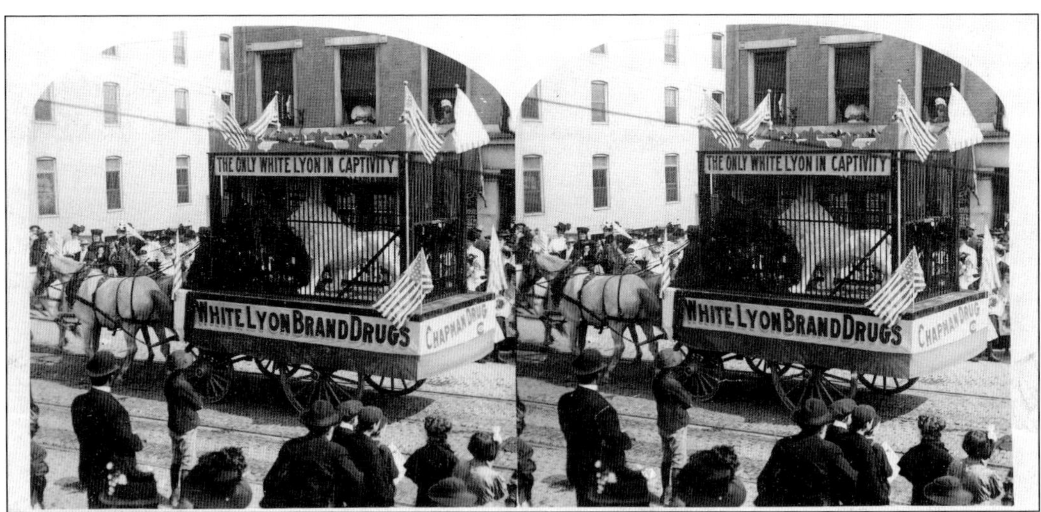

Knoxville wholesale druggist Chapman Drug Company promotes its White Lyon brand circus-style on these stereoscopic photographs from the C.A. Wayland Collection. For many years, the white lion was a conspicuous mascot in front of the firm's store on Gay Street. Pharmacy executive David Chapman later led the Great Smoky Mountains National Park project.

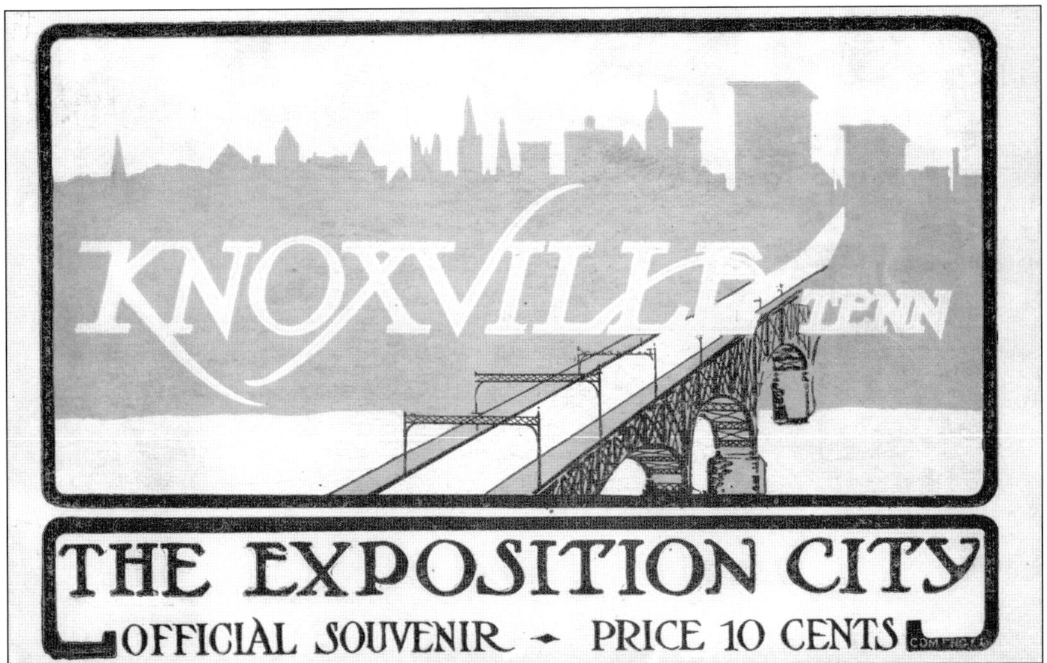

Downtown's skyline welcomed thousands of people to the National Conservation Exposition in 1913 at Chilhowee Park. Following the successful Appalachian Expositions of 1910 and 1911, this conservation-focused extravaganza was, according to the souvenir guide, "national in scope with the South as its special field." More than one million visitors came during its two-month run.

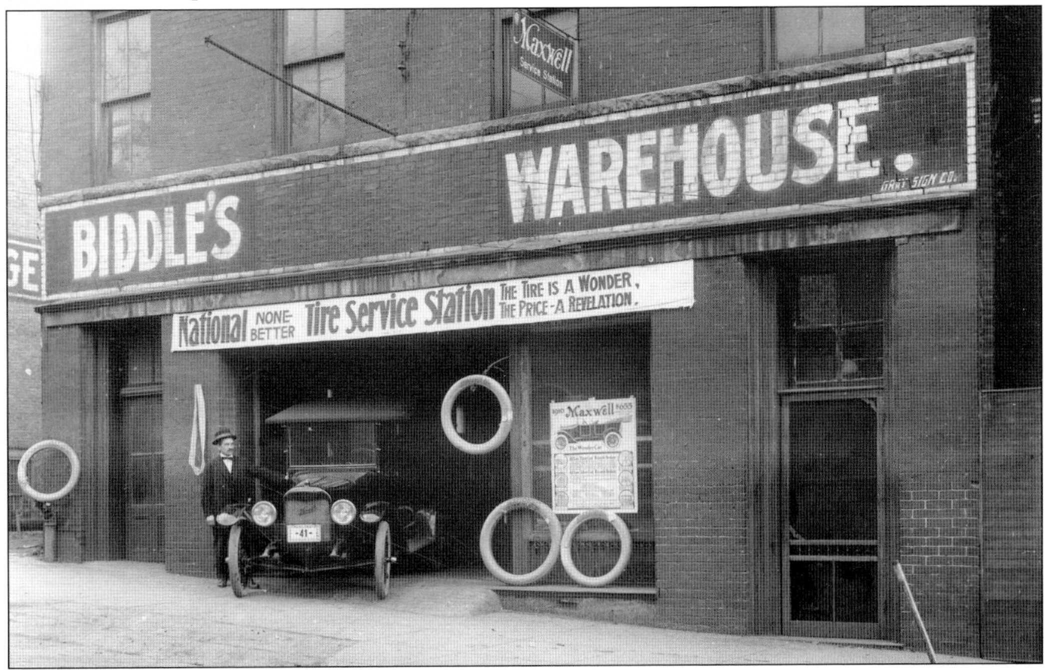

By 1916, Biddle's Auto Company on East Vine Avenue, a former bicycle shop, was a local distributor for the Maxwell automobile. The poster on the wall called it "The Wonder Car." Almost suddenly, automobiles were everywhere downtown. (McClung, Small Photograph Collection.)

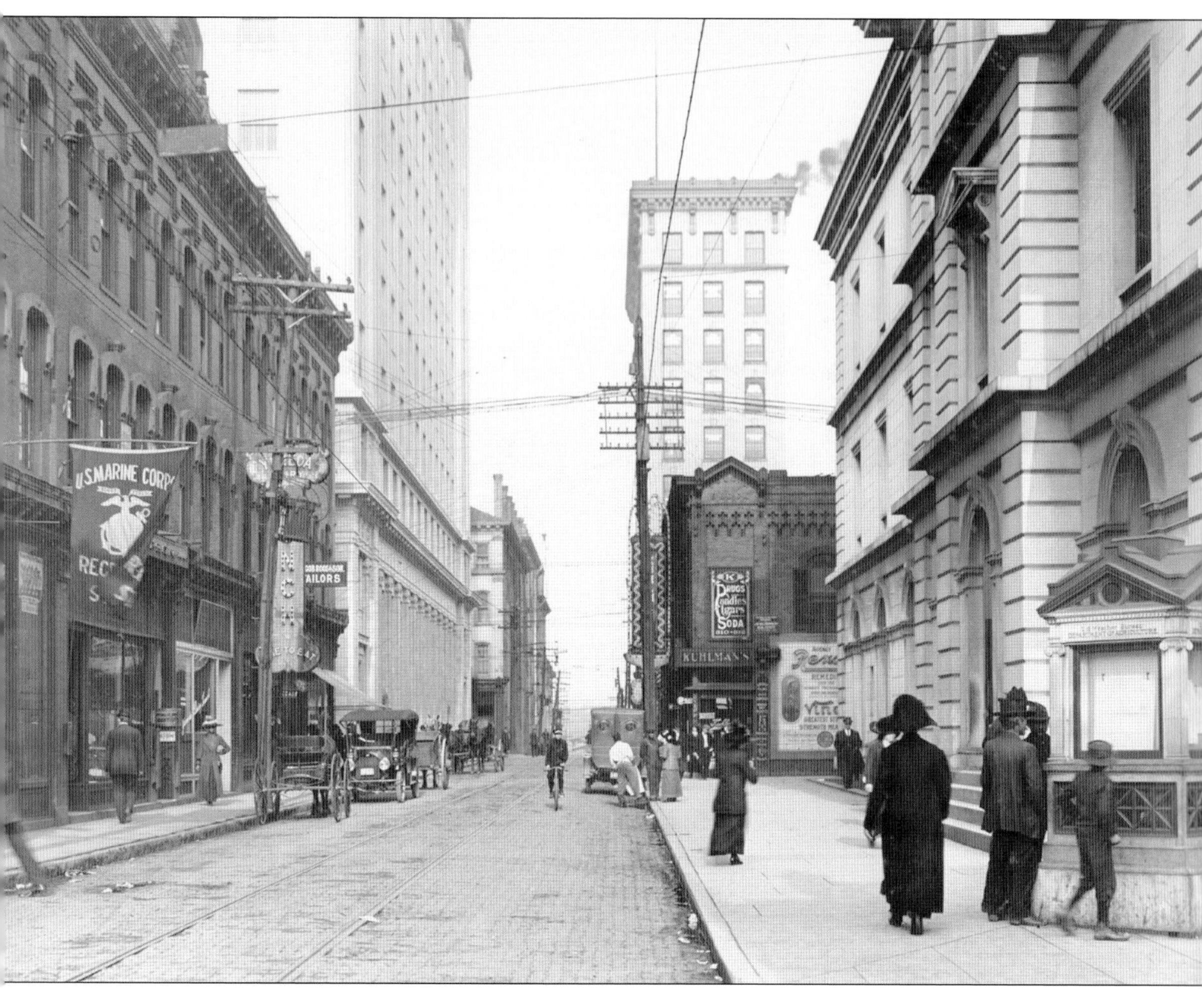

This c. 1914 photograph looking east along Clinch Avenue at the corner of Market Street offers much detail, including pedestrians, cyclists, horse-drawn carts, and early automobiles. The weather bureau kiosk, still standing today by the custom house, was installed in 1912. In addition to providing weather forecasts, it was a popular social gathering spot, serving much like a later office water cooler. Down the street to the right is the old Fouche Building, torn down in the 1990s several years before construction of a new entrance to the East Tennessee History Center, part of a seamless expansion of the custom house. On the left is a US Marine Corps recruiting station, several years before the United States entered World War I. In the distance is the Burwell Building, and barely visible at left on Gay Street, just across from the Holston Bank Building, is the Imperial Hotel, which burned in 1916.

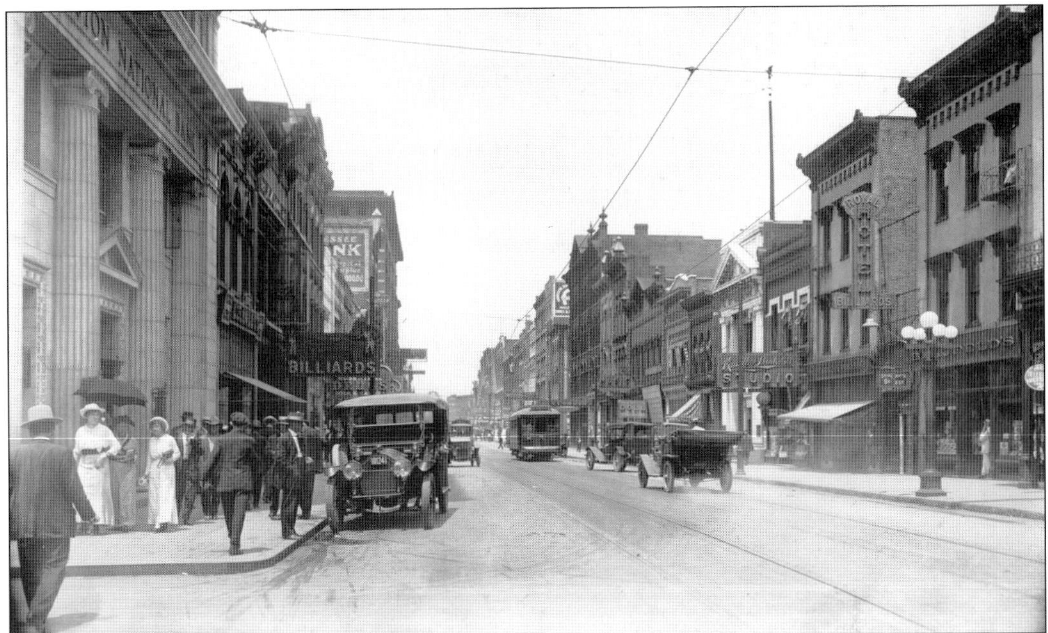

Fronted with a façade of local marble, the Holston Building at Gay Street and Clinch Avenue was still Knoxville's tallest around 1920, when this photograph was taken. The office building once hosted more than 100 separate businesses ranging from powerful attorneys' suites to beauty parlors. The largest was the Holston Bank, which failed in 1931 and reopened as Hamilton National Bank. The Holston is now a luxury residential building.

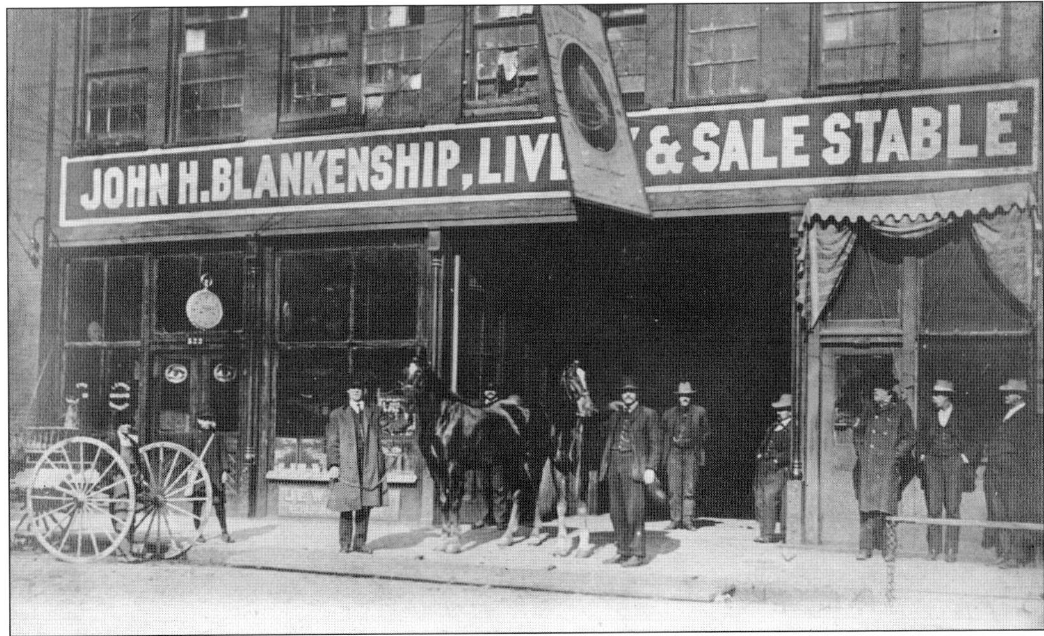

Once, there were dozens of livery stables downtown where horses could be left or rented for a fee. This one on Prince Street (now Market) was at the current location of Krutch Park. Livery stables became less common after the introduction of the electric streetcar and the automobile. This one had closed by 1910. Proprietor John Blankenship (1865–1938) was elected Knox County sheriff in 1914.

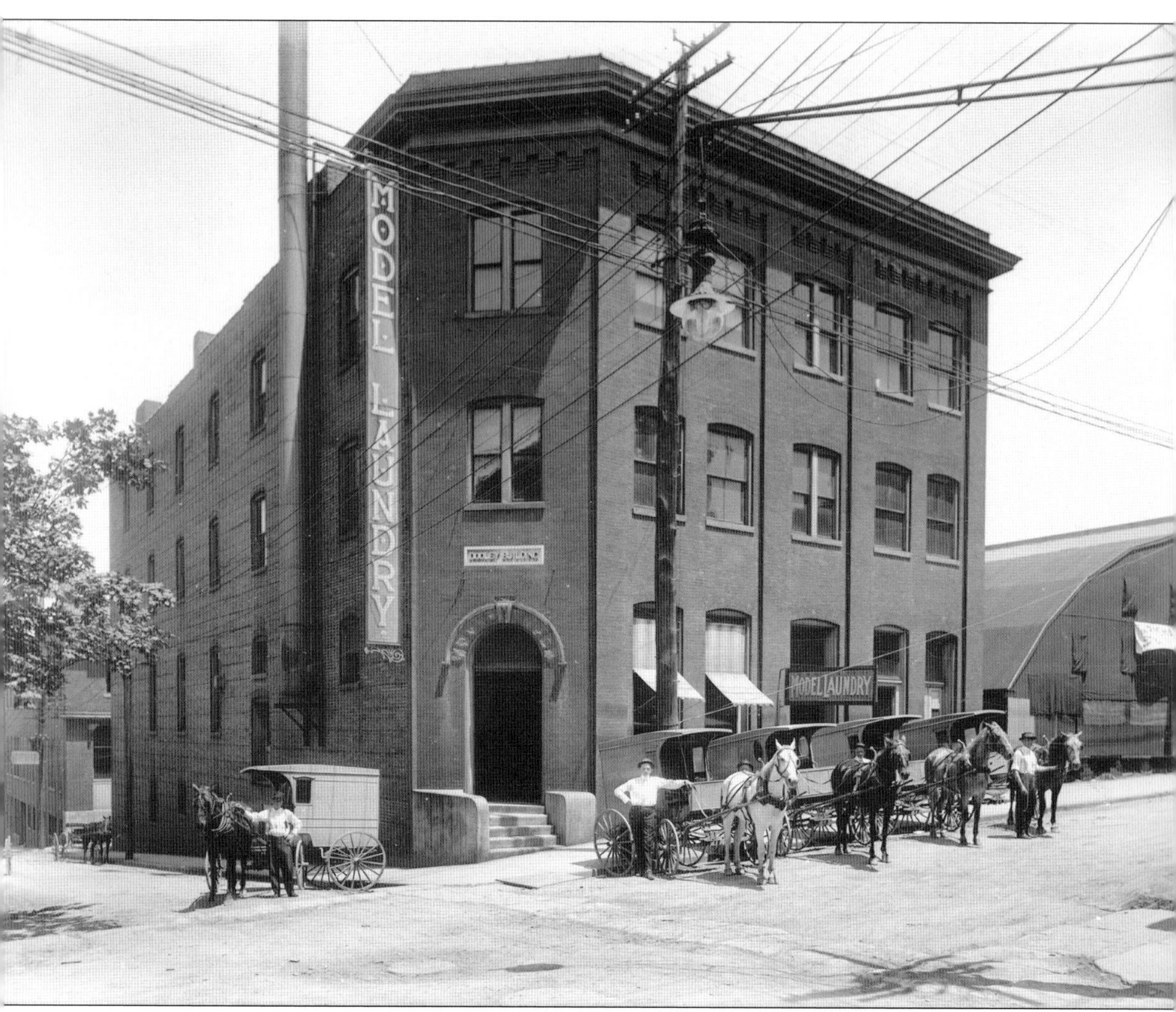

Founded in 1914, Model Laundry, known for big jobs like factory uniforms, started out here in the Dooley Building on the corner of State Street at Union Avenue, close to where James White built his fort. All the buildings on this block have been demolished, replaced by the State Street Garage. With its fleet of horse-drawn wagons, the business served downtown and the suburbs. Its successor, the 1926 Model Laundry building, is still conspicuous just across the Gay Street bridge on Sevier Avenue. The Quonset hut to the right appears to be advertising itself as a dance hall. (McClung, Small Photograph Collection.)

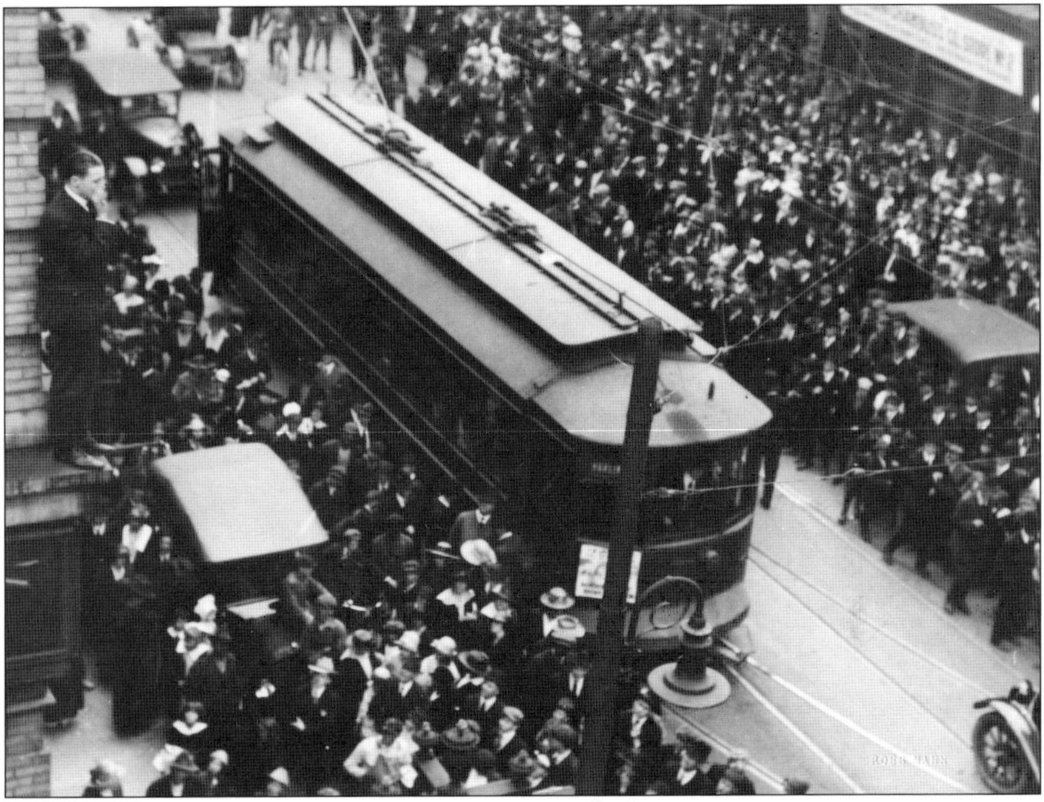

The man on the building ledge to the left, looking over the crowd at the Great Liberty Parade in 1918, is about to do something remarkable. He will climb the 10-story Burwell Building, Knoxville's tallest building when completed in 1908. Known as the "Human Fly," George Gibson Polley boasted 2,000 climbs without assistance, including Boston's Custom House Tower and the Woolworth Building in Manhattan, prior to his Knoxville appearance. (McClung, Small Photograph Collection.)

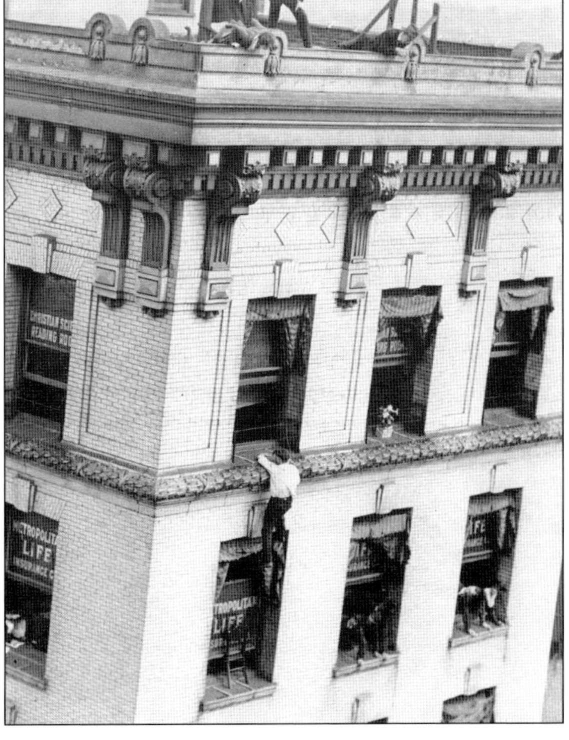

Following the Great Liberty Parade, Polley climbed the Burwell, taking just 30 minutes to make it to the top. He did have one small assist on this climb, a short rope to help him make it over the pediment at the top. On the roof, he performed a headstand with his feet extended over the edge before climbing the flagpole. Police didn't bother him since he had a permit. (McClung, Small Photograph Collection.)

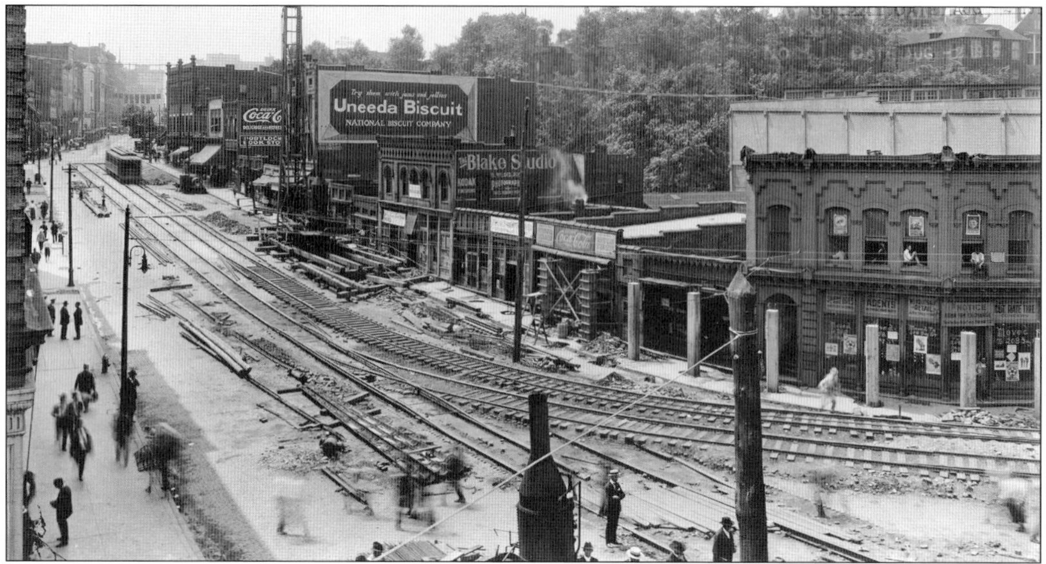

In 1919, the city eliminated the "Death Dip" at the bottom of the 100 block of Gay Street where it met the railroad tracks. The pillars in front of the buildings show where the new street level would be, sending first-floor storefronts underground. Several buildings were rebuilt to meet the new street. At far left is the edge of the Emporium building.

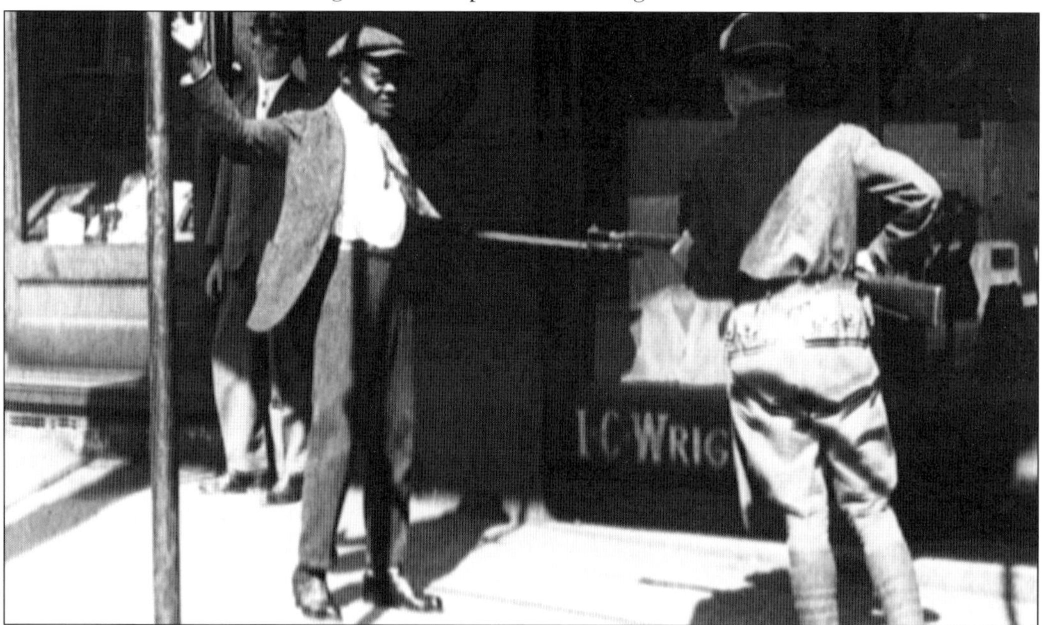

If Knoxville's Progressive era ended on a certain date, it was August 30, 1919, when a murder sparked a lynch-mob riot that resulted in an orgy of destruction downtown and drew state guardsmen with machine guns who for a few hours besieged the African American community. At least two were killed, both by guardsmen. For several days, downtown Knoxville was under martial law. Although the rioters were overwhelmingly white, African Americans were regarded with suspicion and searched. This rare image is a still from a recently discovered 1919 newsreel showing a soldier challenging an apparently cooperative Black man at I.C. Wright's clothing store at 107 West Vine Avenue, at the epicenter of the violence. (Tennessee Archive of Moving Image and Sound.)

Five

Between the Wars

The Roaring Twenties and the Depression Thirties may seem political and economic opposites, but in retrospect, the period between World War I and World War II seems a cultural whole. Nationally, it was an era of jazz music and radio and movie theaters, of bobbed hair and straw boaters and streetcars, and for those who could afford them, automobiles. In Knoxville, the Twenties maybe didn't roar to the same degree as in New York, nor were the Thirties quite as gloomy, because it was the era of the brand-new Great Smoky Mountains National Park, which drew thousands of tourists to Knoxville, and the Tennessee Valley Authority, which from 1933 employed 3,000 people downtown, many of them professionals from across the nation.

During the era between 1918 and 1941, as downtown remained East Tennessee's shopping center, it was also a busy workplace of engineers, planners, financiers, naturalists, attorneys, and idealists making plans for a broad region, creating the wonders of both the national park and TVA's new dams, reservoirs, and natural areas. Downtown also reflected, in a newly obvious way, the adjacent student and faculty population of the University of Tennessee, which before World War I was hardly noticeable downtown—a few hundred students up on top of the hill, hugely outnumbered in the city by millworkers. But the school grew rapidly in the 1920s and 1930s, and by 1940, the student population had soared to 6,000, introducing to downtown a collegiate air as the football team became a national contender for the first time in its history.

Meanwhile, it was also the era of live radio, when Knoxville's WNOX and WROL were drawing talent from across the nation and making stars of some local fiddlers and singers, while the Knoxville Symphony Orchestra—founded by a female conductor—rose to cultural prominence.

Durable attractions like the S&W Cafeteria, the Riviera and Tennessee Theatres, and old Market Square welcomed regional planners, championship football coaches, country music legends, pioneer conservationists, and also thousands of factory workers in a city that was still mainly industrial, making socks, nails, candy, bricks, flour, gauges, and that wonderful new invention, the Dumpster.

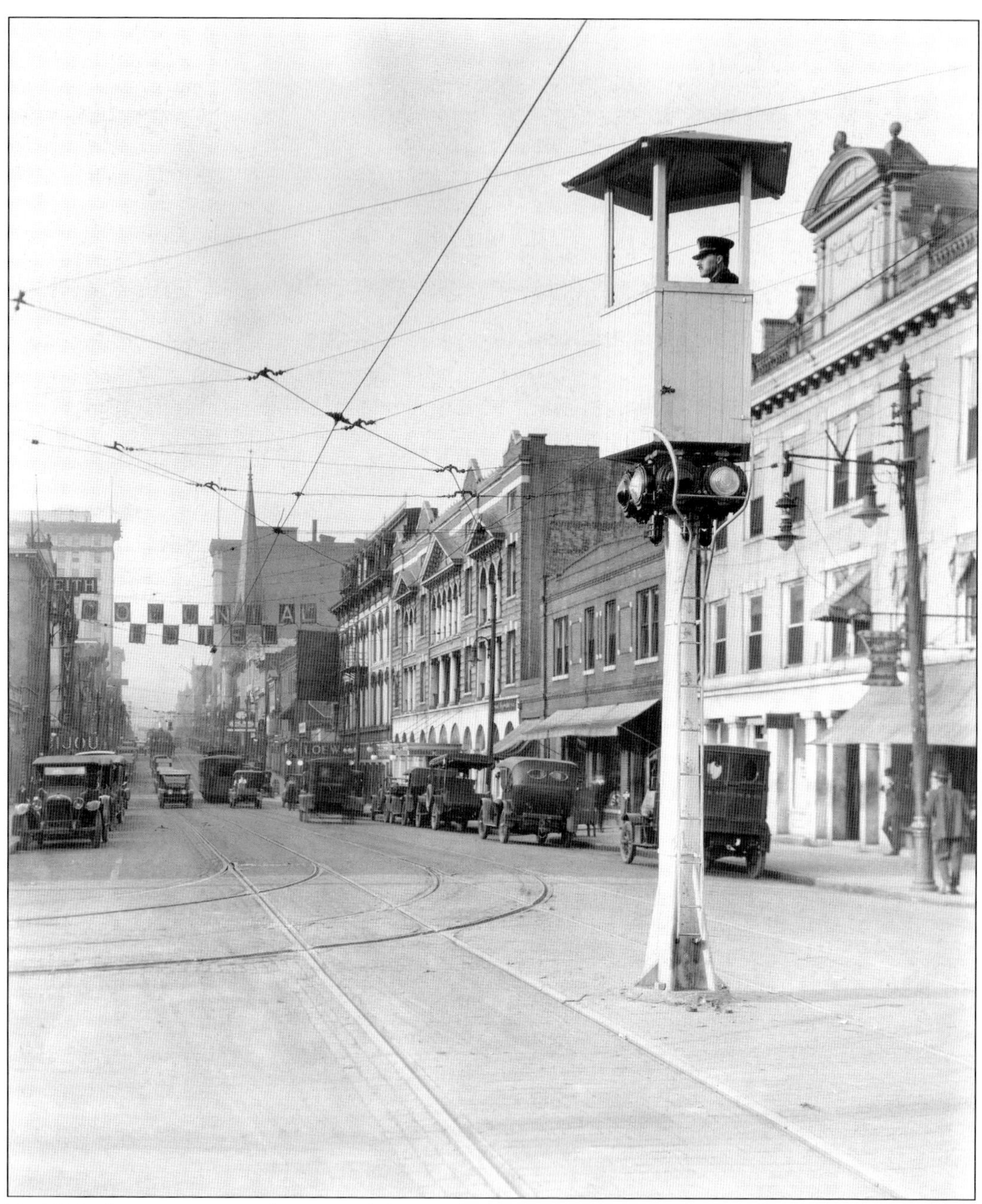

By 1920, there were enough automobiles on downtown streets, and at times so much confusion, that the city erected elevated traffic booths at key intersections to allow policemen to direct the flow of traffic. Automatic color-coded traffic lights became common after 1927. This traffic tower overlooked the intersection of Gay and Main Streets.

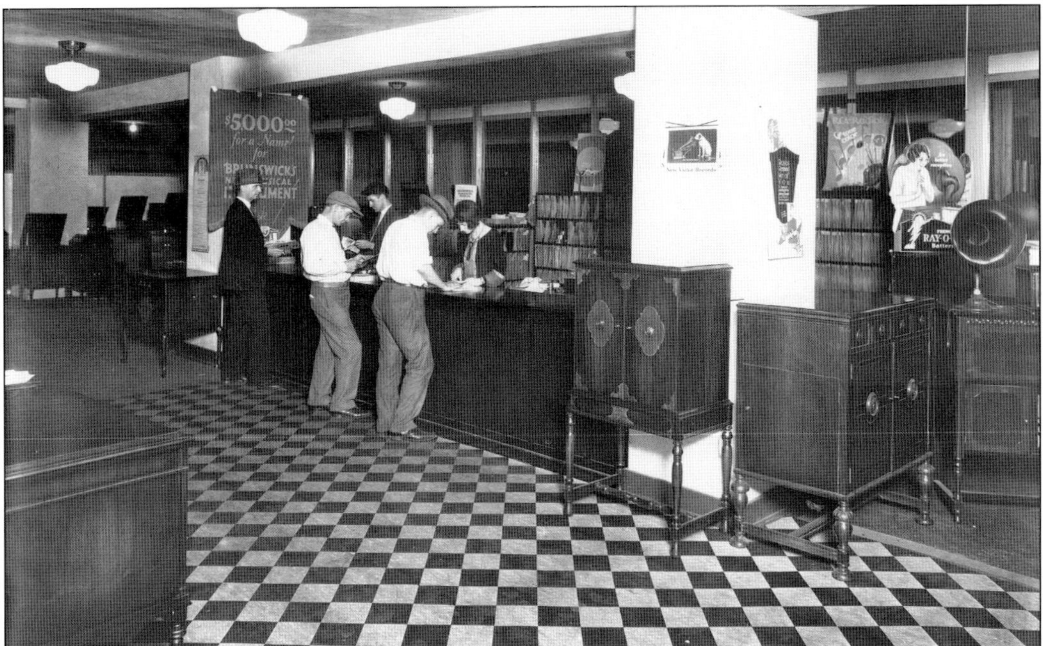

Founded by sons of Swiss immigrants, Knoxville-based Sterchi Brothers claimed to be the biggest furniture company in the world, with over 60 stores, mostly in the South. In 1925, the company built a new headquarters on the 100 block of Gay Street. Phonographs, like these Brunswicks on display, were considered furniture, giving Sterchi a surprising role in the early popularity of country music recordings.

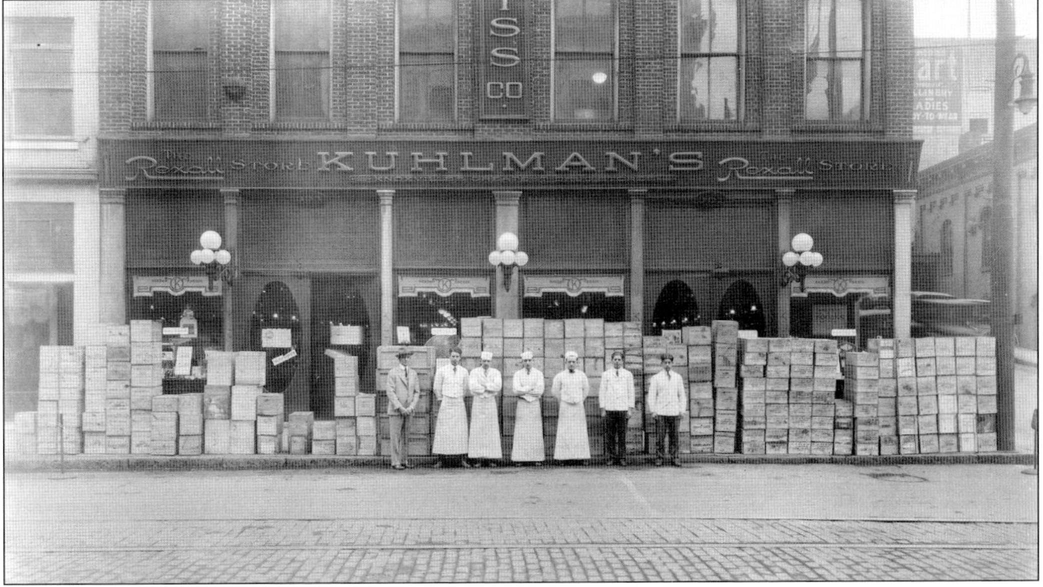

Kuhlman's drugstore had been a downtown fixture for decades before this 1925 photograph captured its soda fountain attendants on the west side of Gay Street at Commerce Avenue. Ads for pumpkin and marshmallow sundaes and Kodak cameras are in the windows. Some of the crates are marked grape juice, others butterscotch, maple walnut, peach, and chocolate. Today, the downtown visitor's center and WDVX Radio are on this spot.

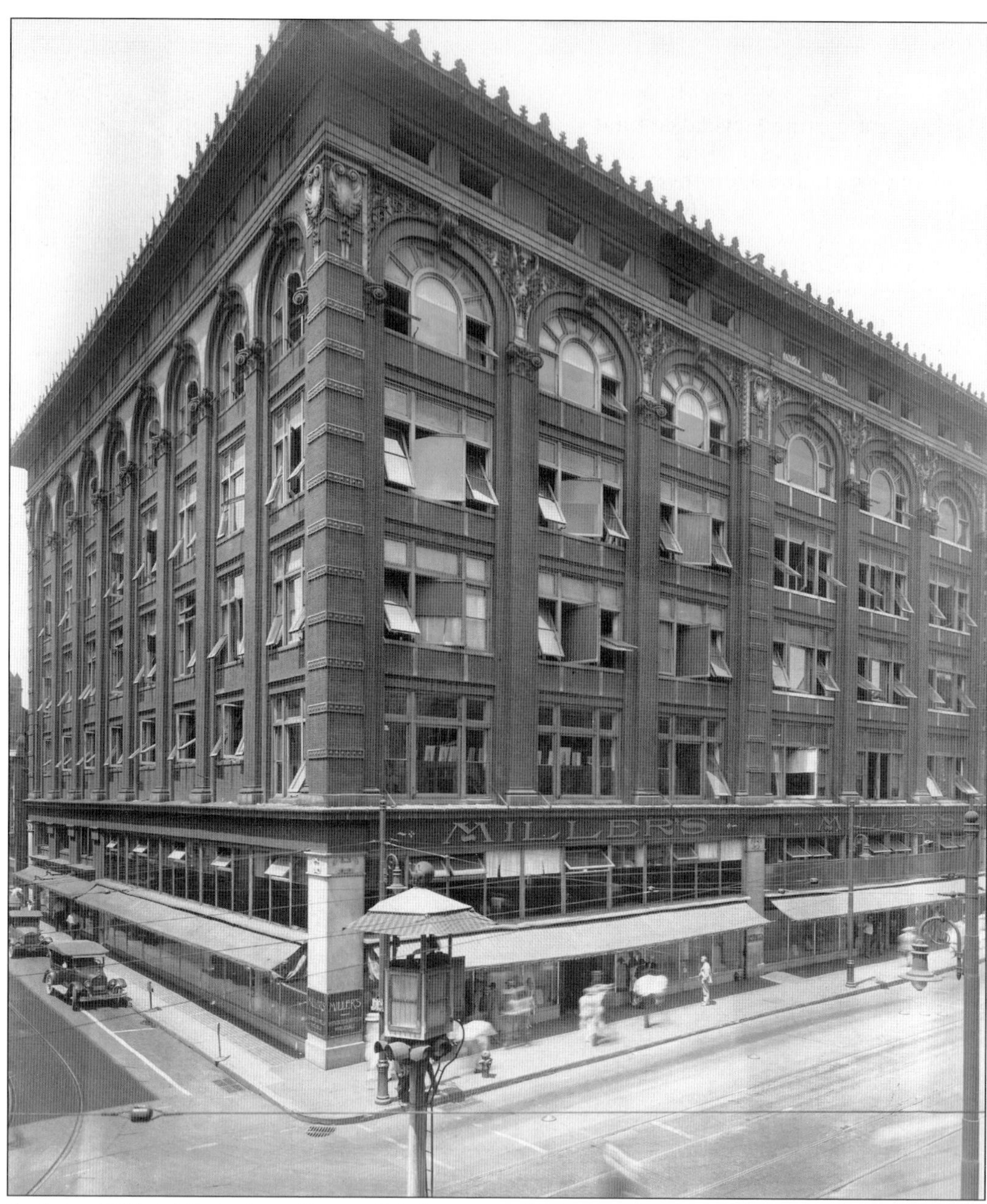

Built in 1905, Miller's, long Knoxville's largest and best-known department store, stood at the corner of Gay Street and Union Avenue. Note the open windows on this summer day in the 1920s. Attempts to modernize the building in the 1970s included covering the façade with reflective glass, destroying much of its original detail. In the 1990s, the building was renovated again, this time by the City of Knoxville and Knoxville Utilities Board. During that effort, Knoxville architect Duane Grieve was able to restore the damaged façade, painstakingly replicating the unusual nude Greek-style caryatids on the upper part of the building (see page 125). Miller's, said to have introduced escalators and charge cards to Knoxville, was such an iconic store that it is mentioned in novels by James Agee and Cormac McCarthy.

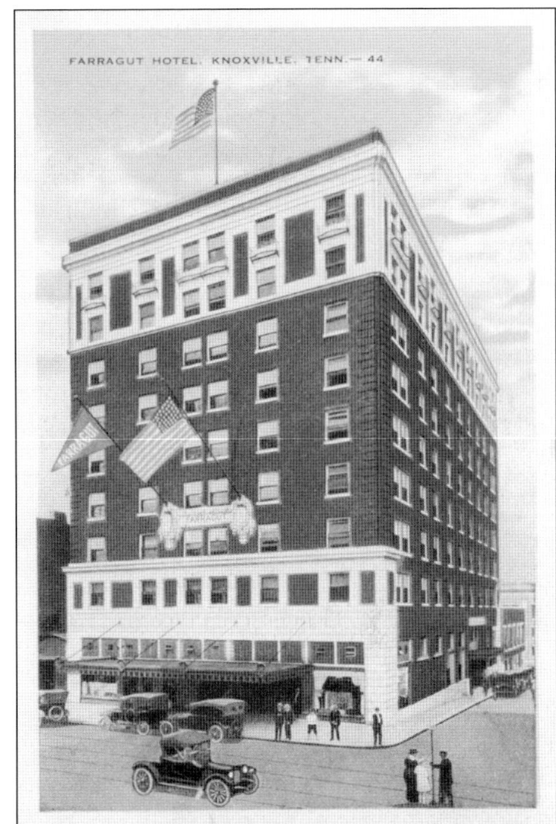

Construction of the Farragut Hotel commenced in 1917, a year after the Imperial Hotel was destroyed by fire. The Farragut nurtured several cultural movements, including the Knoxville Symphony Orchestra, led by Bertha Walburn Clark, who conducted her own "Little Symphony" here; the Great Smoky Mountains National Park, which was promoted by early meetings here; and the Southeastern Conference (SEC), organized in the hotel during a dramatic 1932 convention. (Knoxville History Project.)

Keystone Studios cameramen were at the Farragut Hotel in August 1924, to shoot Park Commission members here visiting the Great Smoky Mountains to determine their potential to become a national park. Col. David Chapman, leader of the Great Smoky Mountains Conservation Association (at right in group posing), was so successful in his efforts that he is now remembered as the "father" of the park.

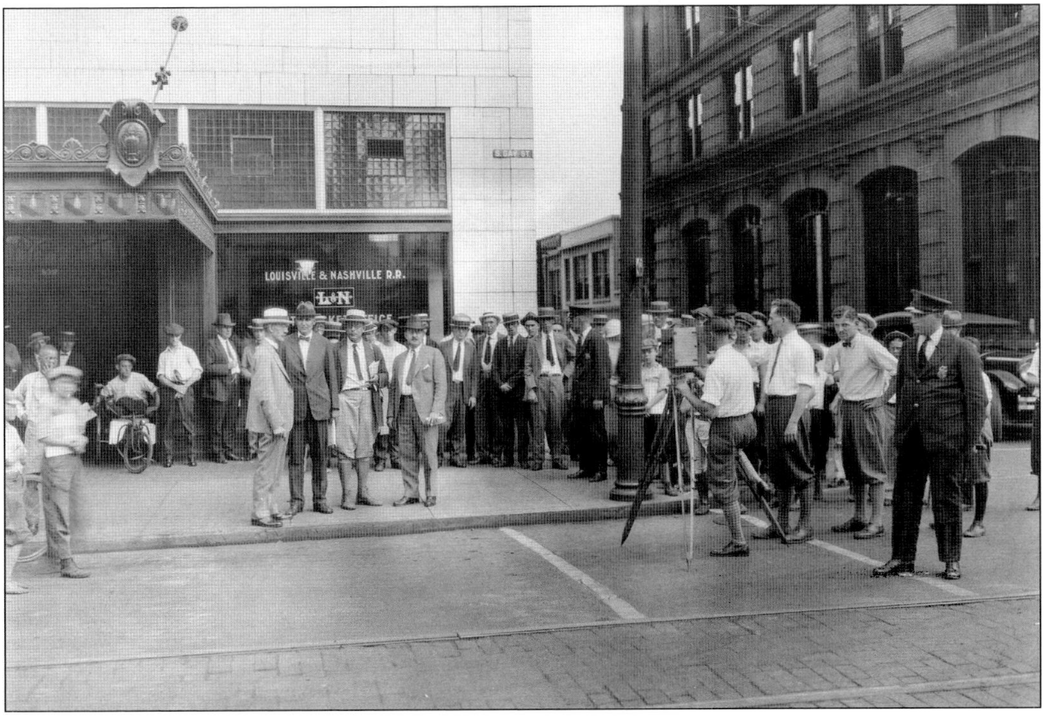

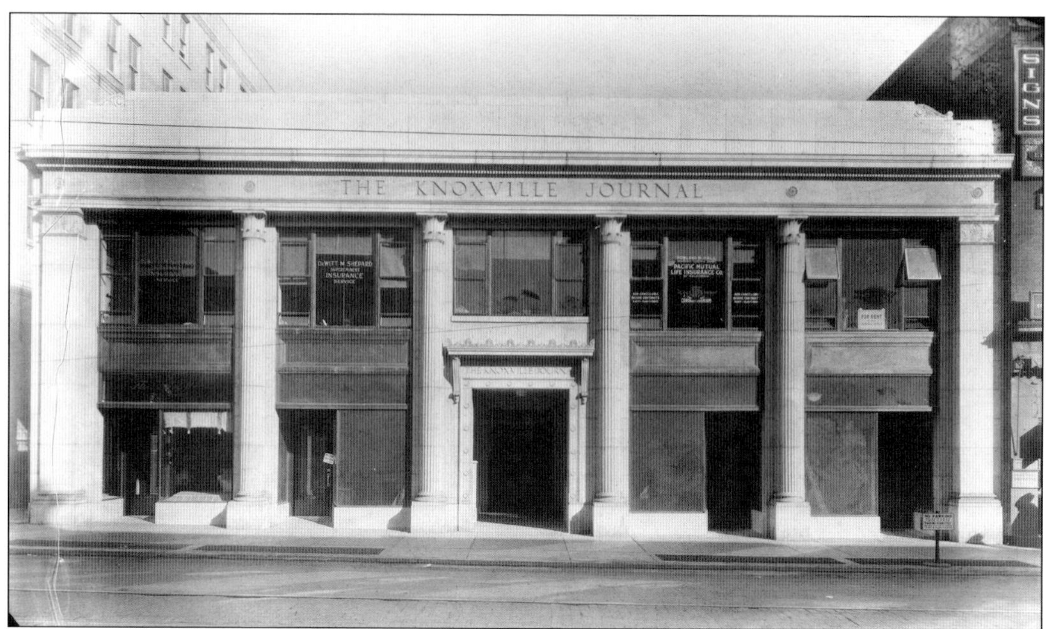

The neoclassical Journal Arcade, designed by architect R.F. Graf and clad in Tennessee marble, included both retail shops and the offices of the *Knoxville Journal*. At the time, the morning newspaper's editor was still the octogenarian Union veteran Capt. William Rule (1839–1928), honored in the painting visible below. Rule was the longest serving editor in the city's history. Twice elected mayor, in 1900 he authored *A Standard History of Knoxville*. (Both, McClung, Thompson Photograph Collection.)

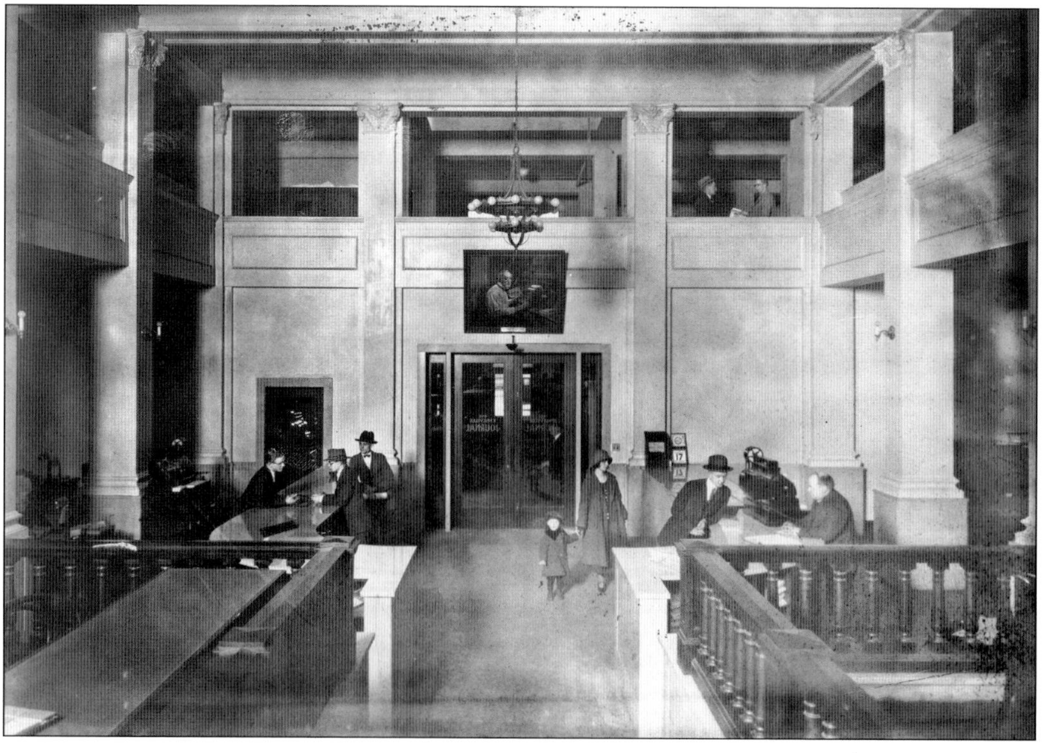

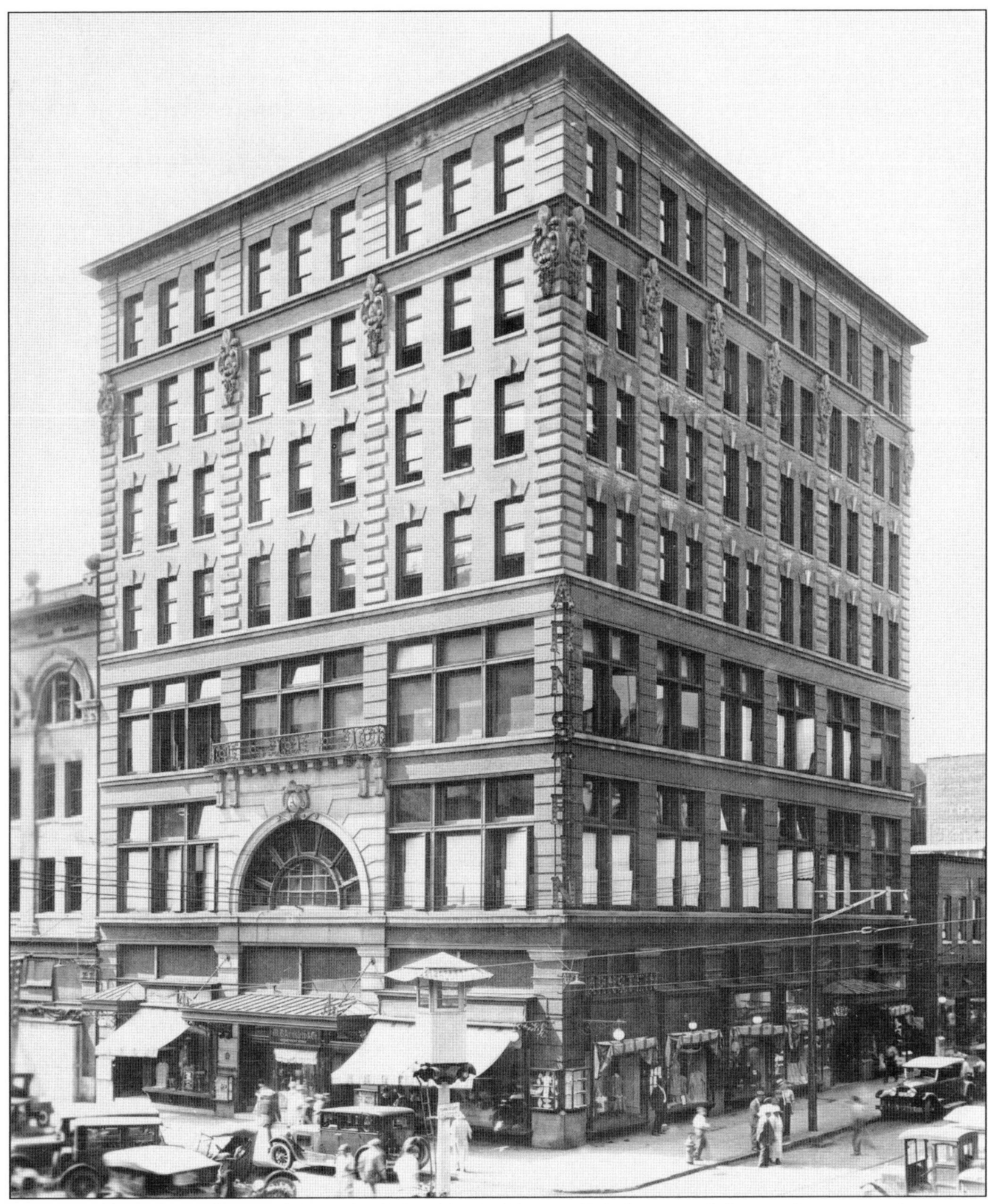

Designed by Cleverdon and Putzel of New York, Knoxville's first steel-frame skyscraper (as it was touted at the time) was built in 1906 by Max Arnstein, a German Jewish merchant who ran what was considered the city's finest department store, especially known for women's fashions from Europe. In 1924, Arnstein's wife, Lalla, became one of Knoxville's first female elected officials as a member of Knox County Court. (University of Tennessee Libraries.)

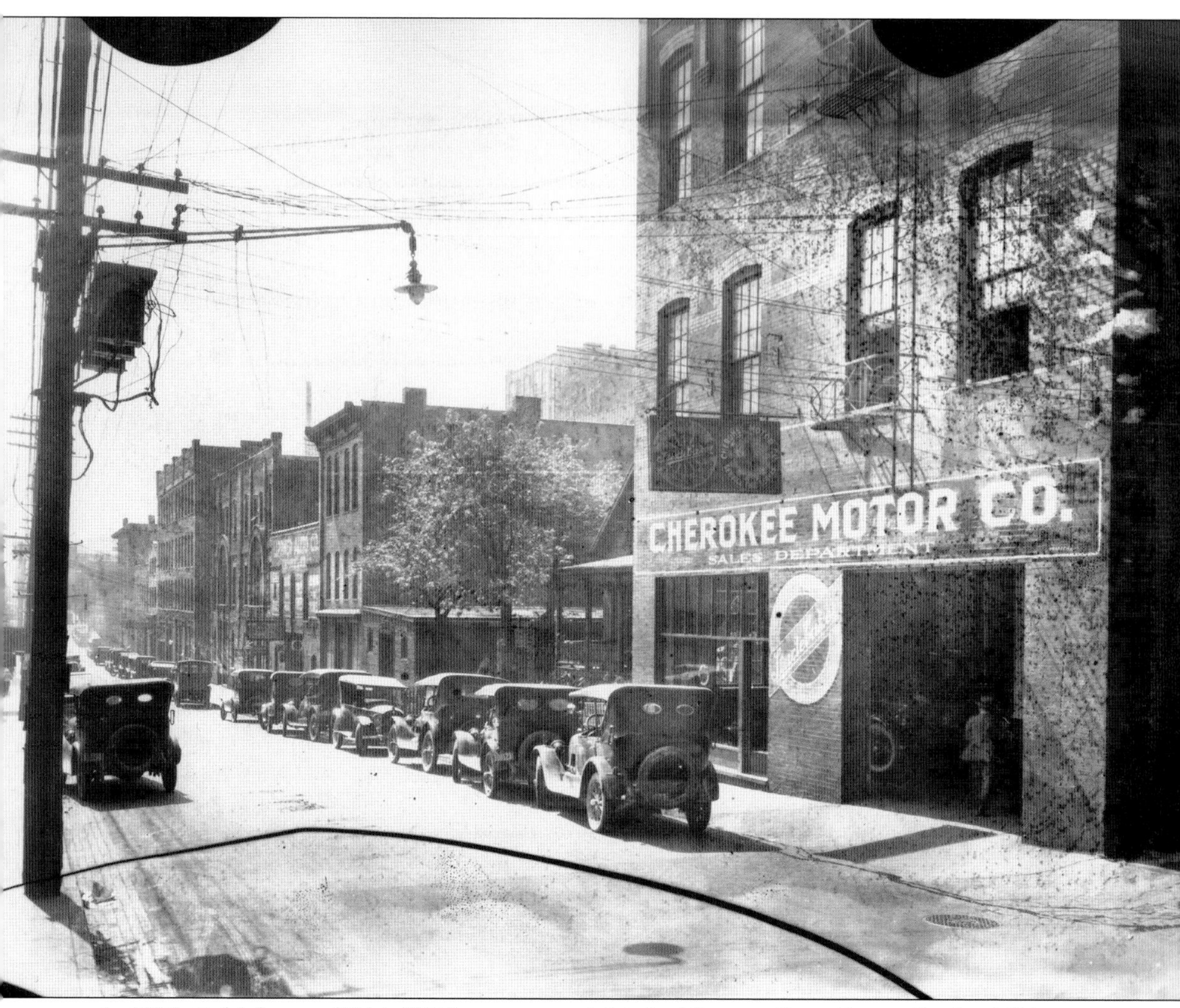

In 1898, Cal Johnson (1844–1925) constructed this building on State Street. By the 1920s, it was occupied by the Cherokee Motor Company, a Studebaker dealer. One of the most remarkable businessmen in Knoxville history, Johnson was born into slavery. As a young man, he earned wages transferring dead soldiers from the battlefield at Cumberland Gap to be interred at the Knoxville National Cemetery. He died a wealthy man, leaving behind a legacy of successful saloons and racetracks as well as a few commercial buildings like this one, originally a clothing factory. The front porch partially visible to the left of the store is the only known image of Johnson's own residence. This long-empty building was remodeled and reopened in 2020 as a residential and commercial space.

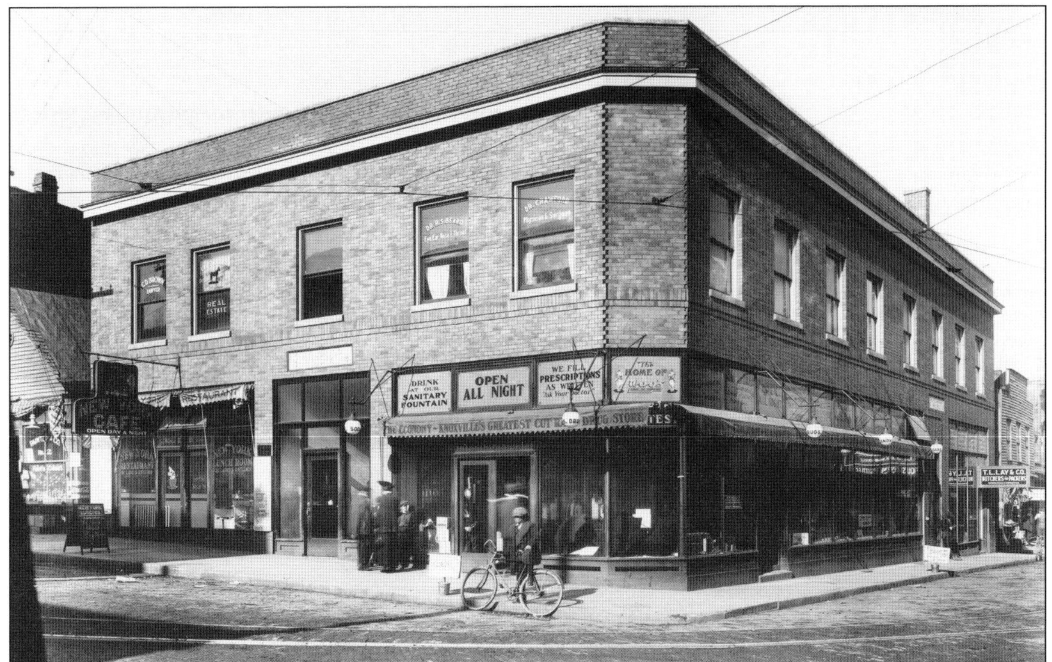

Seen here in 1916 is another building owned by Cal Johnson on the northwest corner of Vine Avenue and Central Street. The Greek-owned New York Café is on the left, with an all-night drugstore on the corner. Johnson himself had an office on the second floor, where an image of a horse advertises his favorite subject. Next door to the right, butcher T.L. Lay later founded Lay's Packing Company.

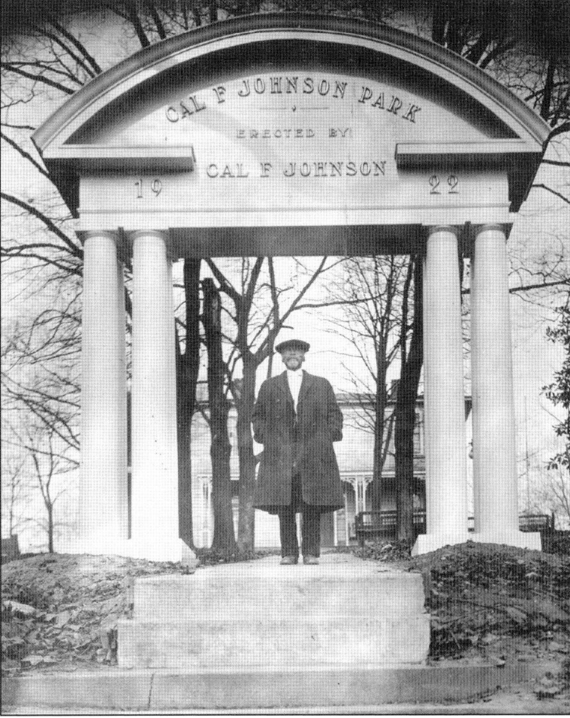

Opened in 1922 on land its namesake donated, Cal Johnson Park was a popular community gathering place until it was affected by urban renewal (1959–1974). The federal slum clearance project displaced many African American families and business owners. In the 1940s and 1950s, poet Nikki Giovanni grew up in her grandparents' home across from the park, which is now the location of Cal Johnson Recreation Center. (Beck Cultural Exchange Center.)

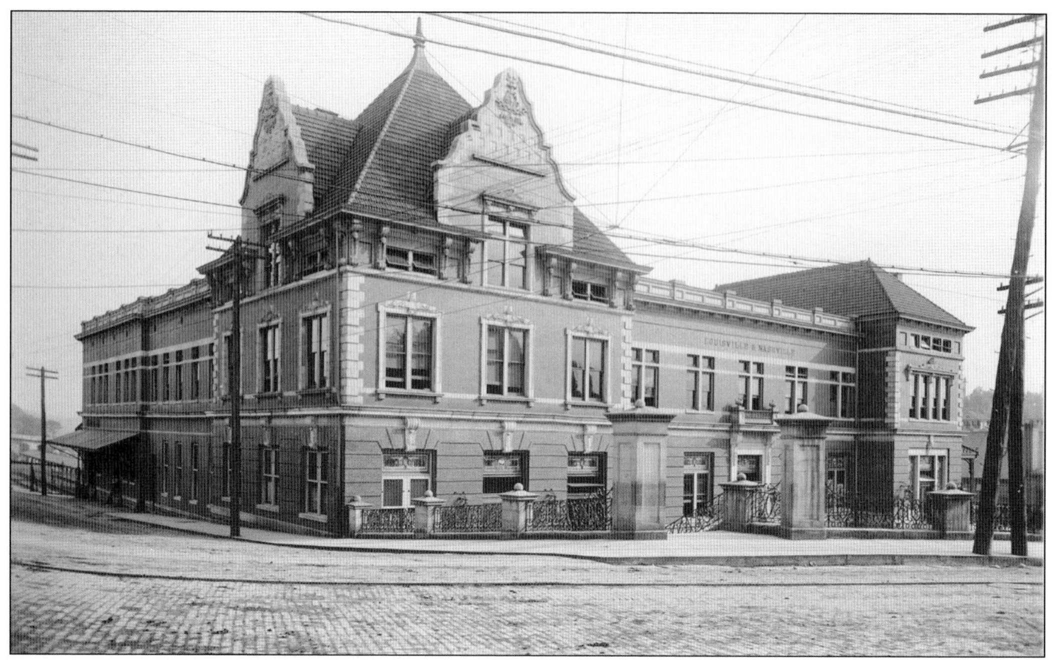

The L&N's passenger station, finished in 1905 and designed to look just a little fancier than the Southern station a few blocks away, is described in James Agee's Pulitzer-winning novel *A Death in the Family*, set in 1916. Renovated to accommodate restaurants during the 1982 World's Fair, it was even more thoroughly updated 30 years later to serve a STEM public high school named for its historic building.

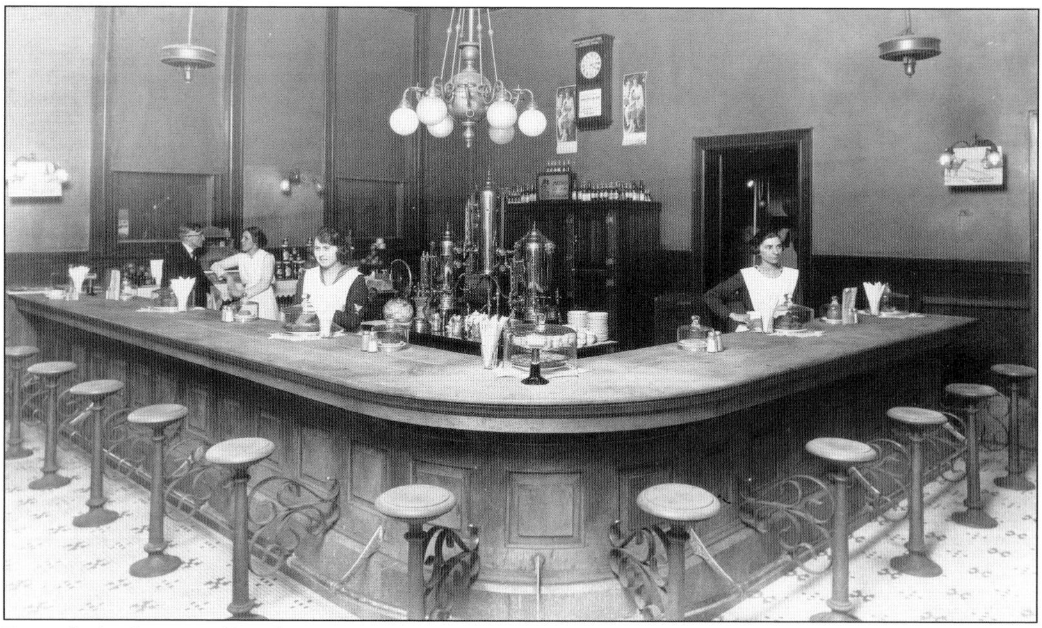

Friendly-looking staff at the L&N's Crescent News Lunch Room, associated with a nearby news stand, offer pastries on the marble-top counter, a very fancy coffee machine, and a variety of bottled drinks. The ads on the walls declare it to be "Like an Oasis in the Desert." Despite the "lunch" in its name, the café was open from 5:00 a.m. until 11:00 p.m.

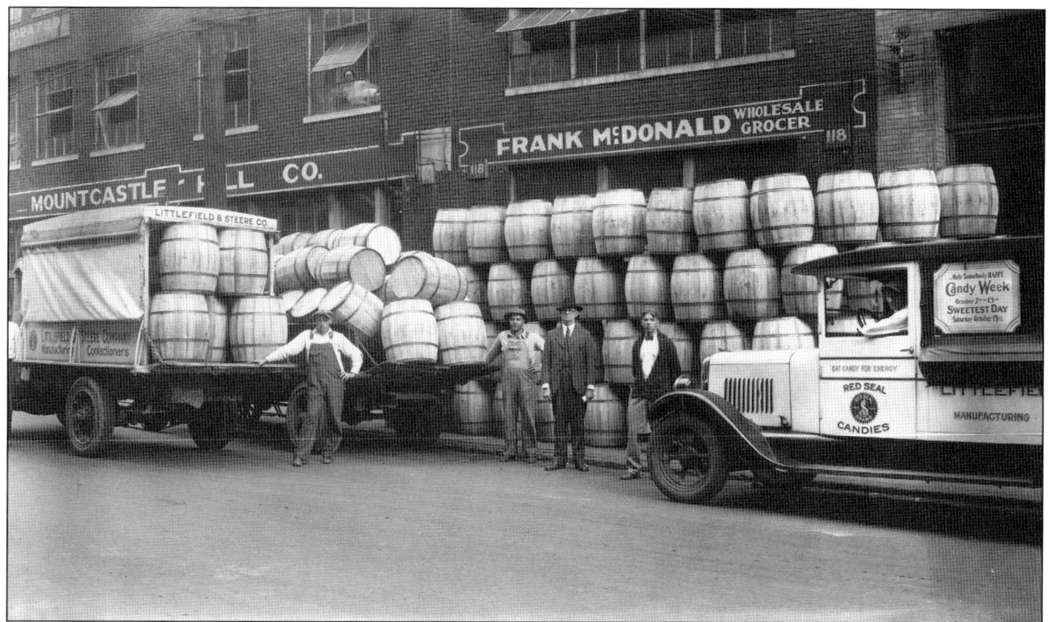

Founded by Henry Littlefield and Arthur Steere around 1890, Littlefield & Steere offered a wide range of sweets for a national market. Above, an early truck unloads at the wholesale house of grocer Frank McDonald, founder of the White Stores grocery chain. Littlefield & Steere built a large, freestanding factory (below) at the western end of the Clinch Avenue viaduct in 1915 where it employed 200 candy makers. The factory closed during the Depression, and the building served as a warehouse until the 1982 World's Fair, when its candy making heritage was revived. A chocolate-making operation survived there into the early 21st century. It is now a luxury residential building. (Both, McClung, Thompson Photograph Collection.)

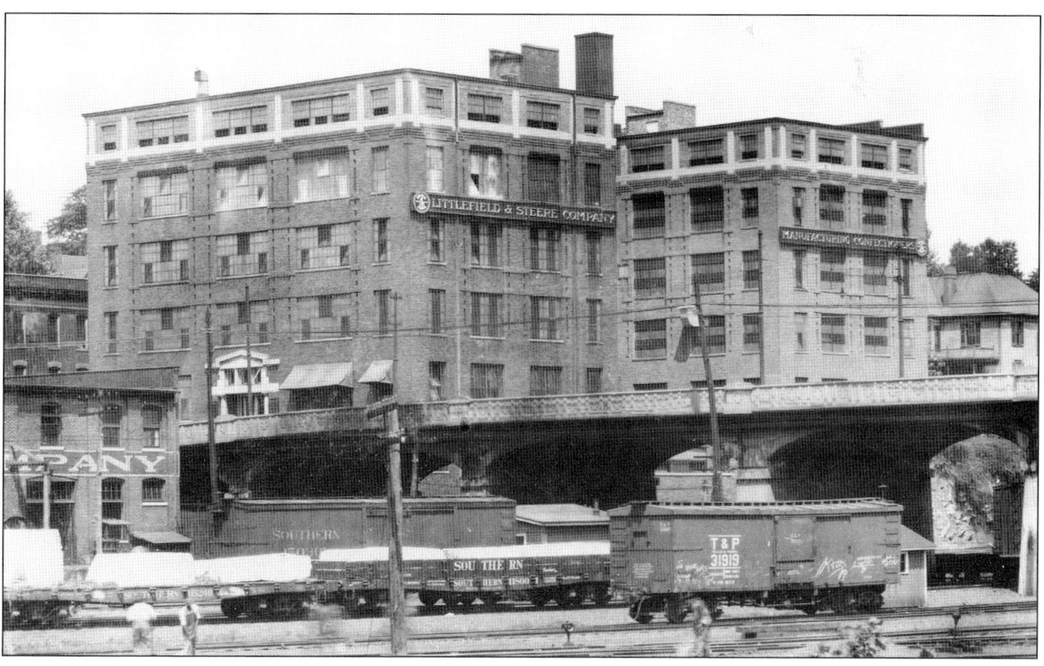

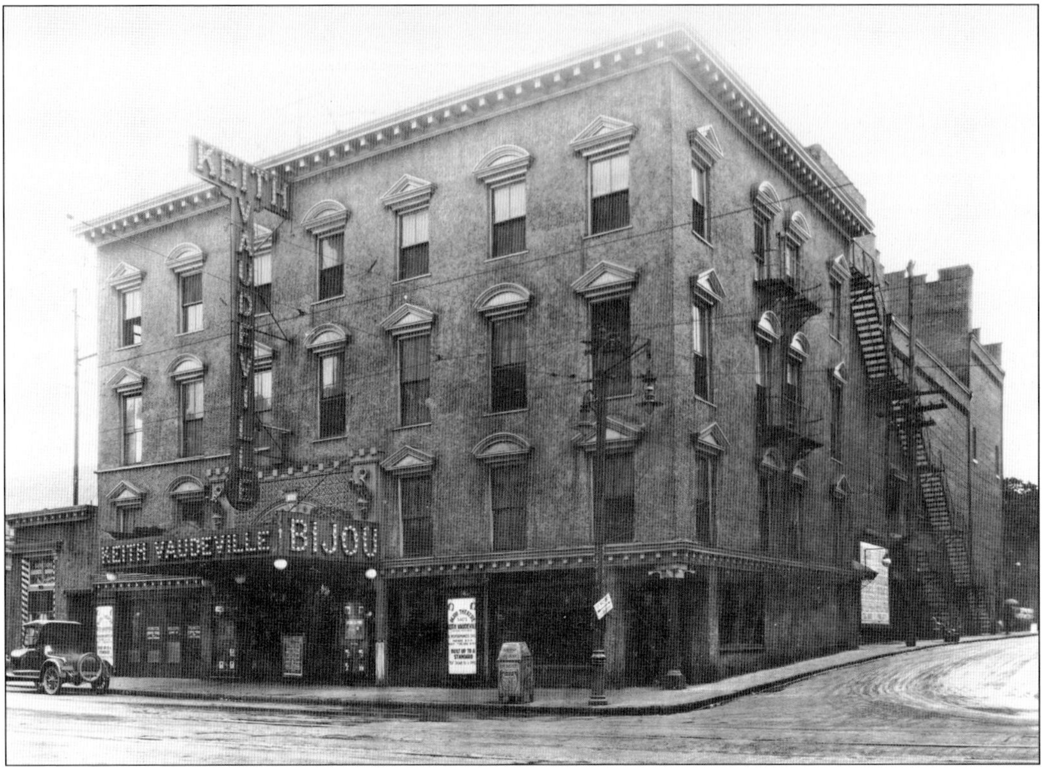

The Bijou Theatre, built onto the back of a century-old hotel in 1909, was a favorite attraction, presenting the Marx Brothers years before their movie career, Russian dancer Pavlova, and singer-comedienne Sophie Tucker, among others. Here the theater is hosting the nationally popular Keith Vaudeville series. At the Bijou, that lively era ended abruptly in 1926, when by a complicated deal involving competition with other venues, the theater ceased performances for five years.

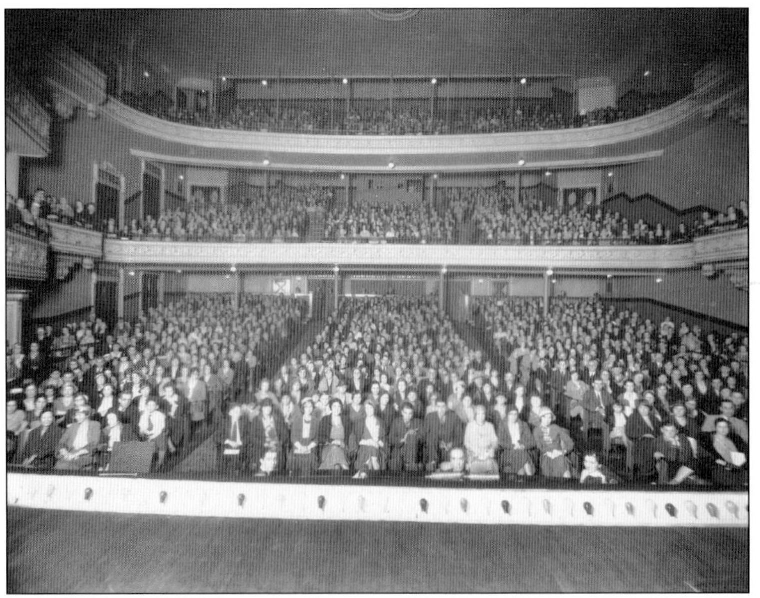

This capacity Bijou audience attending a forgotten function in the 1920s or 1930s appears to be predominantly female. At the time, the Bijou could entertain 1,500, at least twice as many as today. That second balcony, or gallery, was typically reserved for African American patrons, but it is not clear if that was the case at this event.

The former Staub's Opera House became the Lyric Theatre in the 1920s, hosting a wide variety of entertainment, generally dominated by vaudeville and movies but with occasional featured performers like diva Marian Anderson, who sang here in 1927 in a show organized by an African American organization. Will Rogers also performed at the old Victorian-era venue in the 1920s, as did John Philip Sousa and his orchestra. (McClung, Thompson Photograph Collection.)

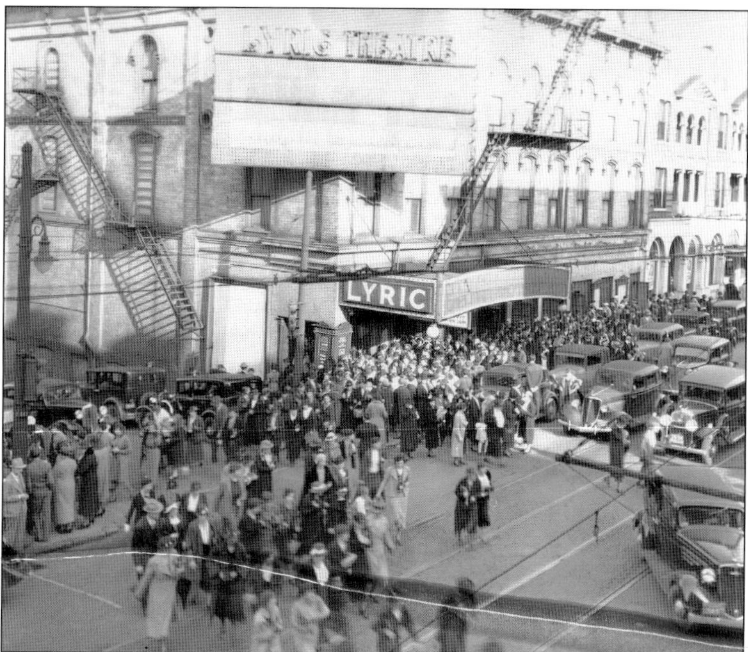

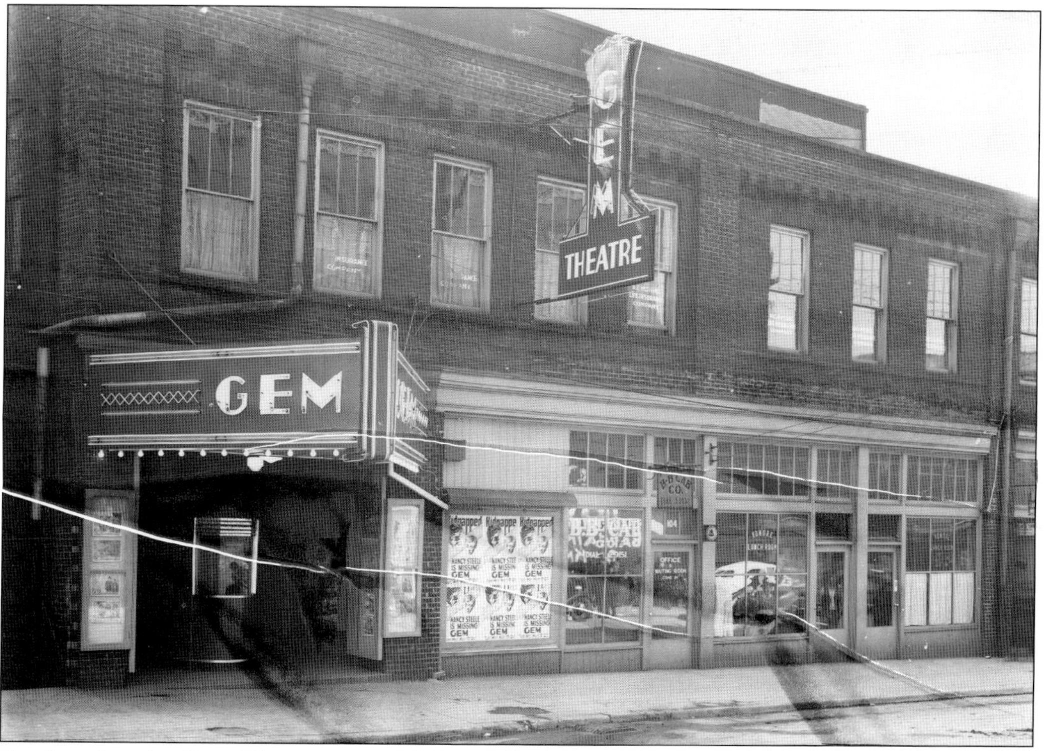

For decades, the Gem Theatre served African American audiences at Vine Avenue and Central Street. Although it often featured "race films" with African American casts, as well as live jazz concerts by Earl Hines, Ida Cox, and others, in this image the theater is advertising *Nancy Steele Is Missing*, a 1937 thriller starring Peter Lorre. To the right are the B.B. Cab Co. and the Vonore Lunch Room, where patrons can be seen looking out the windows.

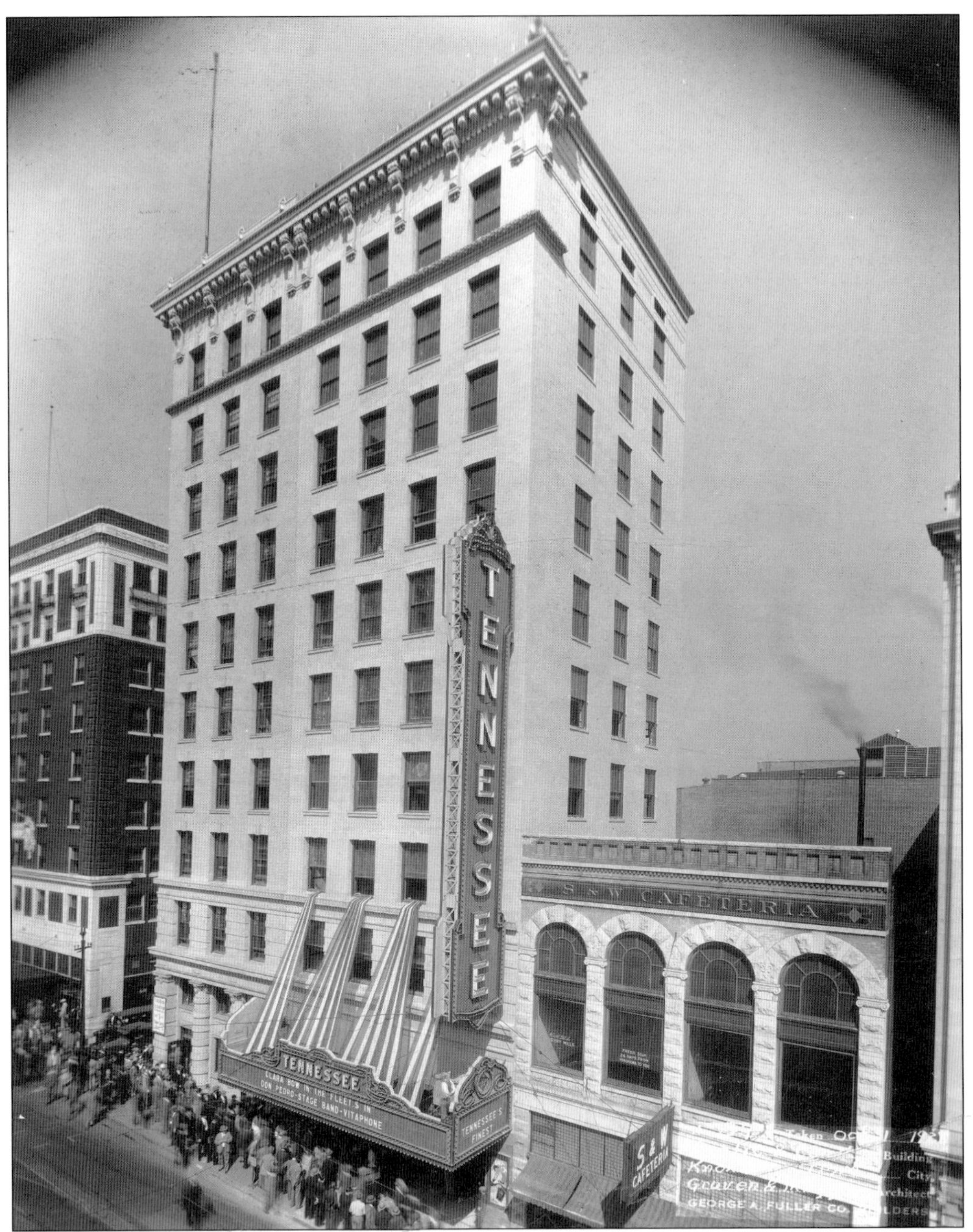

The Tennessee Theatre opened on Oct. 1, 1928, in conjunction with the expanded Burwell, a 20-year-old office building. The new theater's first attraction was *The Fleet's In*, a new silent romantic comedy starring Clara Bow. Like many of the earliest films shown at the Tennessee, it is now believed to be lost. The marquee also advertises the Don Pedro Stage Band, a jazz combo that played at the Tennessee before the movie, with a different set almost every night of the theater's first several months. In those days, an ever-changing multi-act vaudeville show was always part of an evening at the Tennessee as well. At right is the original S&W cafeteria, a small, elegantly trendy chain; in 1937, the S&W moved to a larger space one block to the north. To the left is the thriving Farragut Hotel. (McClung, Thompson Photograph Collection.)

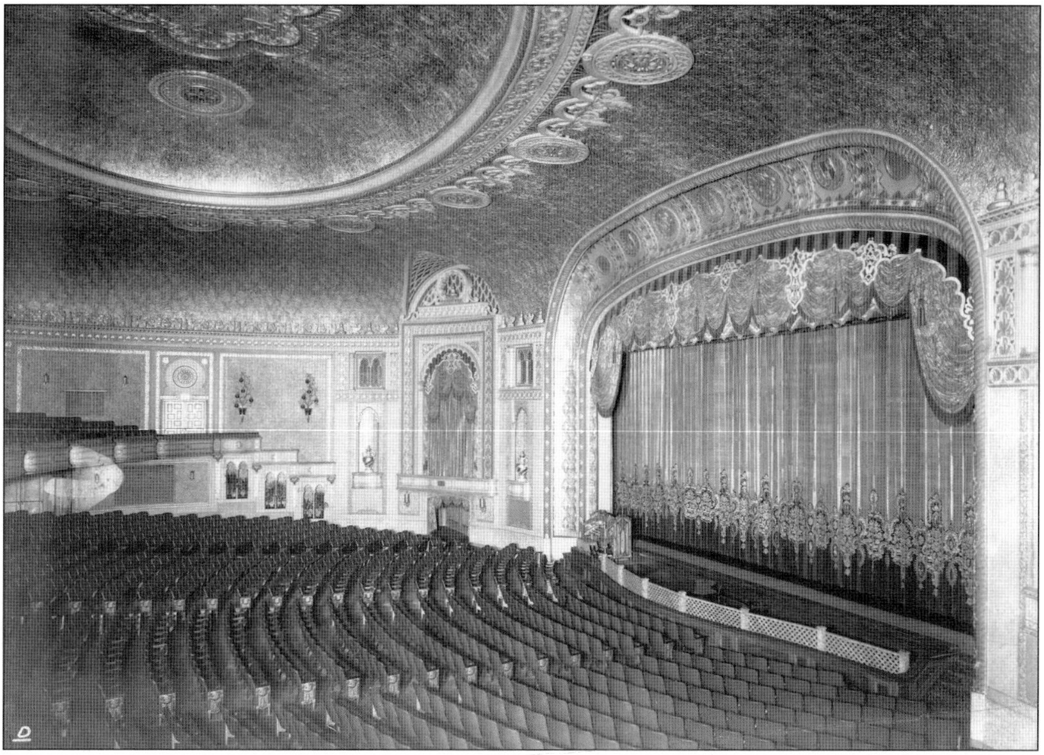

The Tennessee's over-the-top Moorish Revival stage is remarkable for its unusual breadth. Although built mainly for movies, the stage saw an astonishing array of live performers in its early years, including cowboy icon Tom Mix and his rodeo/acrobatic act, Fanny Brice with Ziegfeld's Follies, fiddler Roy Acuff, singer Gene Austin, pioneer jazz guitarist Nick Lucas, Glenn Miller and his orchestra, controversial dancer Fifi D'Orsay, and Cuban musician Desi Arnaz.

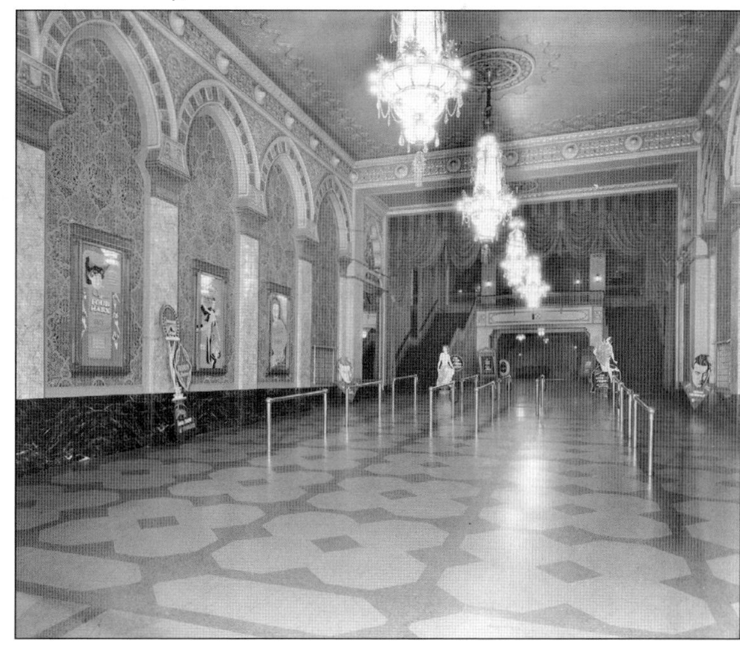

The Tennessee's architects considered the lobby to be as important as the theater itself, and its chandeliers make it seem even more elegant. Since many films visited Knoxville for only three days, the lobby often held capacity crowds who would wait for an hour or more to take their seats. This renovated lobby had its own moment on the silver screen: a scene in Burt Reynolds's final film, *The Last Movie Star.* (McClung, Thompson Photograph Collection.)

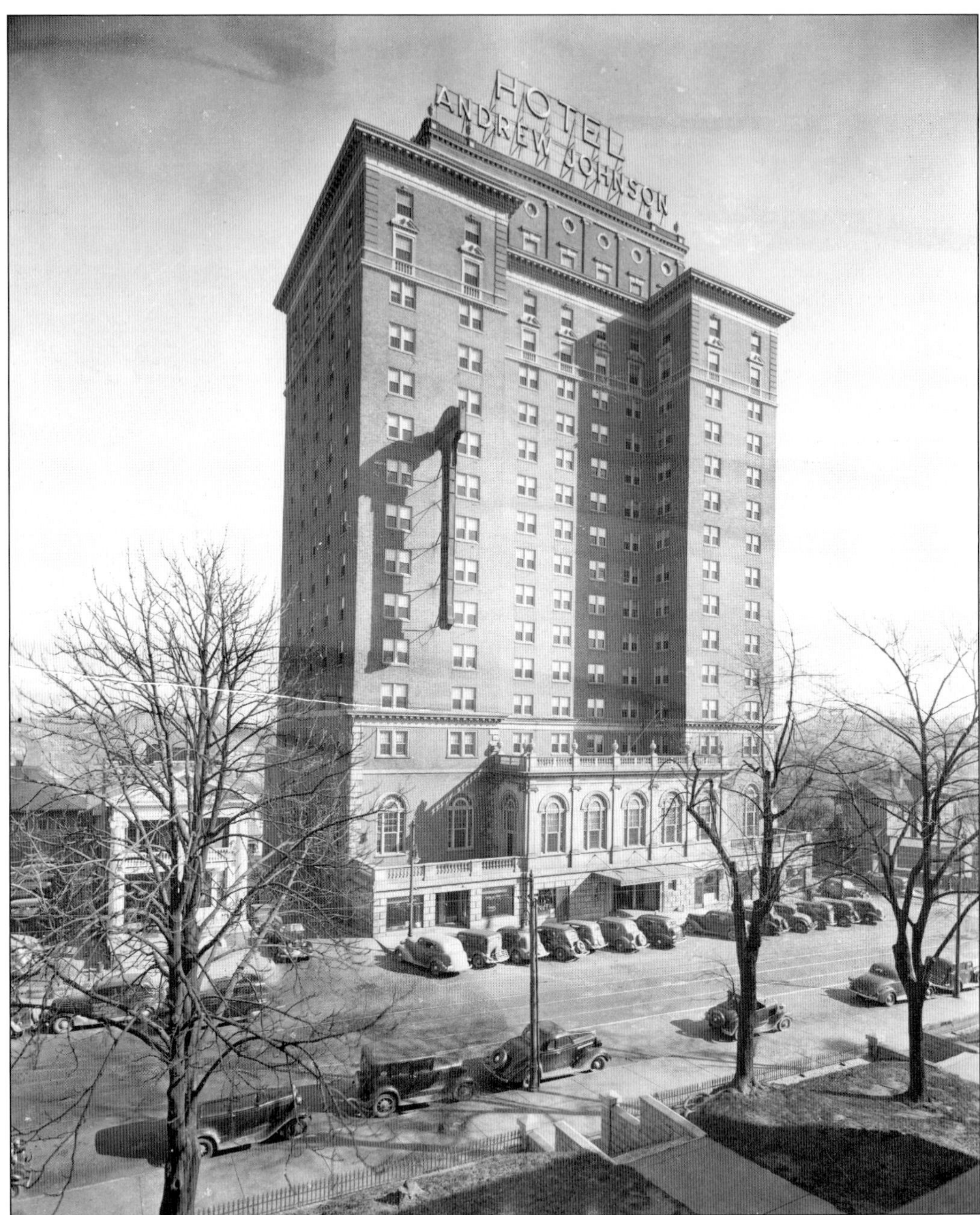

Built in the late 1920s as the Tennessee Terrace, the Andrew Johnson—the tallest hotel in East Tennessee—attracted many early visitors to the Great Smoky Mountains National Park as well as numerous luminaries. Amelia Earhart stayed here in 1936, the year before her disappearance, and gave a newspaper interview in her room. Jean Paul Sartre was here for several days in early 1945 and wrote an essay about American cities. Russian composer Sergei Rachmaninoff spent the night here after the last concert of his career in 1943. Other guests included actor Anthony Perkins, composer Duke Ellington, and photographer Margaret Bourke-White. As a young man, King Hussein of Jordan was the guest at a reception here. Perhaps most famously, and mysteriously, songwriter Hank Williams spent part of the last night of his life here on New Year's Eve 1952.

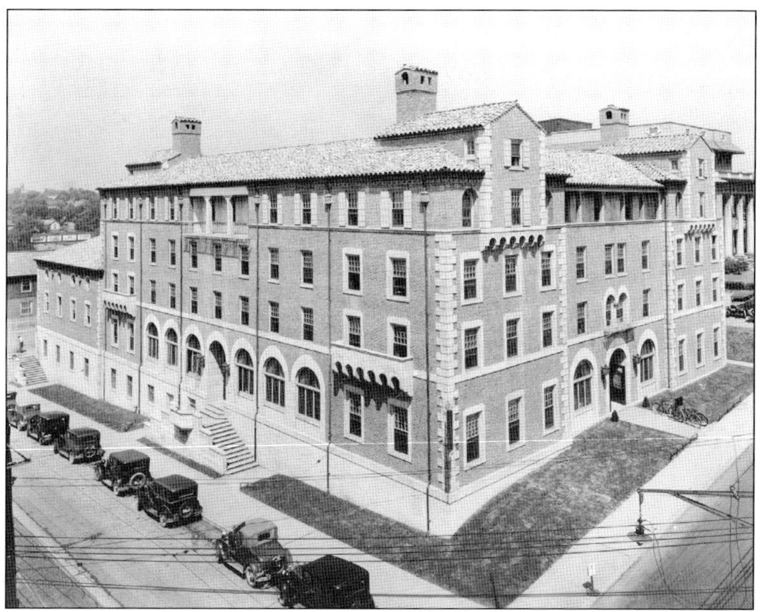

Designed by local architect Charles Barber, who loved medieval flourishes like balconies and arches, the central YMCA was built in 1929. Several pioneer conservationists used it as a residence while spending most of their time in the mountains. In 1944, the FBI captured a Nazi spy staying here. The Y's old rooms have been converted into condos. (McClung, Thompson Photograph Collection.)

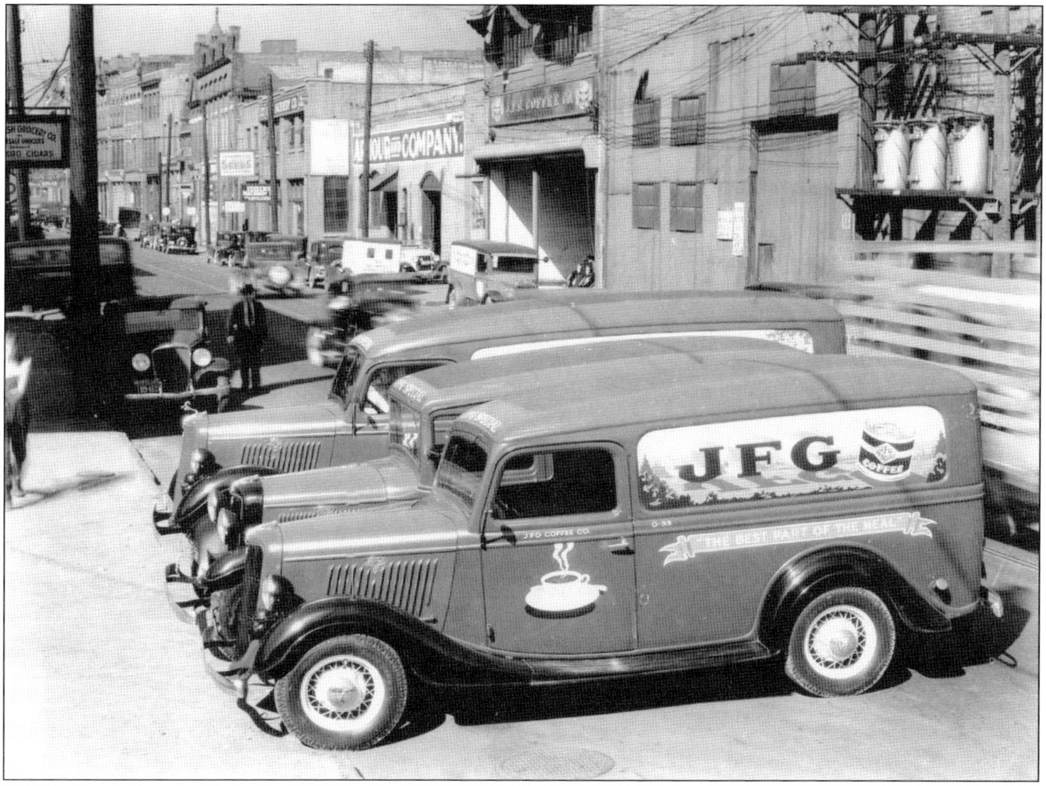

Bustling and ragged East Jackson Avenue hosted JFG Coffee from around 1929 until its move to much larger quarters on West Jackson in 1936. Its neighbors included the Armour meatpacking plant—opened here in 1889, perhaps Knoxville's first corporate presence—and the Iddins Machinery Co. JFG made downtown smell like roasting coffee for 80 years, but in the early 21st century, the company moved west to a modern factory off Sutherland Avenue. (Knoxville History Project.)

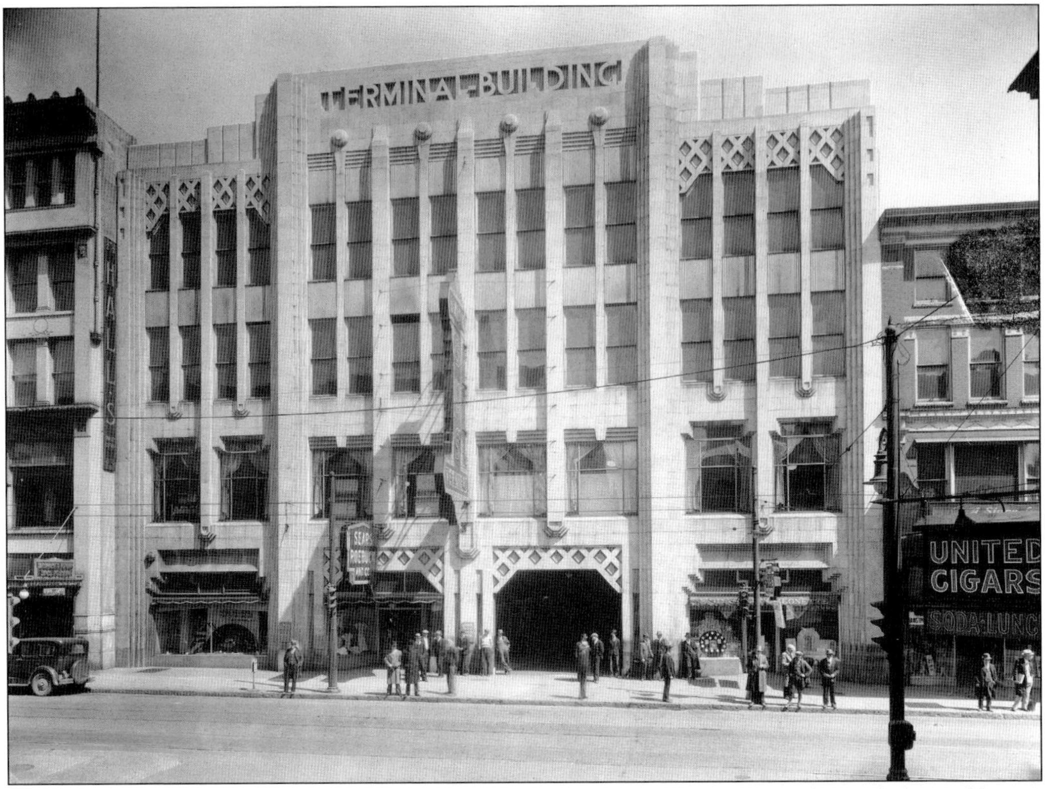

Union Terminal, a stylish marble-front building at Gay Street and Wall Avenue, was a multiline bus station combined with a shopping arcade stretching back to State Street. A Manley and Young design, it was one of downtown's busiest places until the 1950s, when the major bus lines abandoned it to build elsewhere. It burned down in 1974. (McClung, Thompson Photograph Collection.)

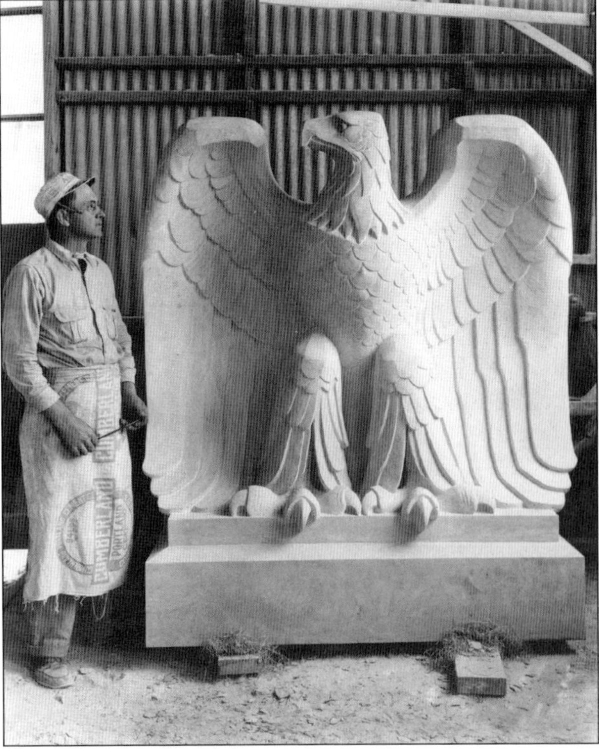

One of the distinctive marble eagles sculpted by Italian immigrant stone cutter Albert Milani (1901–1977) is seen here before its installation high on the façade of the 1934 federal building on Main Street. Although often identified as Milani, the identity of the stone cutter pictured with the eagle is uncertain.

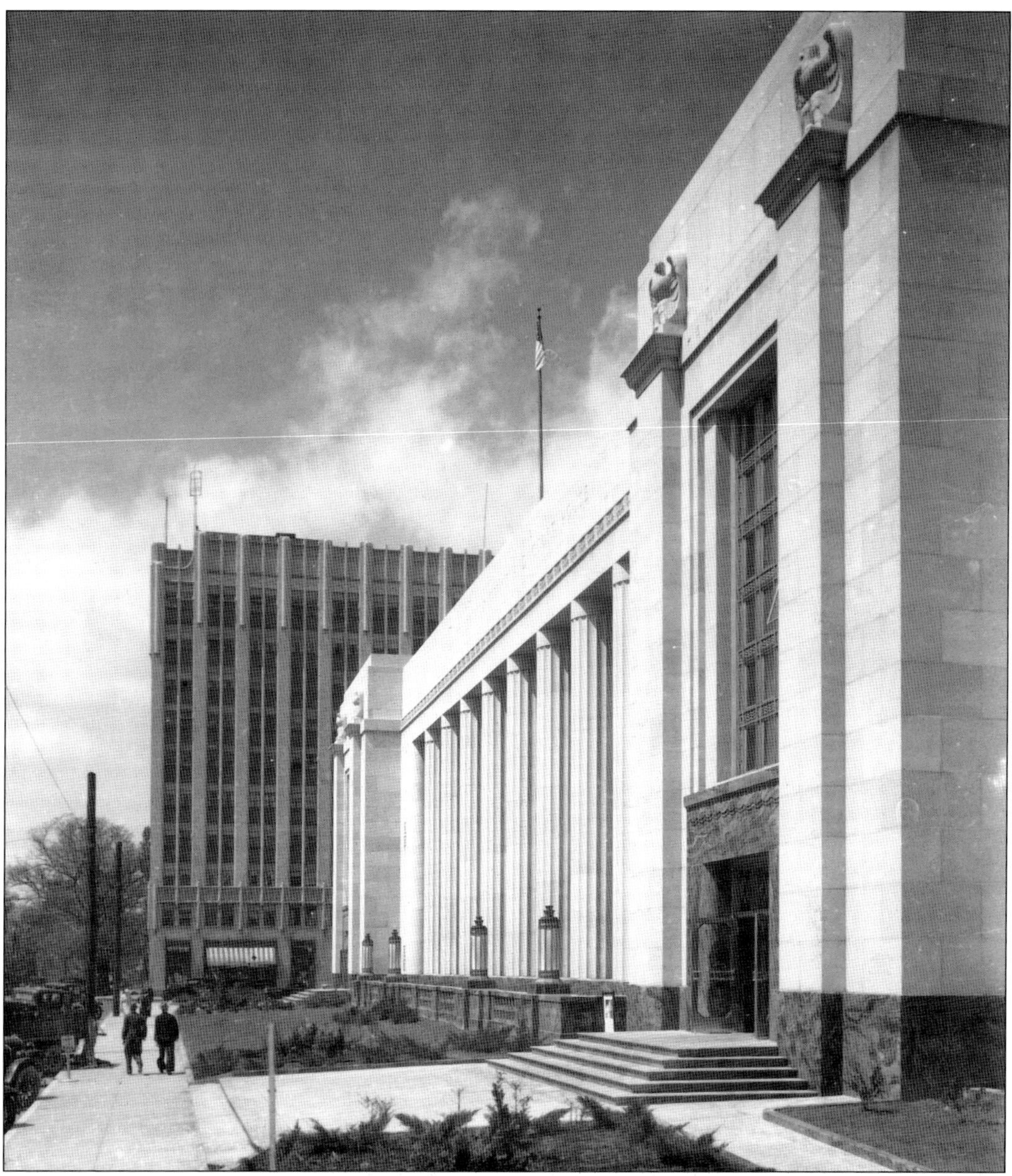

Ironically, Knoxville greeted the Great Depression with the completion of several large new buildings that changed the look of downtown, especially along Main Street. Baumann and Baumann designed the building in the foreground, perhaps the city's most conspicuous use of local pink Tennessee marble, which served as Knoxville's main post office for almost 50 years, with a federal courthouse and judges' chambers. It was here in 1956 that Judge Robert Taylor ordered the desegregation of Clinton High School. Today, its ornate courtroom is used by the Tennessee Supreme Court. It still includes a post office branch. In the background, the Medical Arts Building, designed by the local firm of Manley and Young and completed by Worsham Brothers in 1930, is an elaborate terra-cotta-clad skyscraper. Originally built for medical offices, it is now a residential building. (McClung, Thompson Photograph Collection.)

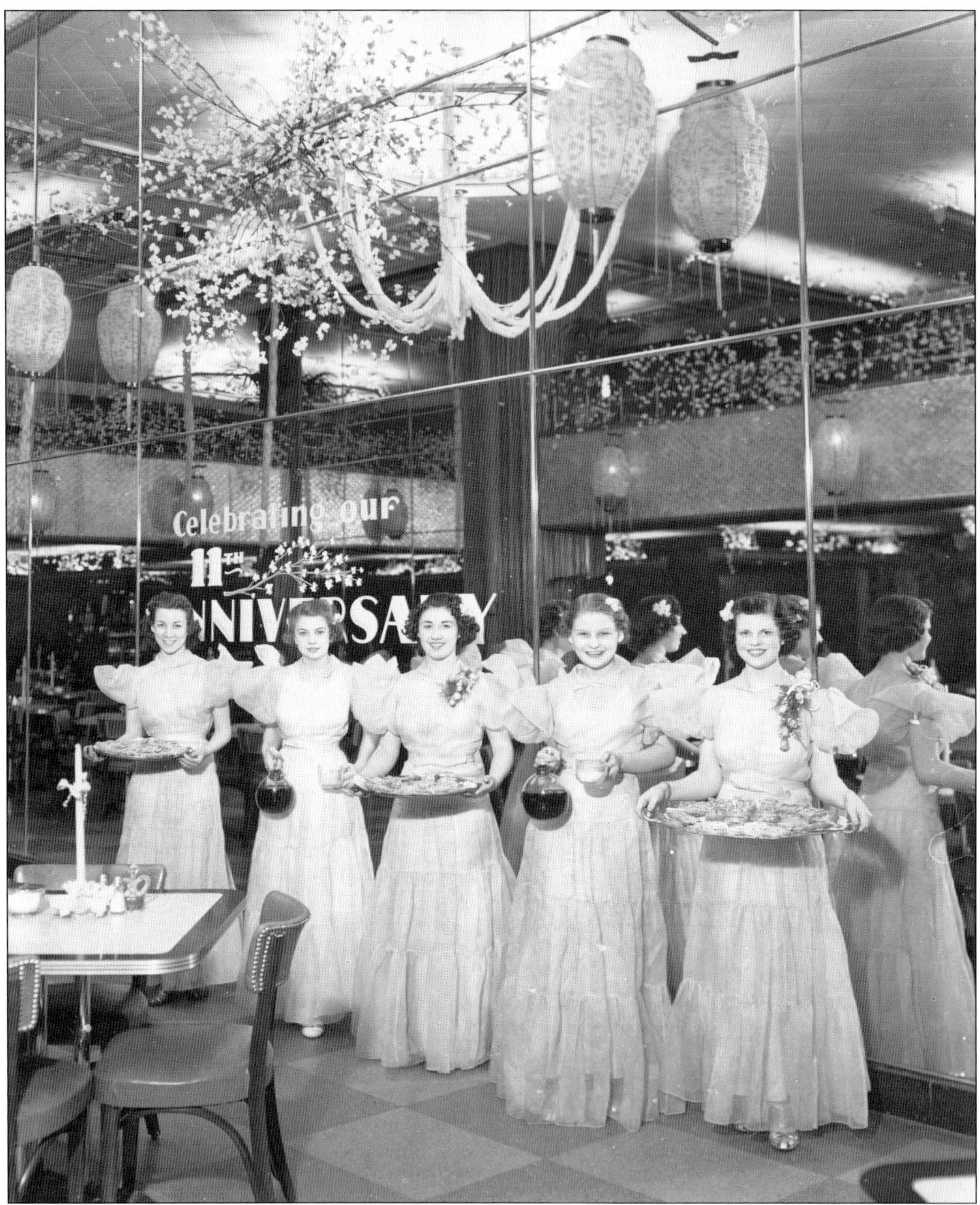

The S&W, an elegant North Carolina cafeteria chain, opened this Knoxville location in 1927 but built its larger and better-known restaurant on the 500 block of Gay Street in 1937. In this c. 1938 photograph, bridelike waitresses standing before the famous mirrored wall seem eager to please. (McClung, Thompson Photograph Collection.)

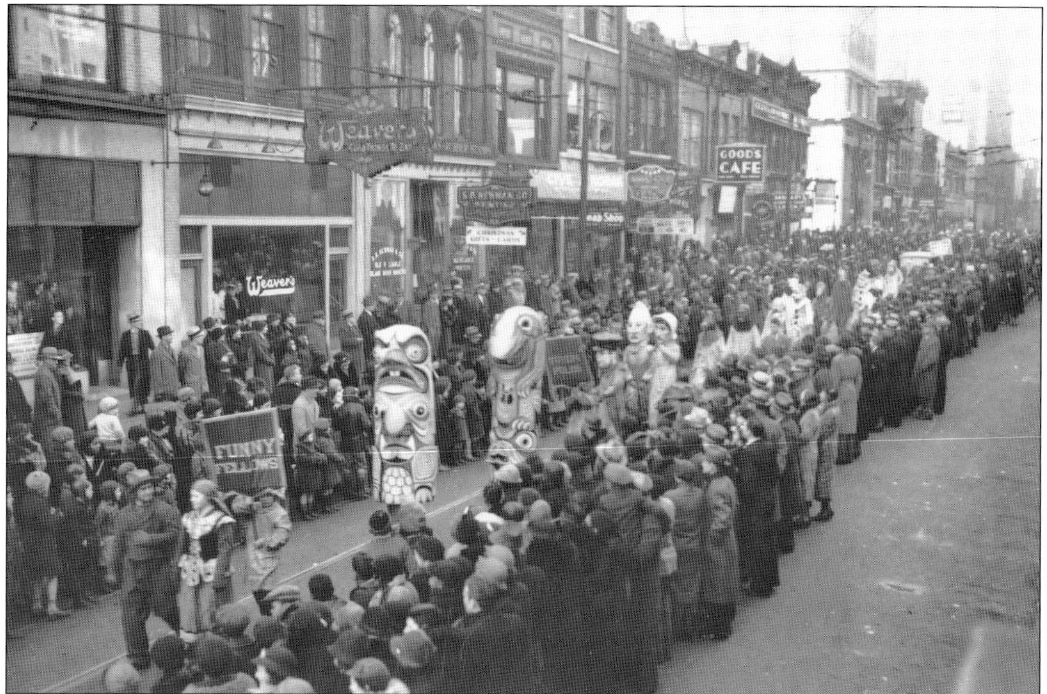

Crowds hailed Knoxville's first Christmas parade in 1928, likely encouraged by the hugely popular Macy's Thanksgiving Day Parades in New York. In Knoxville, the first spectacle, dubbed the Santa Claus Parade, was also held in late November and featured 31 floats decorated with nursery rhyme and fairy tale themes. These photographs from the 1934 Santa Claus Parade show a stream of bizarre-looking characters that might seem better dressed for Halloween, while Santa himself, pulled along by a trio of reindeer, greets an enthusiastic crowd. (Both, McClung, Thompson Photograph Collection.)

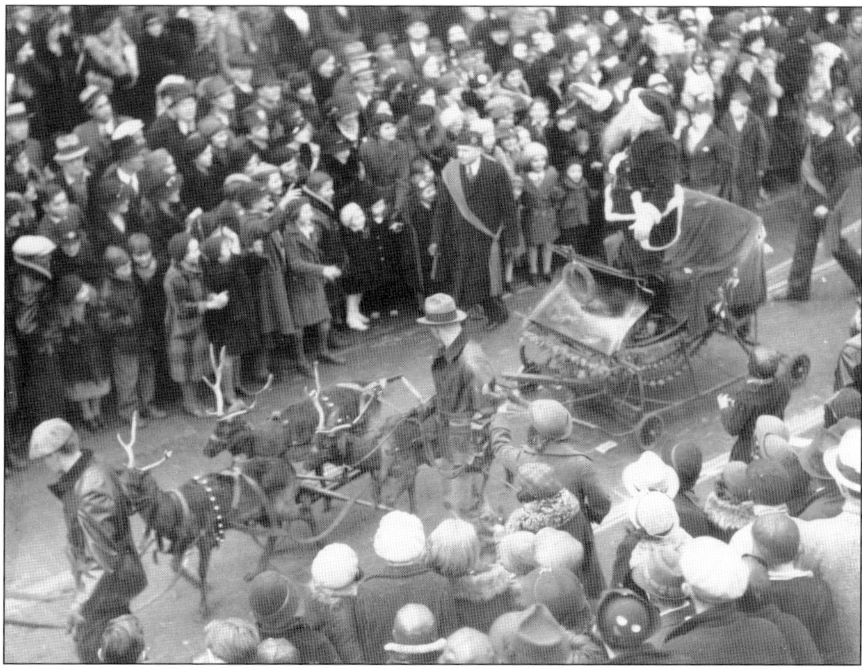

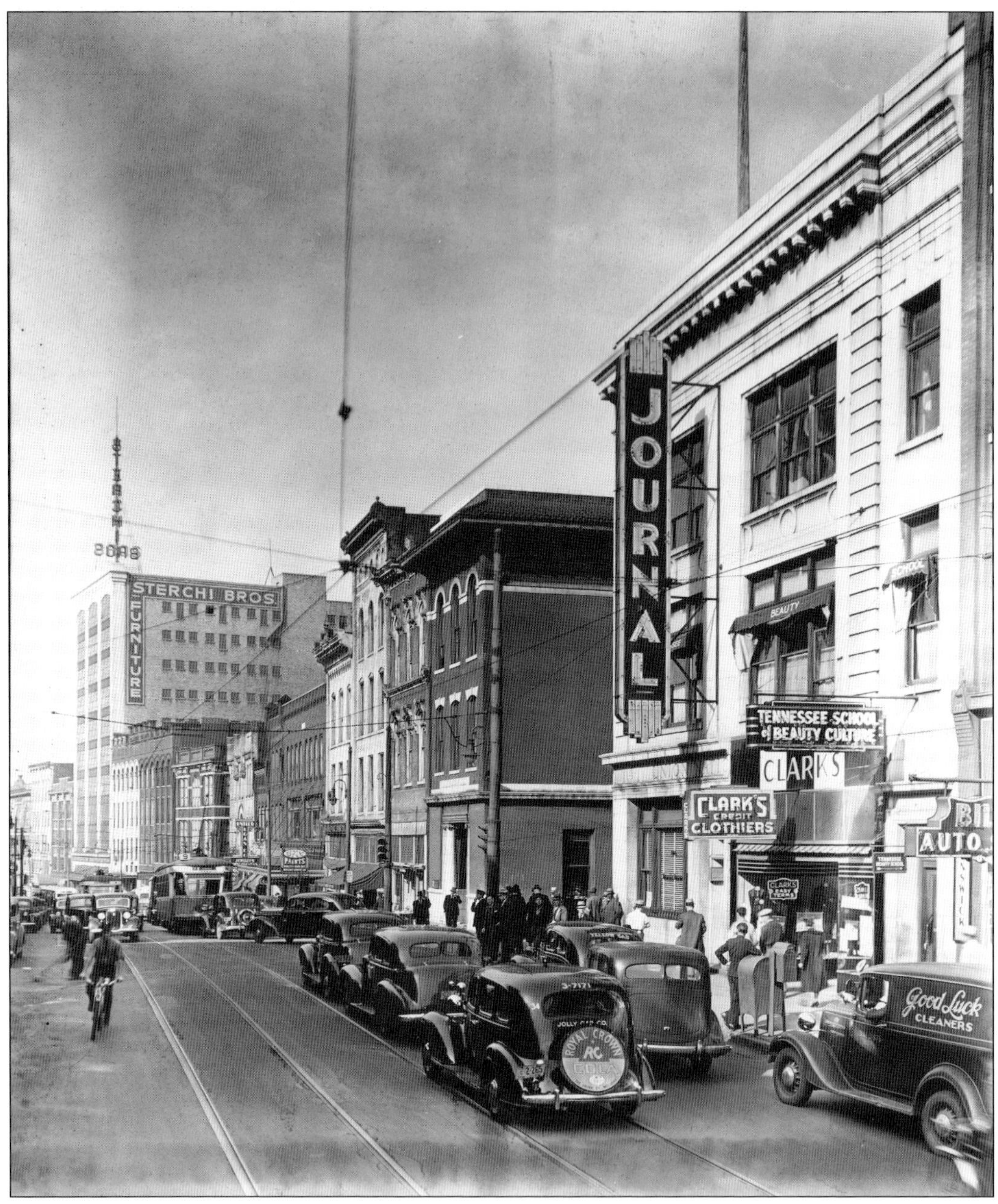

This view looking north on Gay Street shows the building that served for several years as the headquarters of the *Knoxville Journal*, which left its previous building under financial stress. Among its reporters then was the young Lindsey Nelson, later a national sportscaster. Beyond is the now-vanished 200 block of Gay Street, as well as the 100 block, which is mostly intact. (McClung, Thompson Photograph Collection.)

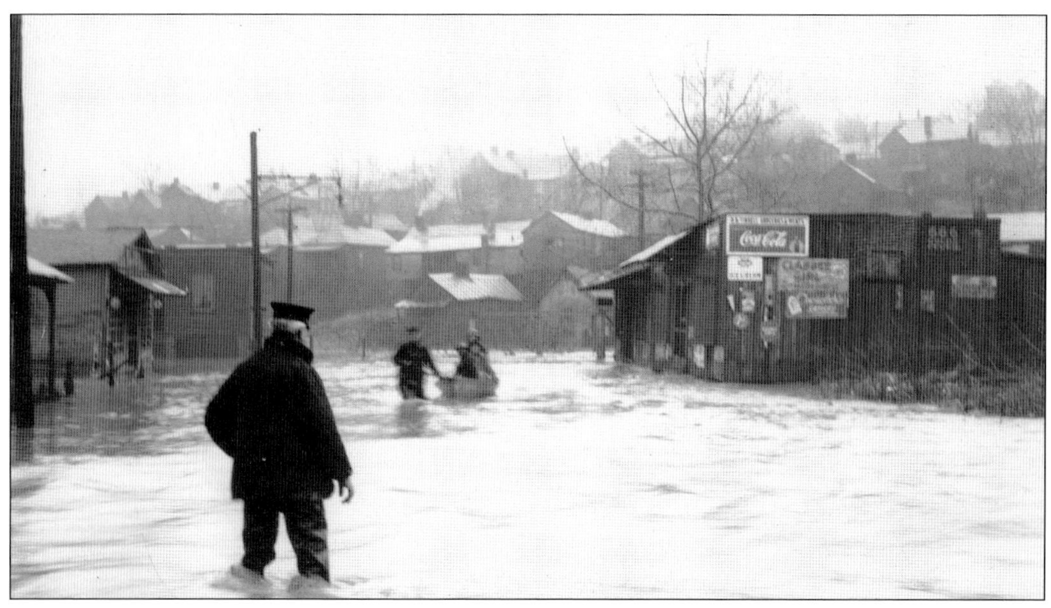

An often-neglected part of downtown was its northeastern corner, known in the 19th century as Cripple Creek but in the 20th century as the Bottom. The lowest part of downtown, along First Creek immediately east of what is now the Old City, it flooded so frequently that land was cheap, attracting Knoxville's poorest, especially African Americans. These two rare photographs by an unknown photographer in the 1930s show the Bottom during a spring flood. Some 20 years later, this area was cleared during urban renewal. Flood-control improvements were successful, but the area was rezoned for industrial use, ejecting the residents, many of whom landed in housing projects. (Both, Cindy and Mark Proteau.)

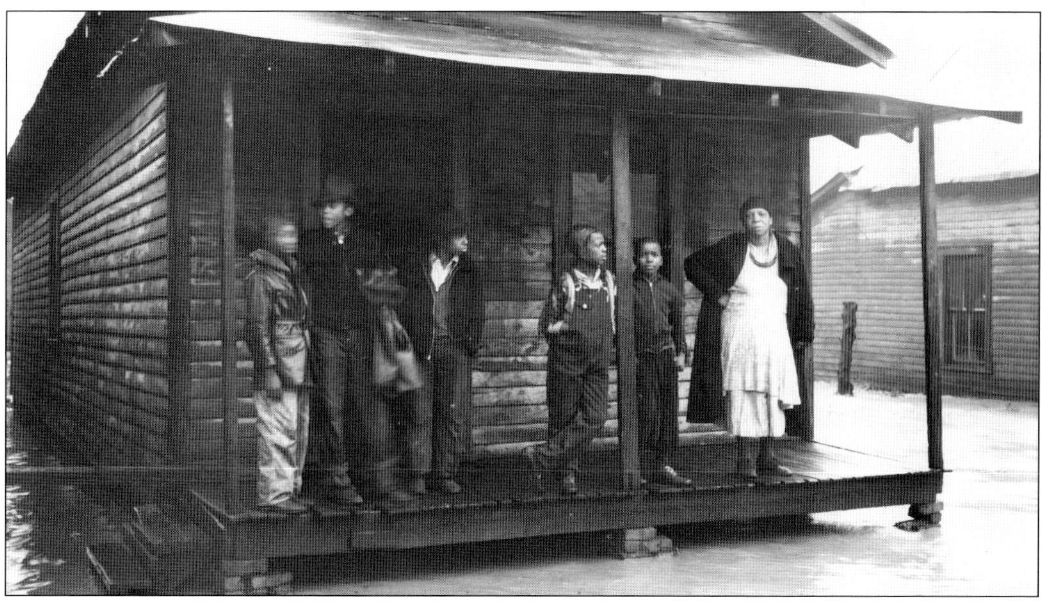

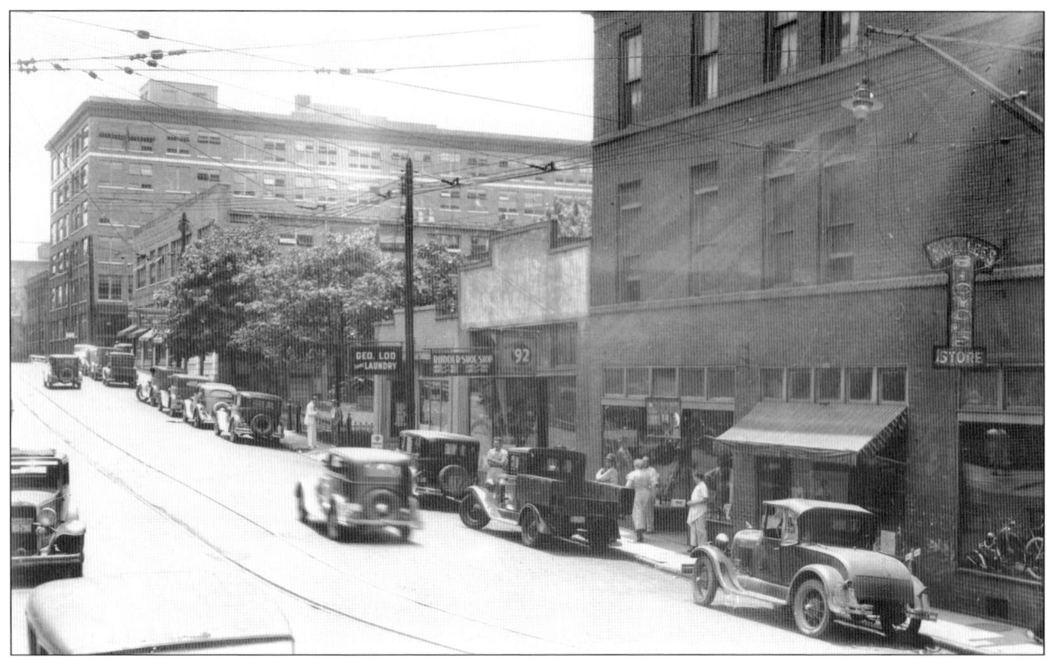

This c. 1935 photograph of Walnut Street, looking south toward Union Avenue and the Daylight and Pembroke (originally New Sprankle) Buildings, includes a rare image of a Chinese-owned business, the George Loo Hand Laundry. Just down the sidewalk are a shoe shop, a billiard parlor, and an early location of Greenlee's Bicycle Store. (McClung, Thompson Photograph Collection.)

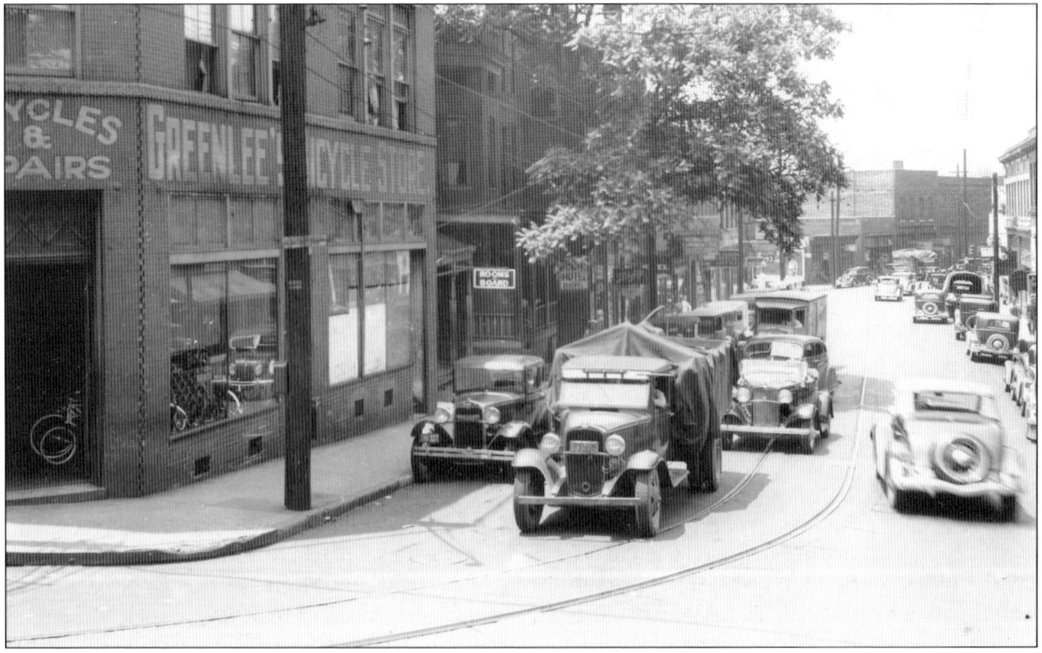

This photograph, taken from about the same spot, peers around the corner down crooked Asylum Avenue to the west. This neighborhood is unrecognizable today. All of the buildings are gone, and the course of the streets has changed. Most of Asylum Avenue was straightened into Western Avenue and Summit Hill Drive. (McClung, Thompson Photograph Collection.)

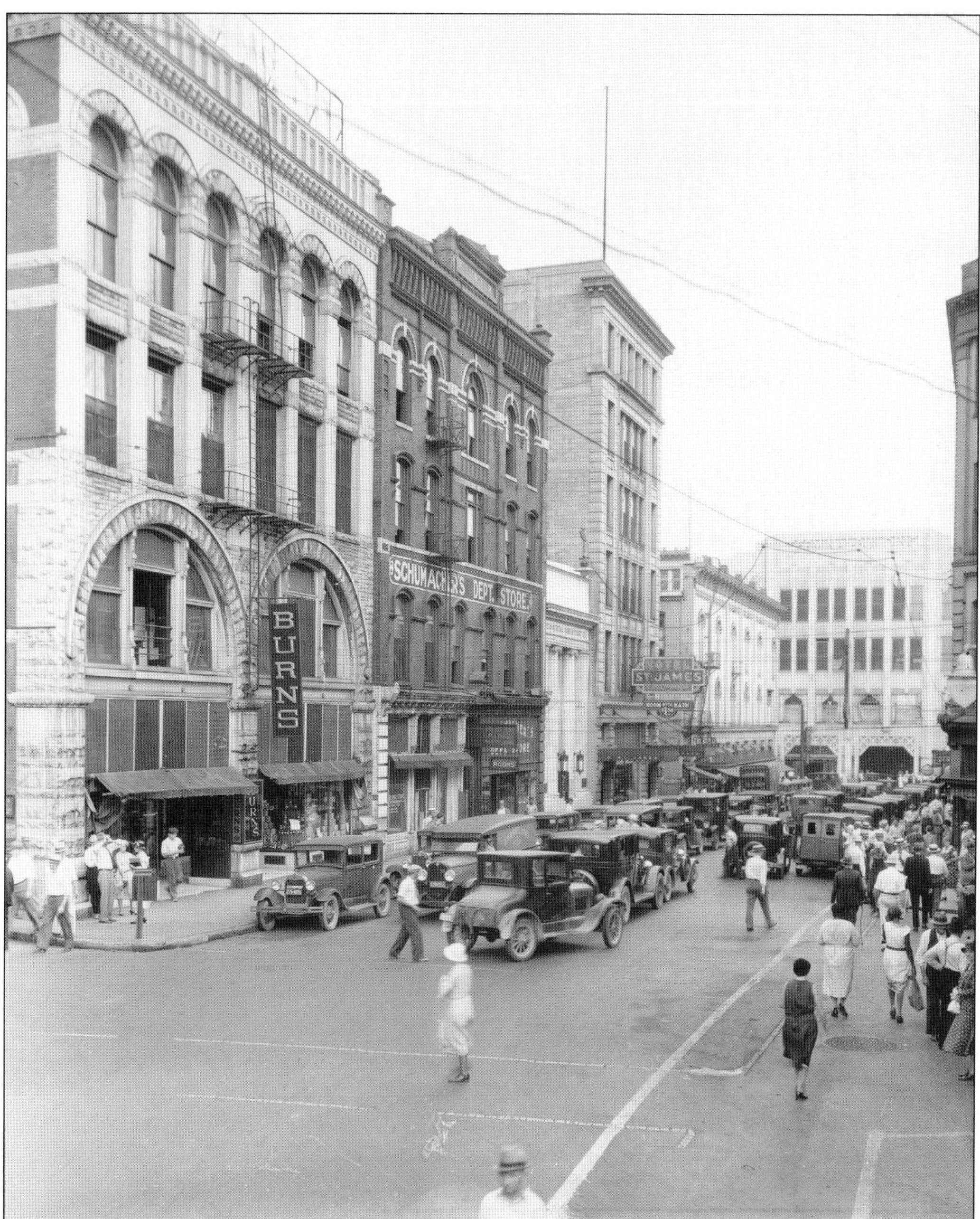

Wall Avenue, at the northern end of Market Square, was a dependably busy scene in the 1930s. T.E. Burns, known for its stone arched façade, was a well-known grocery wholesaler. The tallest building on the block is the Hotel St. James, known for its association with radio station WNOX, whose antenna is visible at top. In 1929–1930, the St. James hosted more than 100 Brunswick-Vocalion recording sessions, creating some of the first recordings of the Tennessee Ramblers as well as the only known recordings of the Tennessee Chocolate Drops and blues singer Leola Manning. This image was used for the cover of the acclaimed box set *The Knoxville Sessions*. The Union Terminal is at the end of the street. Most of these buildings were demolished in the 1970s, some for the Tennessee Valley Authority's new headquarters. (McClung, Thompson Photograph Collection.)

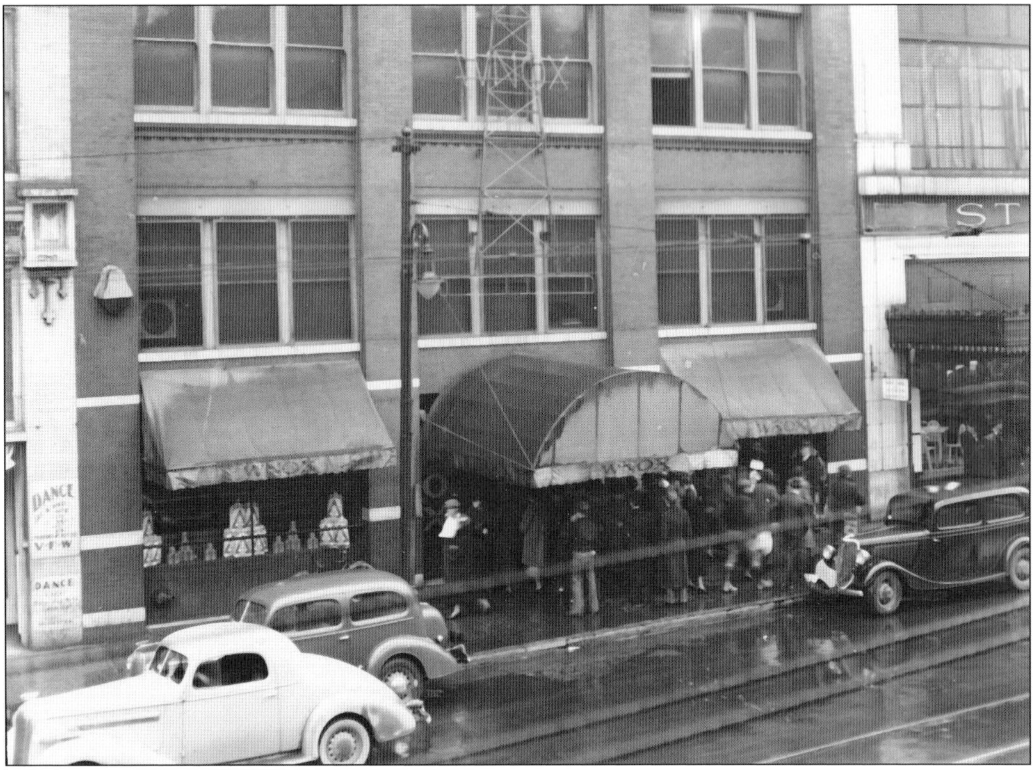

On this rainy day, country music fans wait under cover to get into WNOX studios on the 100 block of Gay Street. During the era when WNOX was located here (1936–1954), its live-audience show *Mid-Day Merry-Go-Round* became famous, launching the careers of Chet Atkins, Archie Campbell, Arthur Q. Smith, and others. (McClung, Thompson Photograph Collection.)

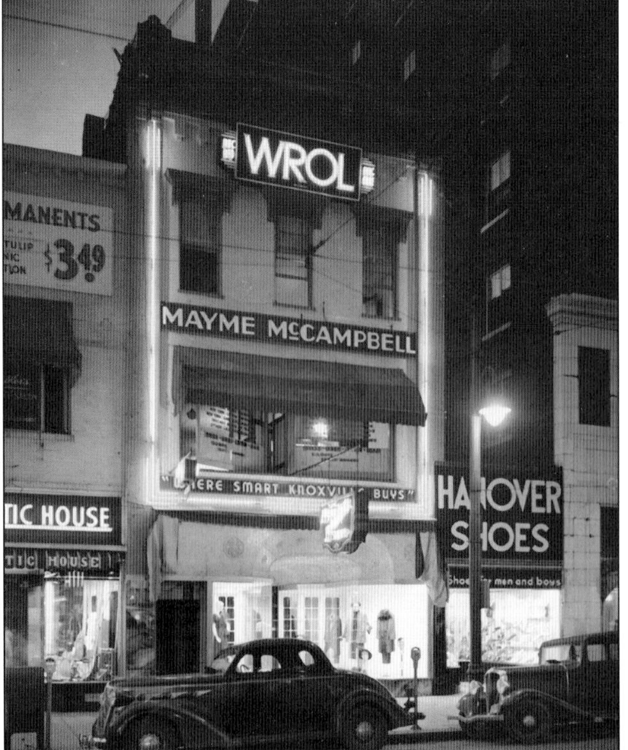

Competing with WNOX in the 1930s was the rougher-edged WROL. Fiddler/singer Roy Acuff probably made his first radio broadcasts from this location near the Farragut Hotel around 1933, years before he became the Grand Ole Opry's biggest star. (McClung, Thompson Photograph Collection.)

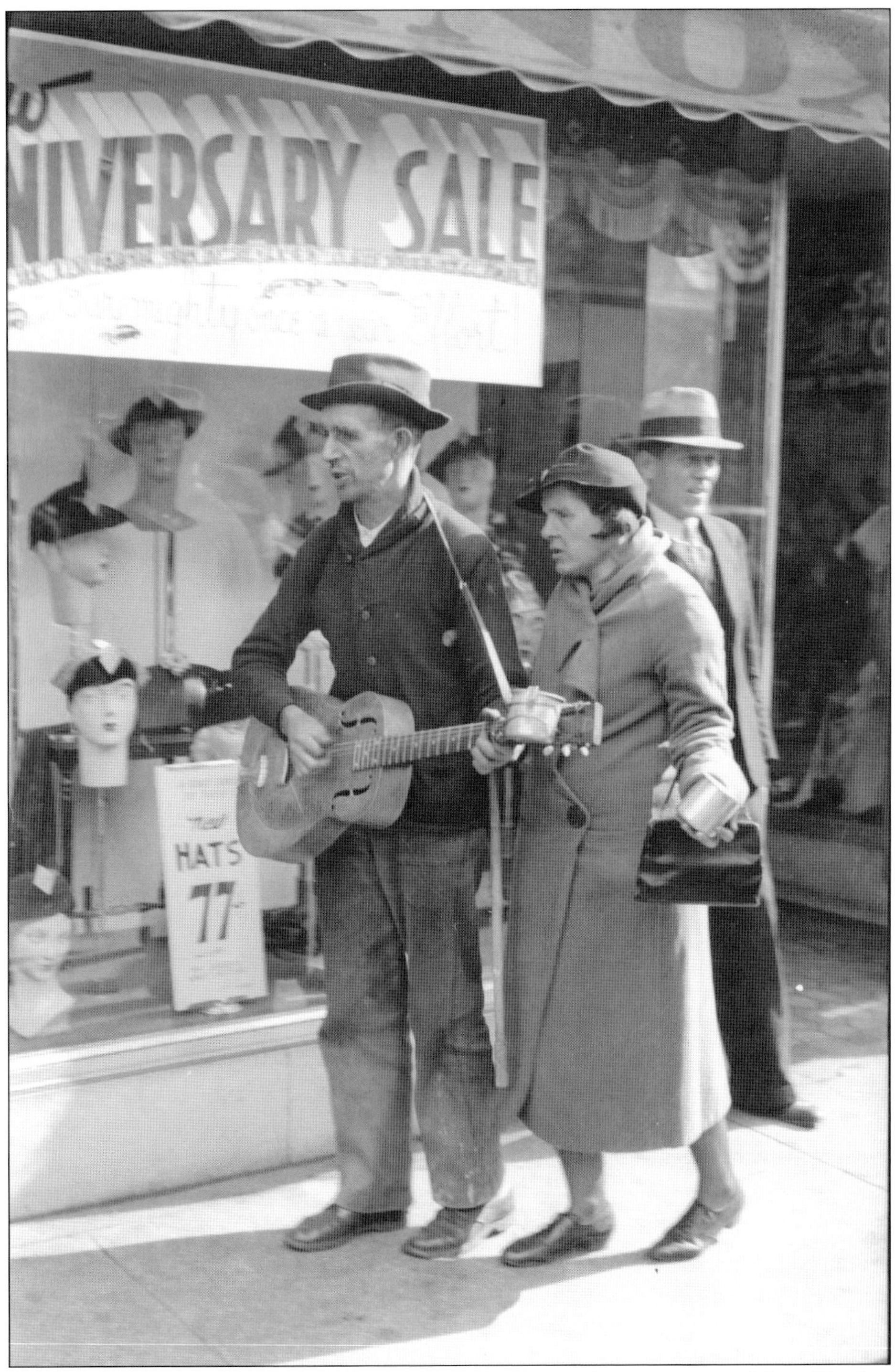

In Knoxville, country music started on the streets, and street performers, many of them blind, offered a soundtrack for a walk around downtown. In 1936, an unidentified guitarist plays and sings, with a tin cup lashed to the neck of his guitar, as his female associate holds out another cup in hopes of a stranger's buffalo nickel or Mercury dime. (McClung, Roger H. Howell Photo Collection.)

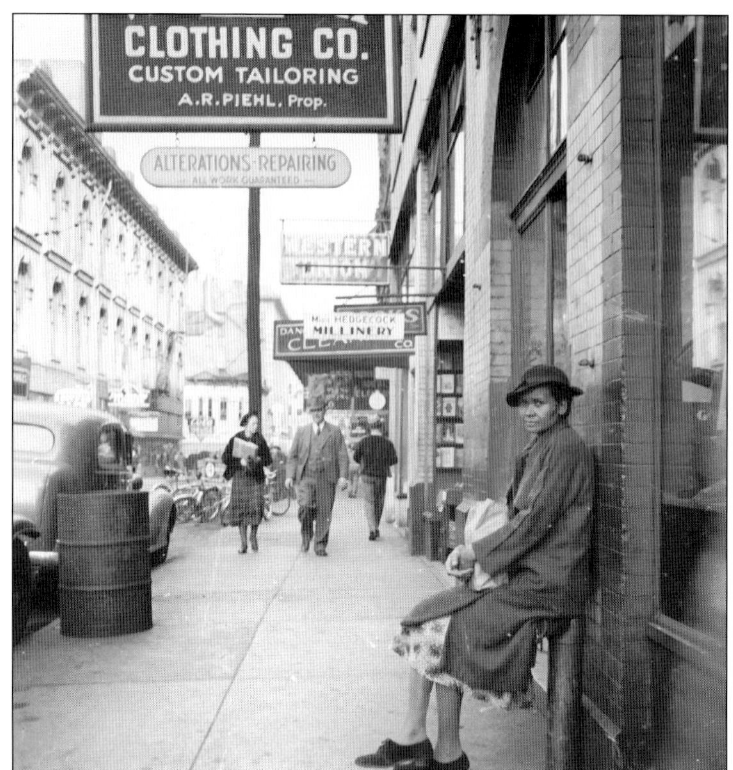

This image, one of several photographs taken by eccentric Swiss journalist Annemarie Schwarzenbach in 1937, shows Union Avenue looking east in the direction of Market Square. Visible are Miss Hedgecock Millinery and the Western Union telegraph office, with multiple messengers' bicycles in front. The familiar Kern Building is in the background. (Swiss National Library, SLA-Schwarzenbach-A5-10/264.)

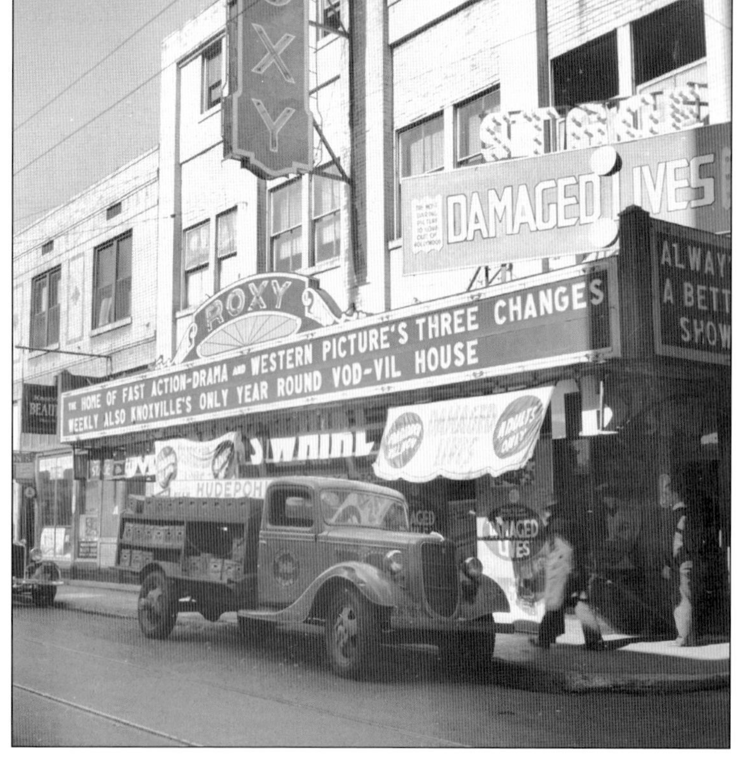

The Roxy Theatre stood near the northeast corner of Union Avenue and Walnut Street. The notably cheap, rough-edged theater showed both cowboy movies and exploitation films like *Damaged Lives*, a 1933 movie about venereal disease (for "adults only," according to a sign). At night, the Roxy featured bawdy comics and striptease acts it called "Vod-Vil." (Swiss National Library, SLA-Schwarzenbach-A5-10/235.)

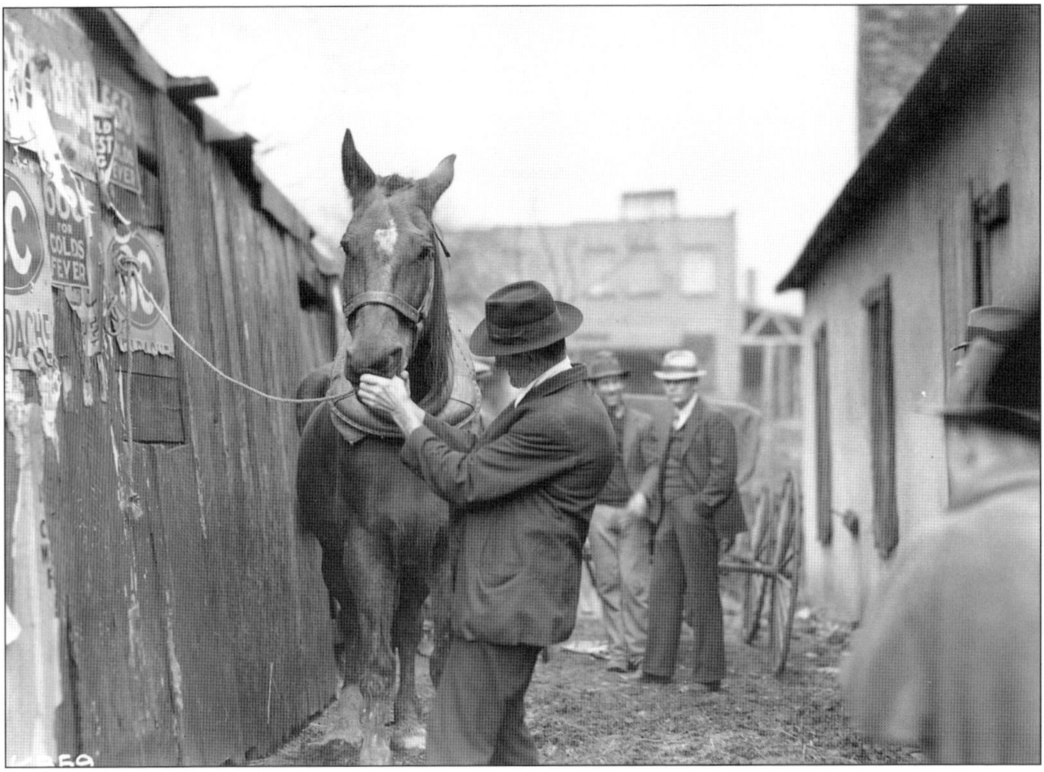

These two 1935 photographs of South Central Street scenes are attributed to Tennessee Valley Authority photographer Charles Krutch, whose monumental images of dams and power plants once earned a display at the Museum of Modern Art. The 100 block of South Central Street was the location of downtown Knoxville's very last livery stable, George Miller's, at 127. Miller converted the space to automobile storage the following year. (Both, Tennessee Valley Authority.)

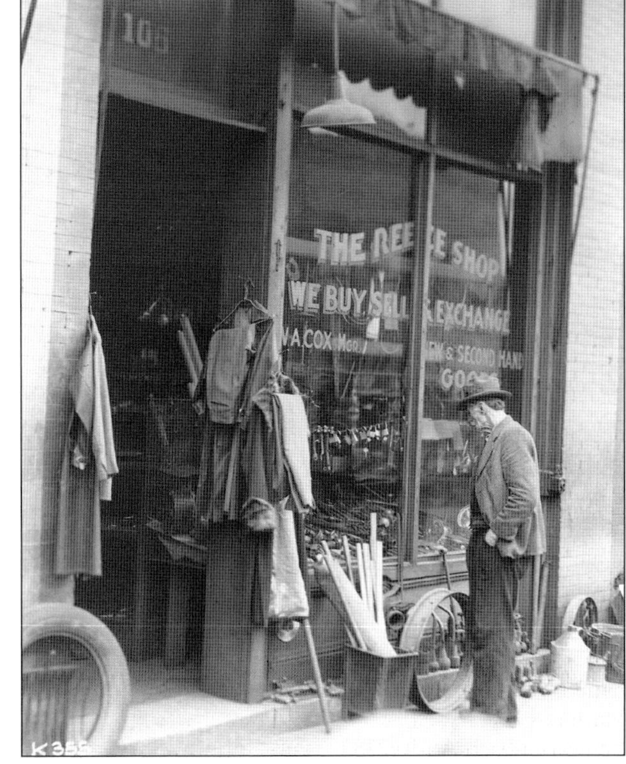

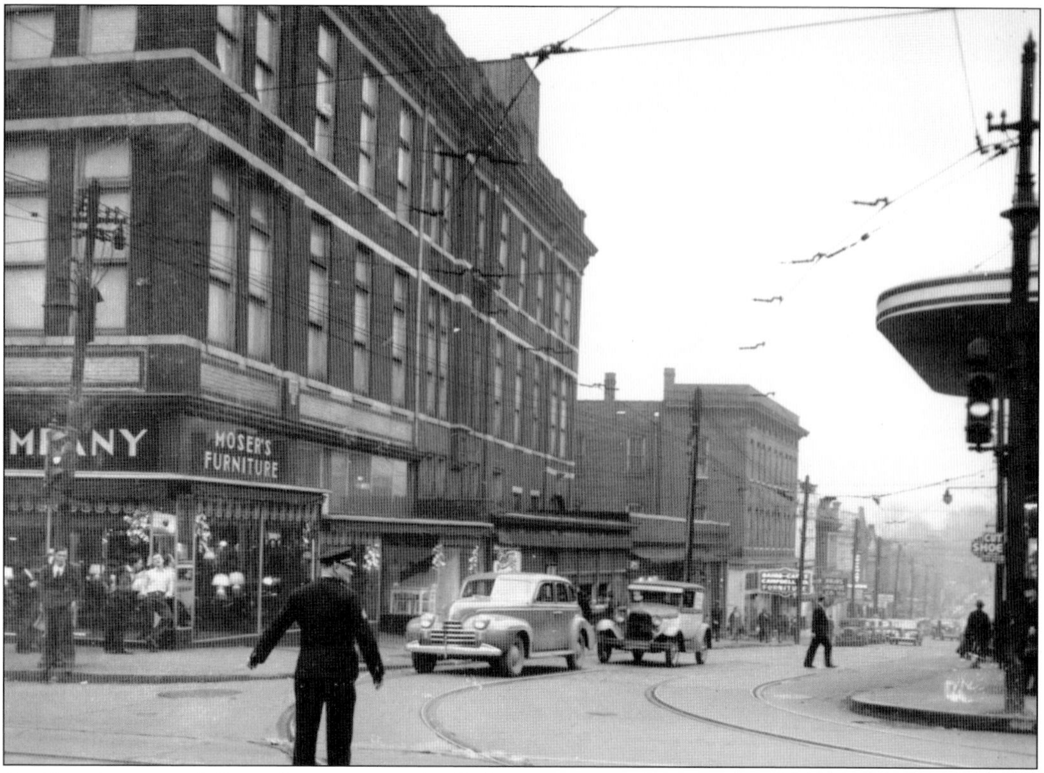

At Gay Street and Vine Avenue was the Rebori Building, here occupied by Moser's Furniture. Built in 1886, it was Knoxville's first public library until it was purchased in 1915 by Italian street vendor Fiorenzo Rebori, an immigrant from Genoa who sold roasted peanuts from dawn until midnight in the low-slung building alongside it until his death at 82 in 1946. (McClung, Thompson Photograph Collection.)

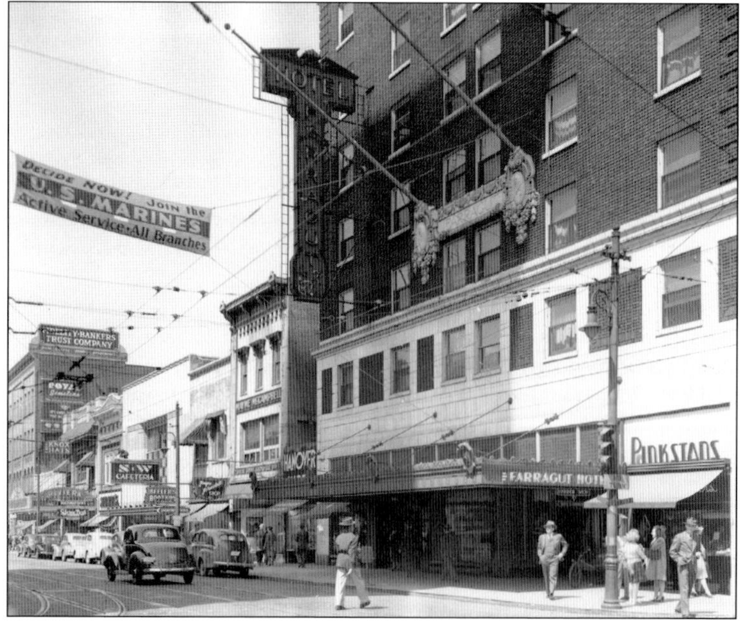

The Farragut Hotel supports a Marine recruitment banner early in World War II. Signs show that the Farragut's lobby included a barbershop, billiard hall, and an L&N ticket office. Down the sidewalk in this 1942 photograph are two wartime attractions, the S&W Cafeteria and the original Riviera Theatre, a 1,000-seat movie house here showing the Betty Grable–Victor Mature thriller *I Wake Up Screaming*.

Six

Mid-Century and Beyond

The postwar era found downtown Knoxville in an awkward spot. Following national patterns, Knoxvillians fled headlong for the suburbs, especially to the west. Retail followed the exodus as downtown stores reopened in malls and strip centers.

Downtown was already in decline in 1947 when travel writer John Gunther declared Knoxville "the ugliest city in America." Urban renewal promised change and yielded the long-wished-for Civic Coliseum in 1961 but also resulted in unplanned loss of community. Others modernized downtown by demolishing old buildings for asphalt parking lots. Bringing the new Interstate 40 right through downtown was less a salvation than it first seemed.

The all-pedestrian Market Square Mall, a 1960 innovation along with the Gay Street Promenade, garnered some interest and offered some hope. A couple of bank-office skyscrapers changed downtown's skyline. But both train stations closed, as did the two remaining movie theaters. The last department stores moved out.

Then, in 1982, downtown Knoxville hosted a World's Fair. In its aftermath, an abandoned warehouse district revived itself as a nightclub quarter called the Old City. A growing homegrown publishing company, Whittle Communications, created some excitement with a palatial downtown headquarters. But when it closed in 1994, much of downtown still seemed empty and hopeless, as even the revived Old City was sputtering. City fathers predicted that some of downtown's hotels would have to close.

Then, somehow, the stars aligned. An array of architects, politicians, philanthropists, entrepreneurs, and developers, some of whom did not even know each other, began working on multiple and mostly unrelated projects downtown in a way that seemed mostly organic and serendipitous. The city restored Market Square, and the Tennessee Theatre, extravagantly restored and improved, greeted new generations, helping to spawn an annual international music festival. Movies returned to downtown in a brand-new cineplex, and affluent residents almost suddenly developed an appreciation for downtown living as, one by one, almost all of downtown's once-daunting vacant buildings filled with businesses and people. Today, more people live in downtown Knoxville than at any time since 1940, and its old buildings resonate with new businesses as sidewalks teem with friends and strangers.

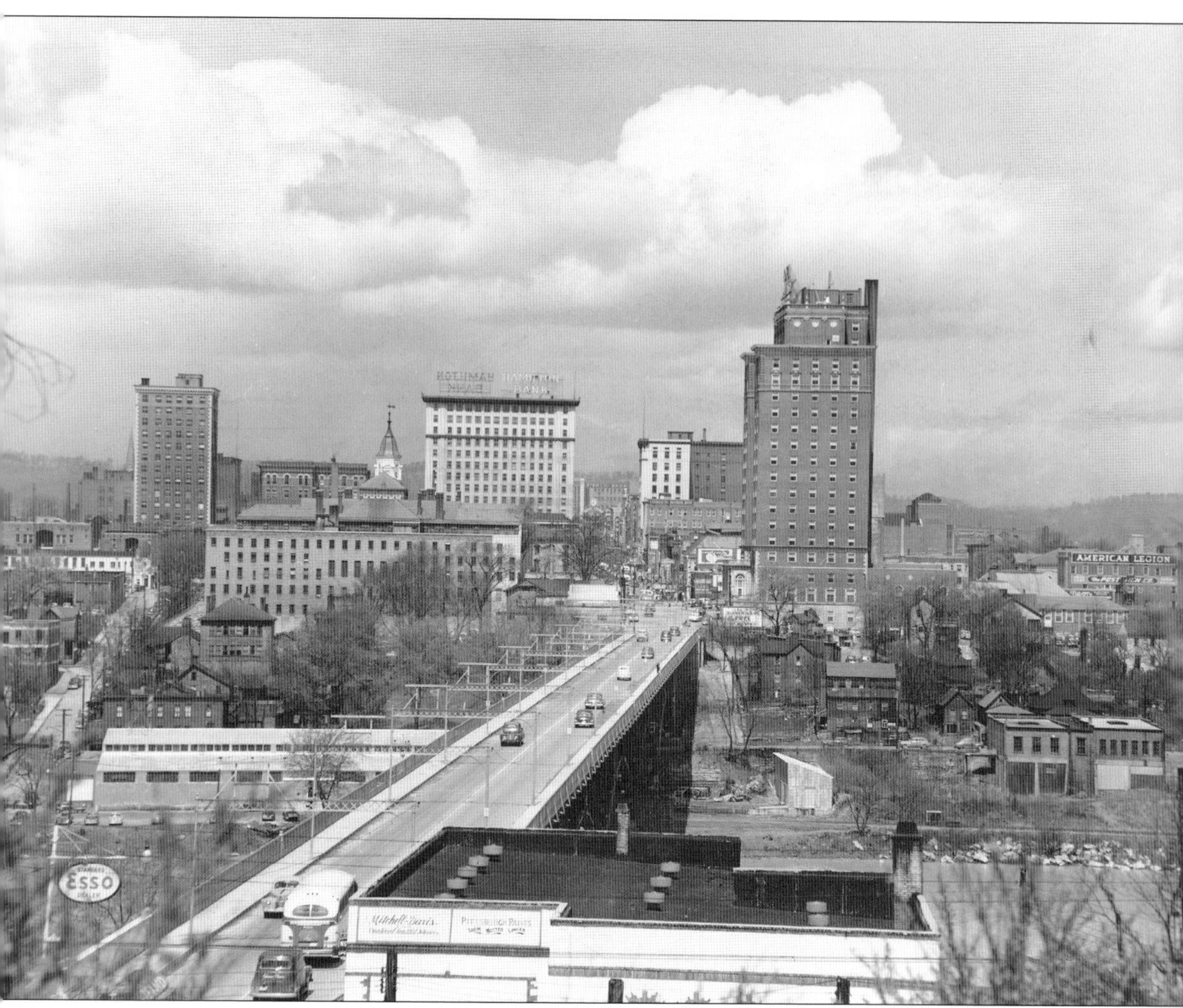

Downtown Knoxville is seen from South Knoxville around 1950. The skyline is recognizable today, though it lacks three skyscrapers built since then. Most of the central business district's buildings then are intact today. (The Empire Building, to the left of the courthouse tower, was torn down in the 1970s.) The Andrew Johnson Hotel was then the tallest building in East Tennessee. However, most of the buildings along the riverfront are gone, replaced with Neyland Drive, built in the early 1950s, and later the City County Building. (Tennessee State Library and Archives.)

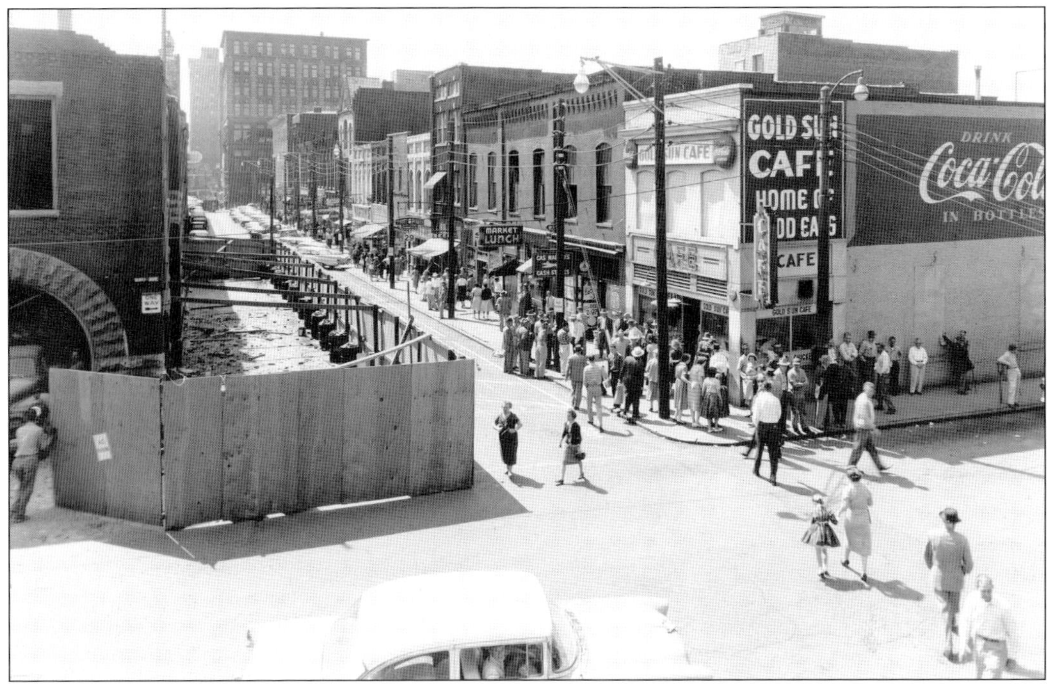

After a decade of contentious discussion, the large and elaborate 1897 Market House was torn down by the city in 1960. (A dramatic fire in late 1959 damaged but did not destroy it; most of its businesses were open the next day.) The Greek-owned Gold Sun (on the right above), opened in 1908, was a 24-hour restaurant that survived the change and was later known as Peroulas. The city considered some merchants' wishes that Market Square become a parking lot, but opted for a proposal by the local chapter of the American Institute of Architects to make it a pedestrian mall, with stylized modernist concrete umbrellas to shade farmers' displays. Initially popular and well-reviewed—it opened in time to herald the first Dogwood Arts Festival in 1961, which received national praise—the modernizations aged poorly and were removed in 1986.

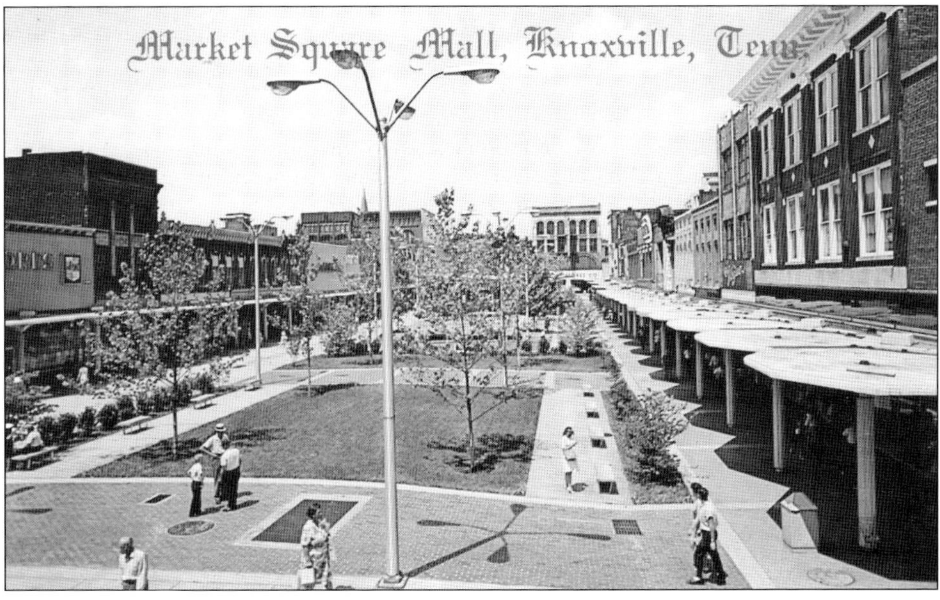

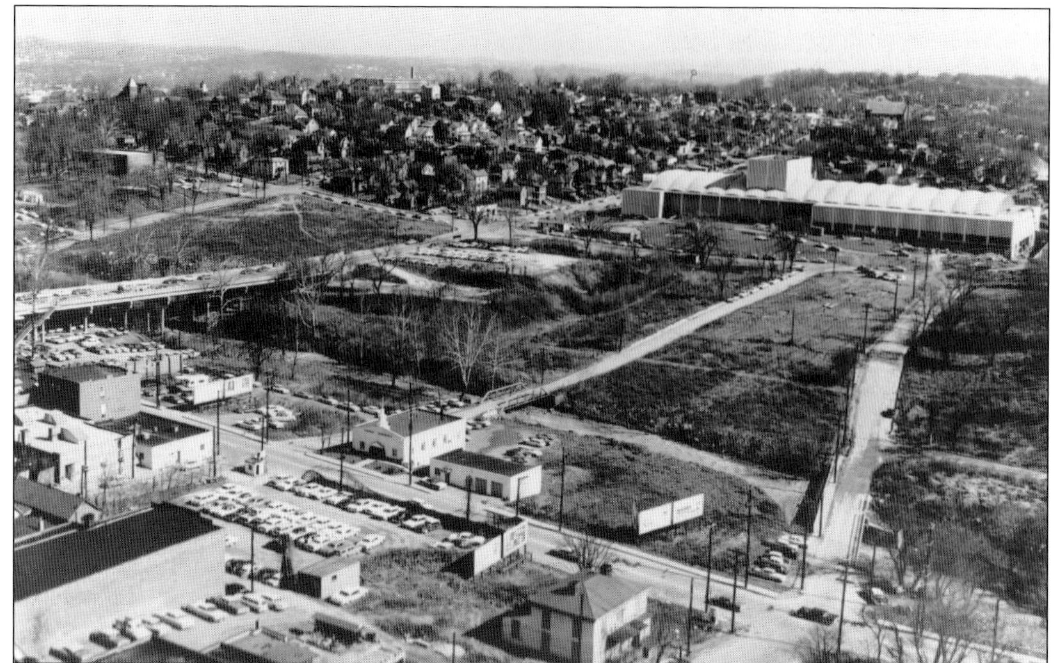

The Civic Coliseum opened in 1961. Enabled by the federal urban renewal initiative, it was downtown's first major new building in 30 years and the realization of a long-deferred dream for a public auditorium. It was also Knoxville's first concert venue to open without segregating the races. From its earliest days, the two-venue facility hosted major performances, lectures, and dramatic productions, as well as Knoxville's first ice hockey team, the Knights. (David Harris.)

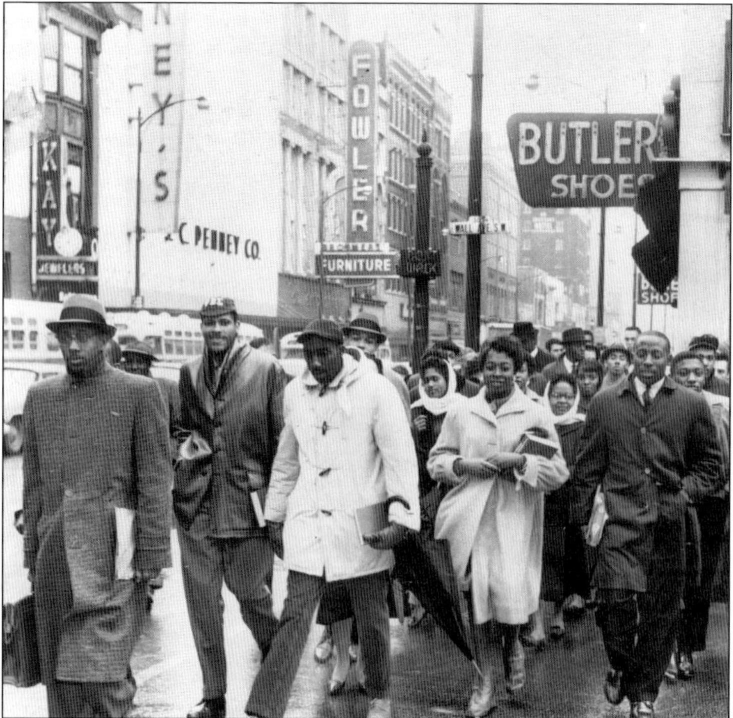

Civil rights demonstrators march north across Wall Avenue on Gay Street in 1960. Among its leaders was Knoxville College student Robert Booker, the tall man second from left with the small cap. Booker was later a successful politician, author, and leader of the Beck Cultural Exchange Center. The demonstrators' sit-ins, commenced just weeks after the first ones in North Carolina, were successful in desegregating downtown's lunch counters without major violence. (Robert Booker.)

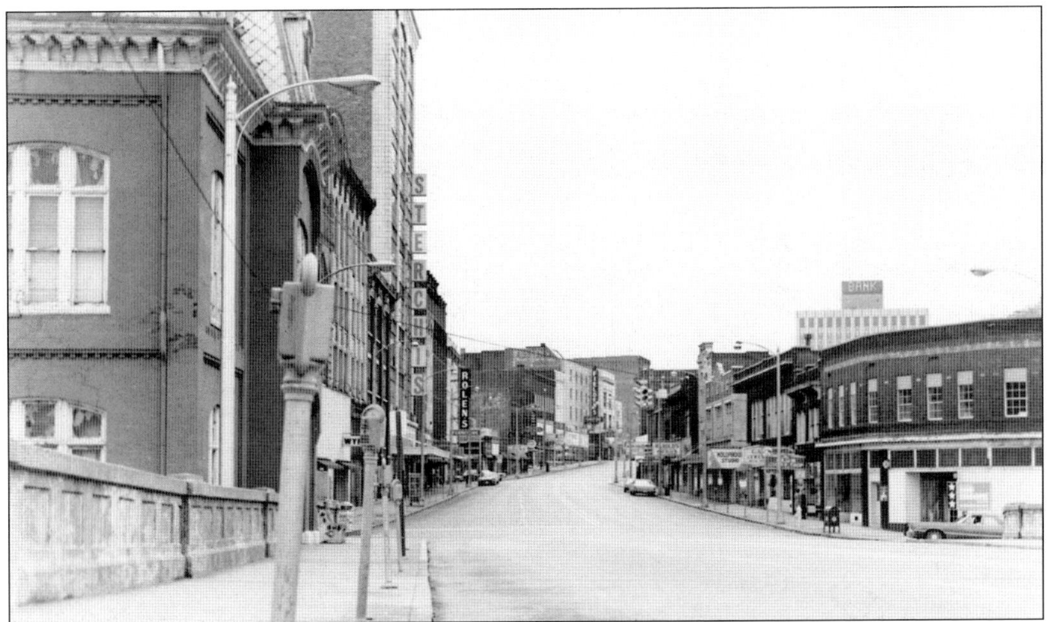

This shot looking south from the Gay Street viaduct in the early 1970s shows the old railroad headquarters building at left, torn down later in that decade, and the 100 block, including Sterchi's, at that time still the headquarters of a major furniture chain and one of Knoxville's tallest buildings. In the background is the densely built 200 block, later removed for the construction of Summit Hill Drive. (Ros Mol.)

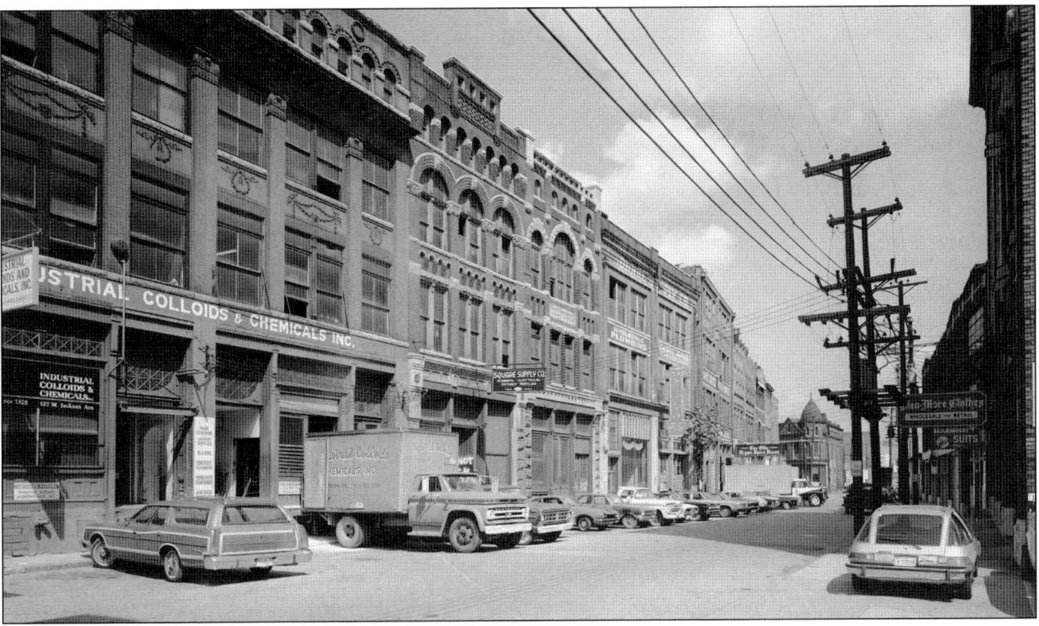

In the 1970s, West Jackson Avenue hosted several businesses, but many of its elaborate old late-1880s warehouses were vacant. The Sullivan's Saloon building in the background was then an appliance warehouse. By the early 1980s, as Knoxville's attention was turning to the neglected district just becoming known as "the Old City," several buildings in the middle of this image had been lost to fire and neglect. (Ros Mol.)

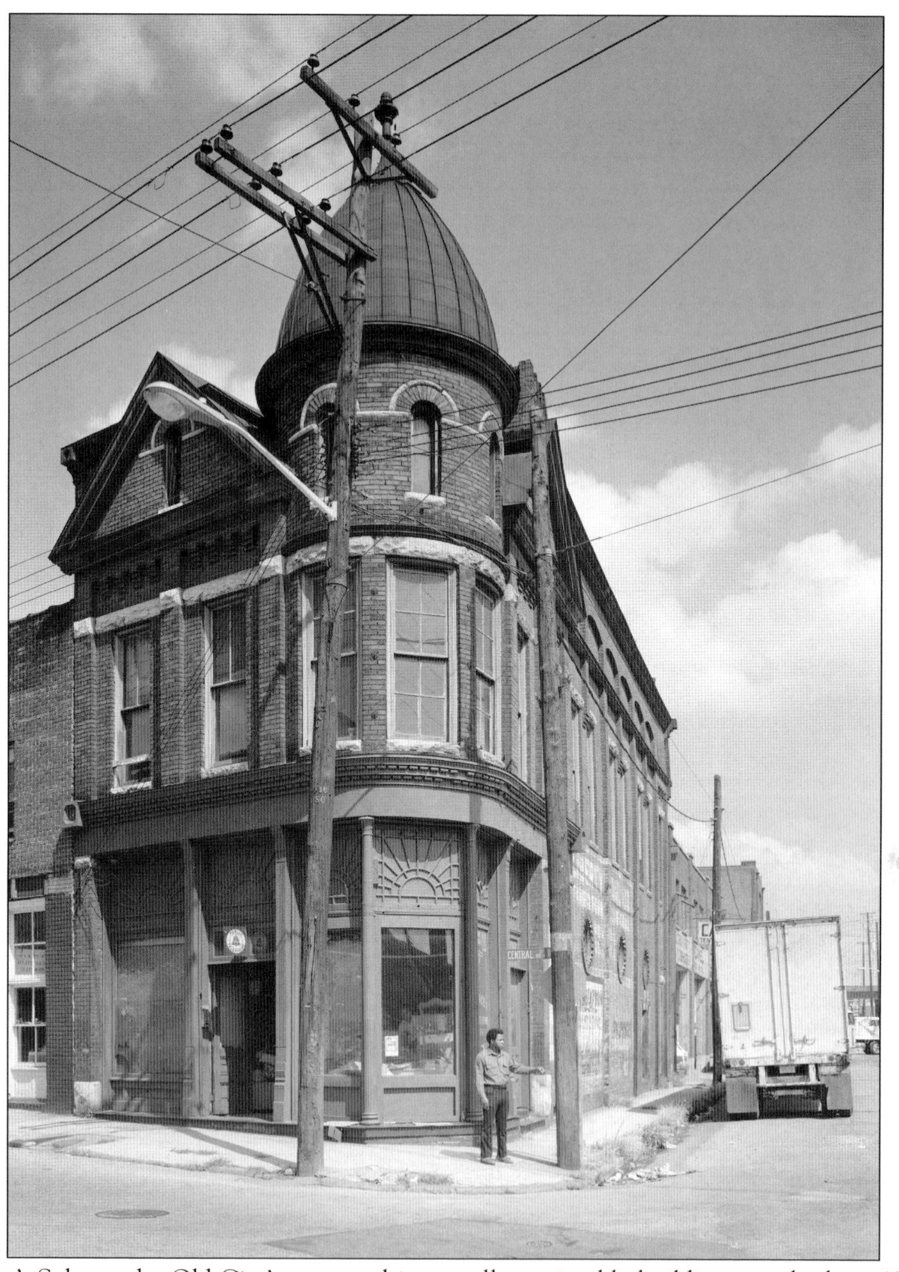

Sullivan's Saloon, the Old City's most architecturally noticeable building, was built in 1888 at the fabled corner of Jackson Avenue and Central Street by Irish immigrant Patrick Sullivan and became remarkable for welcoming customers regardless of gender or race. It was a thriving saloon when this intersection became ground zero for Knoxville's street numbering system. Today, all addresses in Knox County are numbered based on their distance from this spot. Closed by the city's saloon ban in 1907, Sullivan's became home to the Sicilian Armetta family, who operated an ice cream factory here. It had served as a warehouse by the time of this c. 1975 photograph. Its 1988 renovation was a catalyst for the Old City's revival. Hosting restaurants with bars since then, the building has served as a saloon longer in its post-renovation era than it did in Patrick Sullivan's lifetime. (Library of Congress.)

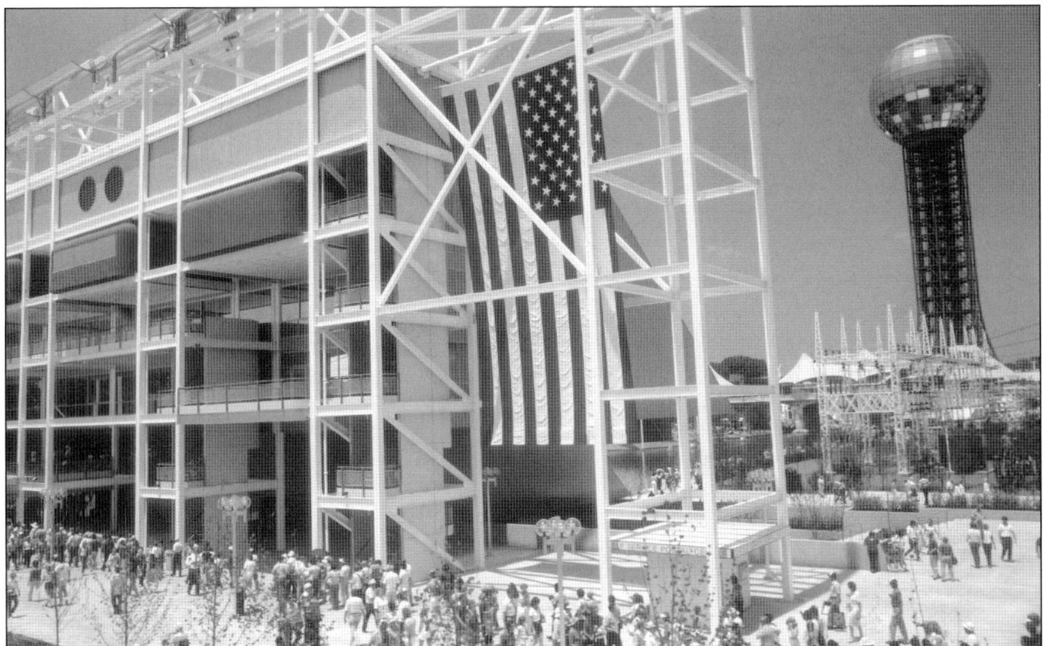

The 1982 World's Fair's modernist US Pavilion was a showcase for American technology, highlighting an early public demonstration of touch-screen technology on a room-sized computer. Although intended to be permanent, the inefficient building and an adjacent IMAX theater were demolished in 1991. At right is the Sunsphere, the fair's signature structure. (James D. Baeske.)

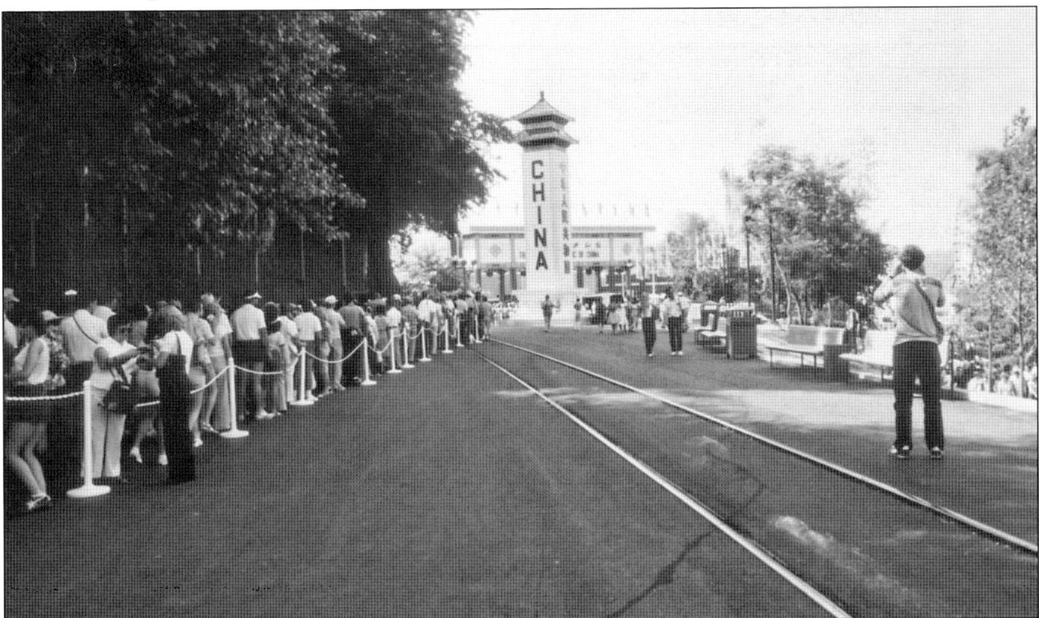

The World's Fair's most popular attraction was the extraordinary China Pavilion. The People's Republic of China had never before participated in a World's Fair. The culture of the once-forbidden nation fascinated Americans, who waited in line for hours to behold its wonders, which included demonstrations by artisans and a rare exhibit of ancient terra-cotta warriors. It was located south of Cumberland Avenue, just east of Second Creek. (James D. Baeske.)

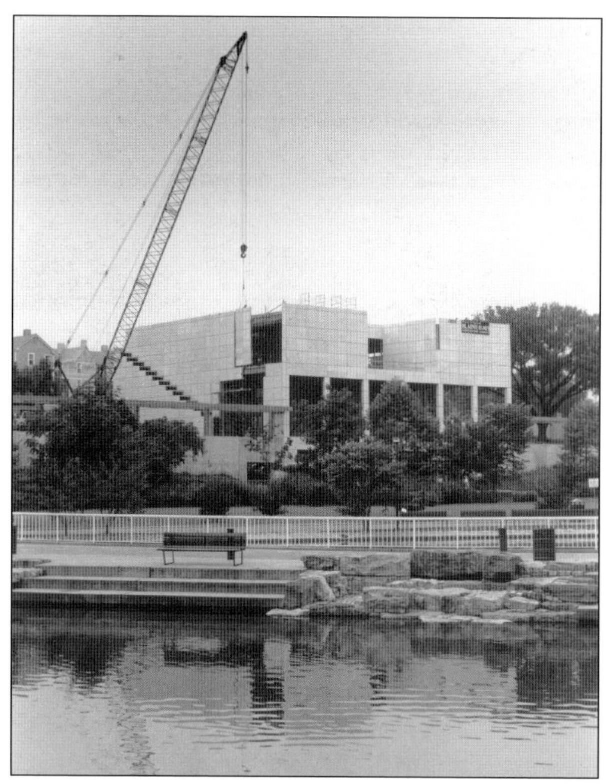

One of the last designs by architect Edward Larrabee Barnes, the marble-faced Knoxville Museum of Art (KMA), the first major new development on the World's Fair site after 1982, was completed in 1990. One of its highest-profile exhibits featured the work of sculptor Auguste Rodin in 1995. Later directing more attention to regional artists, the KMA has acquired the world's largest collection of the work of celebrated modernist Beauford Delaney. (Both, Knoxville Museum of Art.)

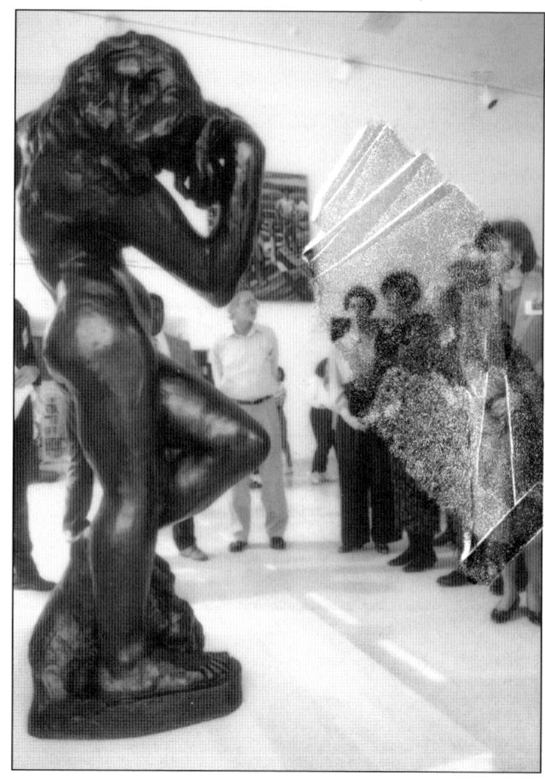

When the beaux-arts Miller's department store building's faux-modernist glass was removed in 1998, preservationists led by architect Duane Grieve were dismayed to discover that much of the building's original 1905 detail was missing, including the four nude caryatids who once fascinated pedestrians. The discovery of parts of one of the missing sculptures enabled a painstaking restoration project that included recasting the figures to be replaced at their original perches above the Gay Street façade. The former department store, closed in 1972, returned as a stylish office building in a major project involving the city and the Knoxville Utilities Board, which moved its main offices there. The major investment encouraged other projects on the forlorn 400 block of Gay Street and prefigured many other preservationist successes downtown. (Both, Duane Grieve, FAIA.)

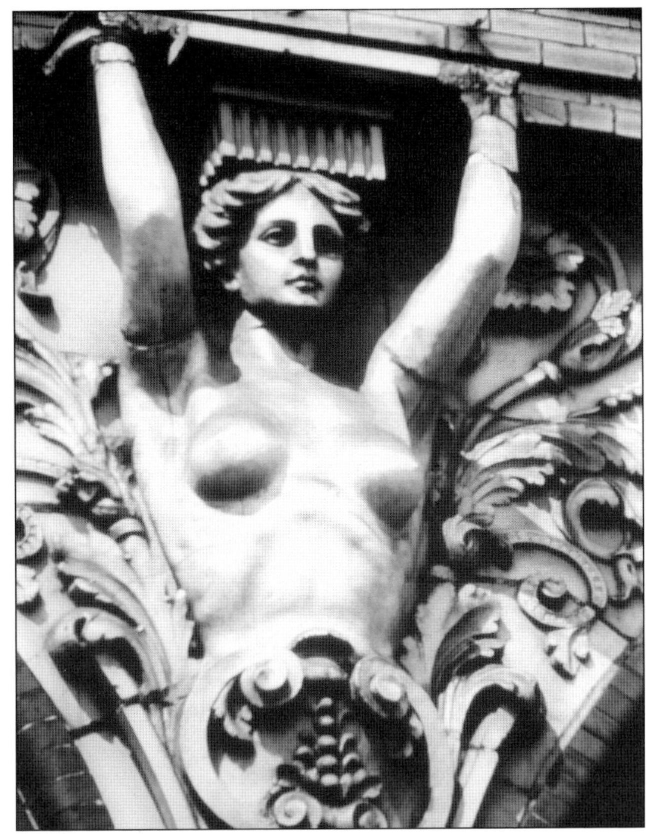

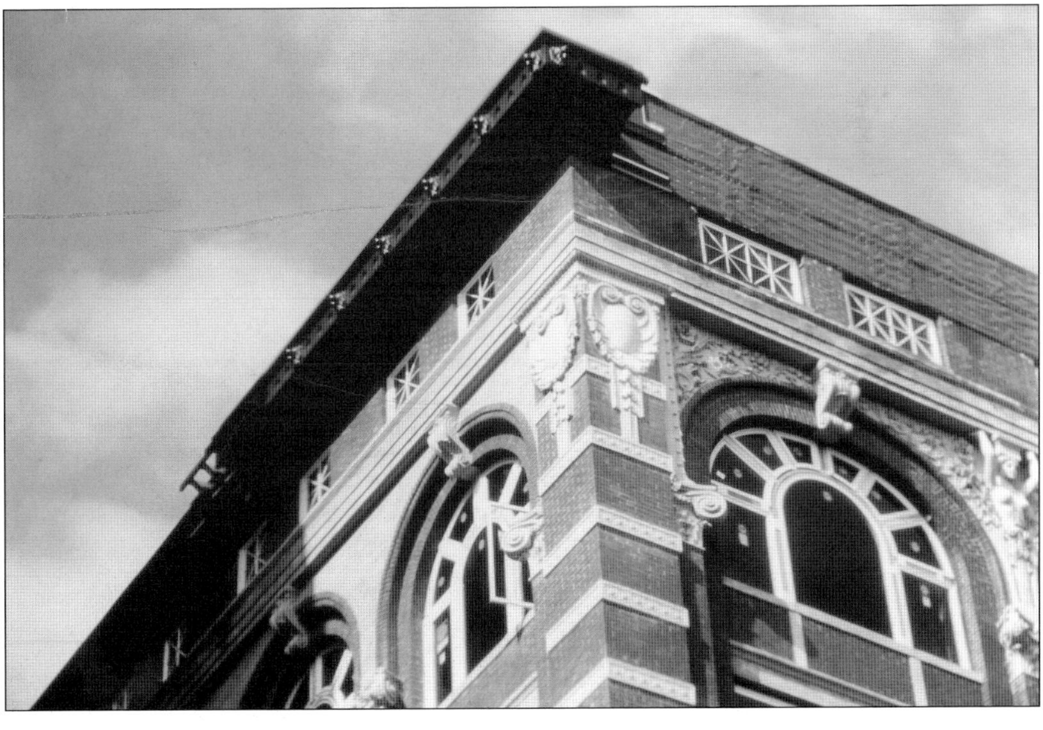

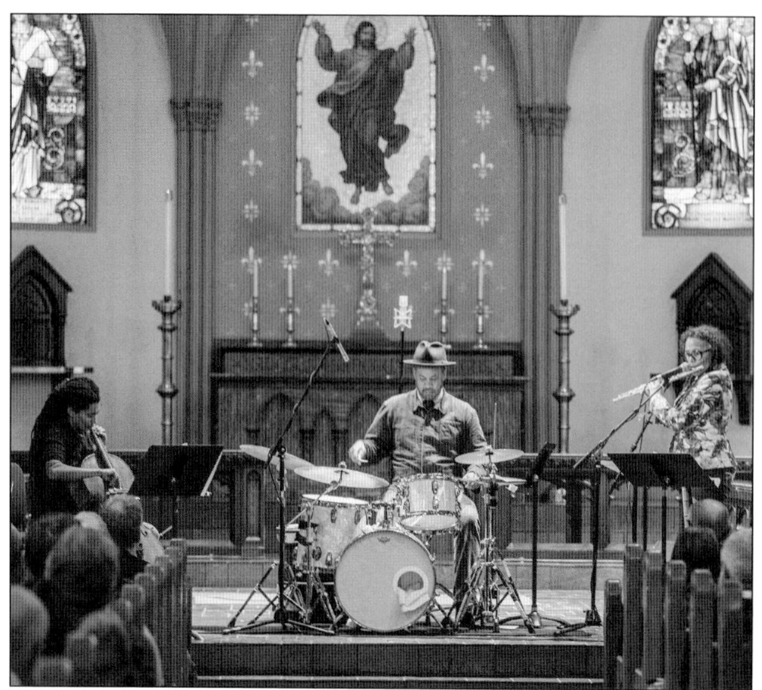

The Big Ears Festival, launched in 2009, is an annual gathering of cutting-edge and legendary musical performers and composers drawing thousands of attendees. International press coverage suggests that it is Knoxville's most prominent cultural event. The Bijou and Tennessee Theatres host much of the festival, but some of it takes place in nontraditional venues, like St. John's Episcopal Cathedral, built in 1892, where Artifacts Trio is pictured here performing in 2019. (insideofknoxville.com.)

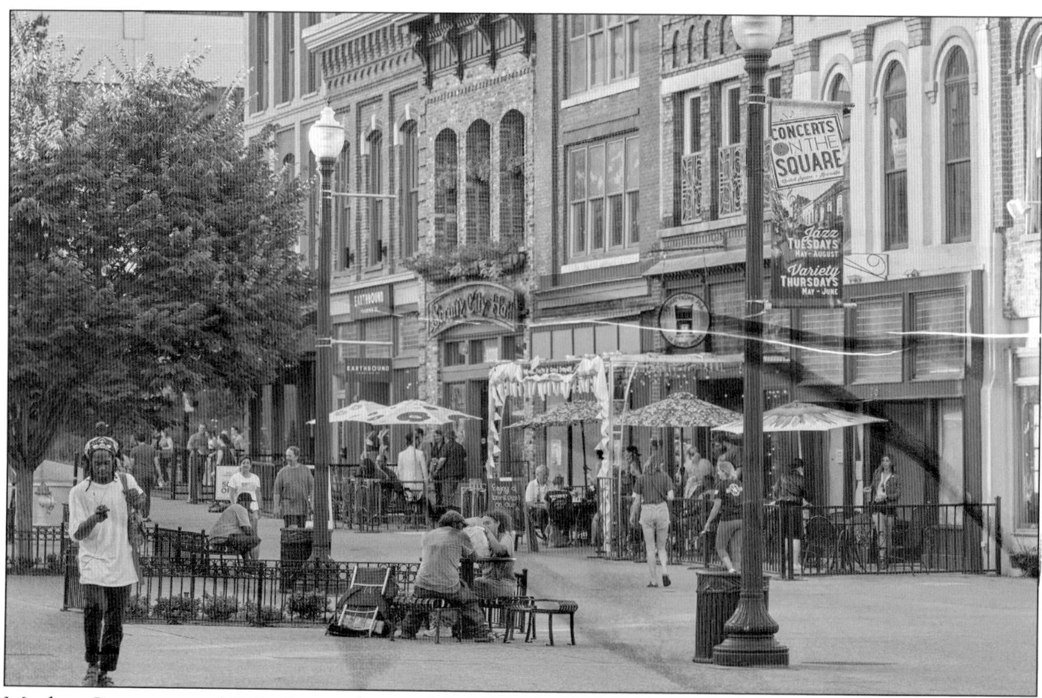

Market Square, established as a farmers' market in 1854, has been a cultural center ever since. Restored by a massive city project in 2003 to emphasize its Victorian architecture, it still hosts a vigorous farmers' market today, as well as occasional concerts and festivals. Its buildings date from the 1860s to the 1920s and serve as home to a lively and ever-changing assortment of bars, restaurants, specialty shops, and residences. (Shawn Poynter.)

About the Knoxville History Project

The authors' royalties from this book support the Knoxville History Project (KHP), an educational nonprofit with a mission to research, preserve, and promote the history and culture of Knoxville, Tennessee.

Established in 2014, KHP engages the community about the city's long and rich story, highlighting the iconic downtown core as well as the broader communities and neighborhoods that form metropolitan Knoxville.

KHP's stories, programs, and publications help residents and visitors understand the city's past as well as its complicated but dynamic heritage.

Learn more about KHP and the history of Knoxville through stories, walking and driving tours, public art projects, podcasts, and other book titles at knoxvillehistoryproject.org.